ATLANTA JEB

T. K. Calhoun is a native Atlantan and fifth generation Georgian. Sheriff Herbert Jenkins A.P.D. praised T.K. as "the bravest boy he ever met." Otherwise he had a normal life. He went to a grammar school named for author Margaret Mitchell. There he acquired a love of poetry after rubbing shoulders with James Dickey's nephew. He graduated from Lovett School where he first published, a poem, and scored the first touchdown in Kilpatrick Stadium. At Mr. Jefferson's University of Virginia he retired from football after his third concussion. He consoled himself at the P.K. Lodge, "doors off the hinges parties." He earned degrees from Dean Tate's University of Georgia, Western and Trinity. As a professor and football coach at Westminster T.K. contemplated a book based on the conflicted and violent events he witnessed in the 1950's. But life's rollercoaster-ride took him from sleeping in a convertible VW to owning a business. He lives in North Florida with his family and Labrador retriever. T.K.'s red-clay heart is a blend pride and angst, Sunday school and scotch – all the symptoms of a southern author – now Atlanta Jeb...

T. K. Calhoun 1955

Published by
Golden Horseshoe Press, LLC

Copyright © 2013 by Thomas Knight Calhoun

All rights reserved.

Published in the United States by Golden Horseshoe Press, LLC
Jacksonville, Florida

This book is based on several True Crimes depicted as witnessed by the author from September 1954 to September 1955. The crimes have been adjudicated. The guilty parties were either convicted and incarcerated on these or other crimes or killed. The law has closed the book and all is past. Participants in the True Events depicted are deceased except the author. The story has been recreated with Fictional characters, including the narrator, father, family, and all others. The names, characters, businesses, organizations, events, and incidents either are the product of the author's imagination or are used Fictitiously. The book contains some violence and some offensive language consistent with the Culture of 1950's.

Cover art owned and produced by Golden Horseshoe Press, LLC

Library of Congress Cataloging-in-Publication Data

Calhoun, T. K.
Atlanta Jeb / T.K. Calhoun. – 1st Edition, © 2013 p. cm.
Golden Horseshoe Press, Jacksonville, FL

ISBN 9878-09898786-2-3

Library of Congress Control Number: 2014948930
Golden Horseshoe Press, Jacksonville, FL

1. True Crime   2. Cultural History   3. Literature

PRINTED IN THE UNITED STATES OF AMERICA

First Edition

Table of Contents

Chapter 1 Lawyer 1
Chapter 2 Crimes 9
Chapter 3 Client 21
Chapter 4 Captain 33
Chapter 5 Weekend 41
Chapter 6 Jeb 47
Chapter 7 Mystery 61
Chapter 8 Hearsay 75
Chapter 9 White 89
Chapter 10 Trying 111
Chapter 11 Shopping 131
Chapter 12 Review 141
Chapter 13 Haymaker 149
Chapter 14 Deal 161
Chapter 15 Maid 167
Chapter 16 Vacation 183
Chapter 17 Gauntlet 201
Chapter 18 Magnolia 213
Chapter 19 Roadkill 241
Chapter 20 Rogues 253
Chapter 21 Convicts 271
Chapter 22 Clue 285
Chapter 23 Revenge 297
Chapter 24 Crossfire 311
Chapter 25 Respite 329
Chapter 26 Promise 337

"Out of the mouth of babes...Thou ordained strength"

- Psalm 8.2

Chapter 1 Lawyer

Cousins called me "Atlanta Jeb" to distinguish me from the other Jeb's in the family. I'm the one referred to in police reports as "Mr. McKnight's minor son" or "a minor child represented by Mr. Wallace." I was directed to never speak of events even to my mother or siblings, as this would break the seal of confidentiality with my lawyer, who protected my identity. Stan Wallace represented me and or my father five times in criminal proceedings from 1954 to 1959. Some found fault with Stan's handling of matters, I never did. He wanted to do more. He said he could write a book, give speeches and be mentioned in TIME and LIFE magazines, though not the cover. It was certainly in his interest to go public. He would joke our story was so incredible that we should offer the criminals immunity from prosecution to verify my role in events. No thanks. This is what I witnessed beginning in the fall of 1954.

Dad, Hank McKnight, did not plan to teach me about moonshiners, murders, assaults, burnings, and other things a boy should not see. Dad had trained as a youth to be a cavalry officer and thought the solution for any problem was to charge and "give them the steel" – his saber blade. He would lead by example and his son would follow. The charge of this Light Brigade of two would make havoc if not history.

A lanky six-footer with gray eyes and light brown hair, Dad graduated at the top of his class from the cavalry corps at Hampton Military School in South Georgia. He studied engineering and played football as his father did at

Georgia Tech. He worked in Atlanta until World War II started; he passed on the cavalry to become a Navy pilot. After seeing Japan from the air, he went to Yale Law School and married a fraternity brother's sister from Chicago. He brought his bride, Kate, to Atlanta, a city with a reputation for well-mannered people and beautiful homes.

Like granddad, Dad was quite a storyteller. I could hear a good story told and retold at cocktail hour or as Dad talked on the phone. As small boy, I sat unnoticed on the stairs to the second floor where I could see and hear the men sitting at the dining room table through the banisters. In winter I leaned against the wall and felt the warmth of the radiant heat from the furnace below the stairs. In the summer a breeze from the window air conditioners passed by as the cool air headed down the stairs. I might have been hungry waiting for dinner on the stairs, but I was comfortable. One evening I heard the news that shook our world like a tornado snapping the tops out of tall pine trees. I would have preferred a tornado, less damage.

Dirk Lockhart had been invited over for cocktails. The dining room table was set with an ice bucket, decanter, water pitcher, napkins, two glasses and two ashtrays. Dirk, was a lion of a man. Tall and heavyset, he had a daunting presence. He was several years older than Dad and wore gold-rimmed glasses. He was one-quarter Creek Indian and his lined face had a faint redness like sunburn. Dirk was from a family of lawyers and regarded as an excellent jurist. Dad appreciated Dirk's born in a Georgia courtroom opinion.

Dirk arrived and after a quick greeting the men went into the dinning room. They still had on their dark suits from work. Each man sat down and splashed bourbon from the decanter into an ice filled glass. They twirled the ice on top with their fingers to cool the whiskey. Neither man poured from the small glass water pitcher. They lighted their cigarettes and the aroma of matches and tobacco wafted up the stairs. They settled back in their chairs and cocktail hour was on.

"I don't know what Judge Jackson was thinking." Dad began, "He decided for my client in my commercial case and asked me to remain in the courtroom. Then Jackson named me the state's appointed counsel for two criminal defendants and handed me their folders. The judge said to meet my client and return with a plea. Agents from the Georgia Bureau of Investigation had one of my new clients in the hallway outside his courtroom."

"What did he give you?"

"A moonshiner and a murder case. I couldn't believe it, my first criminal case in seven years of practice. I left the courtroom the agents had GBI on their jackets and an old man in handcuffs."

"So what are you going to do? I'd plead them guilty and move on. No offense, but you didn't get these clients because the judge thought they had a case."

"You mean, what did I do? I had to do something right then. The moonshiner said he was innocent."

Before Dad could continue Dirk burst into roaring laughter, "I'm sorry. I could have told you they were innocent."

"My client was over sixty years old and looked seventy. He smelled of smoke and an outhouse. I thought the GBI wanted to give us some privacy and then I realized they just wanted to avoid the stench. The old man said he was across the highway and the law only grabbed him because he was the closest one to the still."

Dirk laughed again and slapped the table with his large lion paw hand as he spoke, "He was the closest to the still because it was his damn still! The smoke on his clothes was from stoking the wood fire under his cook pot. As far as the other he may have soiled himself. A number of them do, he knew what was coming. The prisoner stairwell is tiled floor to ceiling for easy cleaning. Next case."

"The GBI's agent said the same thing. I gave them my client's version. The GBI man said the highway my client referred to was a four-foot wide wagon trail. They found the pull pin to spill the moonshine still warm in the old man's coat pocket. I told him to plead guilty and hope for the best. Lawmen have arrested him seven times and he served three years in the pen, all for moonshine. I told him if we tried the case he would lose and get a longer sentence. Could I have done anything else?"

"No, heck, no, I said 'next case.' The question is why didn't he do something else? He gets caught every time. There is big money in it. I would say three quarters of my criminal practice had a moonshine component. This fine bourbon we're sipping cost about a twenty-five cents to distill a fifth of a gallon. Add bottling, retailing and taxes and we're paying five to eight dollars a fifth. Moonshiners can make it cheaper and sell it for not much less and keep all the profit. Most Georgia counties are dry so moonshine is more convenient. Bootleggers often have that good outlaw Robin Hood mystic. Believe me, there is nothing good about it. The sheriffs are good men but the GBI has to get involved. In small counties everyone is related including the sheriff, the judge, the jury, and the moonshiners. Nobody wins in a family feud. The GBI and the Feds bring them to Atlanta to get convictions. What did he get?"

"Five years. I guess he'll do his time on the inside, he's too old for a road gang," Dad said shaking his head. "I felt awful. I have never been around someone sentenced to jail."

"And your murder case?" Dirk sensed he should not dwell on the old moonshiner's chances of surviving his prison sentence.

Dad paused to empty his glass and fix another drink. "The defendant is a young Negro woman named Ida Mae Reivers. Her case was up before Judge Hightower three years ago. I don't know how Judge Jackson got it."

"Doesn't ring any bells. Knife or gun?"

"Butcher knife. She claims it was self-defense against her husband. She moved here from Houston County and worked as a shirt presser. In her statement she says that her late husband took her earnings, beat her, and sold her to his friends. In their statements the three friends say they gathered in the house earlier in the evening. They claim Mrs. Reivers was a prostitute and gambler and when they left the house she was arguing with her late husband over money. Her friends say the husband was "no damn good" and the profanity is recorded in the police report."

"I have heard it used in court. And her friends do not refute the statement of his three friends as to what happened - in what you have given me so far."

"The deceased had one arrest for gambling. My client was nineteen. He was thirty-four. Her police report states they met at a church. She notes her Auntie told her not to date him."

"So what did you plead?"

"I pleaded ignorance on her lawyer's part. I asked the judge for more time, the file was an inch thick. I have read it now. Her first lawyer advised her to plead guilty to manslaughter. She did not have an eyewitness to support her claim of self-defense. She could lose a murder trial and risk hanging or life in prison. The judge gave me until Friday to meet my client. She has served three years of a ten-year stretch. Another lawyer has prepared an appeal for a new trial alleging Mrs. Reivers did not sign the deal. I was assigned the appeal, pro bono. If she gets the new trial, it'd be for murder. Neighbors heard the fight. What do you think? Self-defense?"

Dirk fretted, "Can you get rid of it? Don't even think about asking me to take it."

"By Friday? I have an interview at the jail at ten o'clock tomorrow morning. All I have to do is file the appeal. I don't have to proceed, she could get a real criminal lawyer then."

"OK, Hank, go see the woman and call me tomorrow after three o'clock. Hundreds of people in prison accepted plea deals to take murder down to manslaughter. Unless you can give Judge Jackson screaming proof of the first lawyer's total incompetence, I mean like he's committed to the asylum at Milledgeville and you can prove he's still there, then the matter is closed."

Dad thought for a moment, he had Dirk's answer. But like a student trying to get his test score changed he wanted to make one more pitch. "You don't think it would be incompetence if the sentencing deal was not signed by the prisoner?"

Dirk raised an eyebrow at Dad's persistence, "A lawyer would be incompetent to try the case on the facts you gave me. She would hang. You have nothing to refute the statement given by the three men. You would need an eyewitness; two would be better. No judge will free a woman who stabbed her husband to death because the neighbors said he was "no damn good." There would be an epidemic. A thousand Negro men, white ones too, would show up for butcher knife removal at Grady Hospital. They already handle at least thirty knife wounds a night. You have to come up with something a heap better than what you have."

"I thought she had a better case. I guess not."

Dirk looked incredulous, "The neighbors heard but did not see a fight? They said the husband was "no damn good?" Are you serious? My wife could kill me and get her friends in the Daisy Garden Club to say I was "no damn good." They wouldn't be all wrong either. Would you take that case for Alice?"

"No, I guess not."

The aroma of baked ham and yellow squash casserole drifted into the dining room. Mom called, "Is Dirk staying for supper?"

"Thanks, Kate, I can't stay. And I don't want Hank telling my wife he is defending a husband killer, she'll get ideas." He laughed and drained his glass, "Thanks for my, if Alice asks, one drink. Remember call after three. Bye."

"I will call. Be there or I might take Alice's case, pro bono."

"Hush Hank, y'all shouldn't joke about such things." Kate said as she brought plates and silverware to the table.

Chapter 2 Crimes

Nate Reivers was a powerfully built Negro with a square jaw, and flat nose. He stood over six feet tall. He earned his broad shoulders and muscular arms in Atlanta's River Brick Yards by throwing bricks into a steel form until four hundred and ninety-five bricks stood ready to bundle with steel bands. Brick-slingers received their pay in cash Friday afternoon. Gamblers, thieves, moonshiners, and prostitutes waited to ply their trades as the men left the property. Using his fists and knife, Nate caught the attention of moonshiners. He had the demeanor of a coiled rattlesnake and intimidated others with his reptilian stare. By age thirty he was the big NIC, Nigger In Charge, of his home turf. Nate and his gang of three lived the sporting life financed by moonshine, gambling, and loan sharking.

Ida Mae Norris called her country home Egypt. She was large and strong for a young woman. She was a "country darky," a poor Negro from a rural area distinguished by the marks of poverty and characterized by an impossible family situation. She never knew her father. She was abandoned by her mother and raised by her Auntie. Like many rural poor people, Negro or white, she grew up on a dirt road in an unpainted house. Her aunt also raised four unrelated boys as Ida Mae's brothers. Ida Mae suffered all the indignities and maladies of those circumstances. Worse, she suffered bullying and sexual abuse at the hands of her "brothers" and their friends. Driven by the desire to escape, she graduated from the colored high school and attended a colored nursing school for a year. To get the money to finish school, she moved to Atlanta and worked as a shirt presser. She met Nate in the church where she sang in the choir. Nate knew Ida Mae had no family and friends. She knew him as a churchgoer and a Saturday night dancer. He hid his criminal connections from the impressionable country girl. She was his prey.

Nate proposed to nineteen-year-old Ida Mae Norris and in June of 1951 her sole living relative, the Auntie who raised her, came from South Georgia for the church wedding. Ida Mae was blinded to Nate's true character by her passionate desire for her own church going family: a husband, children and a real momma – her in the middle. The new Mrs. Ida Mae Reivers could not imagine the plans Nate had for her. Nate wanted the added income he thought prostitution would bring. He did not see himself as a pimp but he could only add to his gang by increasing his territory or getting more money from the area he controlled. Ida Mae's legitimate income enabled Nate to rent the larger house he wanted for his new enterprise. Ida Mae was not a looker; she had a pleasant round face and a stout frame. She would do for a start. And once he broke her, she had the size to intimidate other women.

Ida Mae was young but not stupid. After a few months of marriage she discovered the real Nate. Her dream for a family would not die and she hoped to change him. They lived in an unpainted shotgun house with electricity, running water in the kitchen, and an outhouse. They used firewood for cooking and heat. The neighborhood was called Buttermilk Bottom and it smelled like anything but buttermilk.

On a Friday evening Ida Mae found Nate and his three gang members, all Negroes like Nate, drinking shine in the dim light of a single light bulb hanging from the ceiling in the front room.

"Hey baby, give your man a kiss," Nate said, not rising from his chair. He wore his drab, street clothes.

"Later." She passed close to his chair to avoid the three men on the new-to-her worn sofa.

Nate grabbed her, "Well you better have some cash today or we gonna call on your boss."

"You right, Brick Man," said Blue Shoes, who wore black shoes, green pants and suspenders. Along with Willie Rat and Boot Head, Blue Shoes lounged on the sofa. Blue's narrow face seemed askew of his head. He was a pitiless young man with a reputation for the remorseless use of his knife. Like Nate he had worked in the brickyards and was the tallest and strongest of Nate's gang. Willie Rat was next in the informal pecking order of the gang. He was the most talkative and social member of the gang. He was style conscious and used pomade to slick back his hair. People who were afraid to face Nate came to Willie Rat. Boot Head was as large as Blue Shoes but awkward in every sense of the word. Some thought his jutting jaw looked like the toe of a boot. He had a room temperature IQ and was prone to emotional fits. Willie Rat often had to spend time explaining, "what it is" to Boot Head.

"I wish you was a brick man," Ida Mae said, not resisting Nate.

"Them mean-ass brick bosses push a man too hard. You don't want me run down, do you? Honey?"

"I don't want you in jail."

"Brick Man too smart for no jail," Boot Head spoke, stroking his jaw.

"Where's the goddamn money?" Nate demanded.

"I got it hid. Let me go in the back. I'll bring it out to you."

"How 'bout I get it?" said Nate, emptying the purse on the coffee table. Ida Mae's butcher knife clattered out alongside the usual contents.

"Wooo! Big-ass knife, Ida Mae!" exclaimed Willie Rat as he leaned forward to see the knife. He smiled and his face crinkled around his long pointy nose, the Rat nose. "What's a big girl like you need a knife for?"

"I got a right to defend myself from peoples what would steal my pay."

"Like Brick Man?" laughed Blue Shoes.

"Ask my four brothers if I can fight," said Ida Mae, not backing down.

"Your Daddy told me you wasn't a patch to your bothers," Blue Shoes continued.

"Fool, my Daddy don't stay around here. You don't know him no how."

"Where do he stay?... You don't know where your Daddy stays 'cause you don't know who your Daddy is neither." Blue retorted.

The men laughed. Nate clapped. "Mens, y'all got some work to do."

Each man picked up a brown paper grocery sack full of pint mason jars of moonshine and went out.

"Blue Shoes, Willie Rat, Boot Head?" she exclaimed. "Why can't you find some friends what got real names?"

"Baby, I done told you, these is our street names so the wrong people don't recognize us."

"They is the wrong people. They's no-good. Instead of being 'the big NIC' you gonna be lead nigger on the chain gang. And don't be spending every cent we have. My Auntie says you got to save for a rainy day."

"Woman! Go on with your bad self. You giving me a headache."

Ida Mae walked down the dark hallway past the two bedrooms to the kitchen. She removed the pay envelope from her purse's lining. She added eight dollars to the roll hidden in the Quaker Oats container. She left fourteen dollars and change in the envelope to give to Nate.

The clapboard shack had been retrofitted with electricity and running water. A refrigerator and a small water heater were the only appliances. Ida Mae hid her Zenith clock radio in a cupboard so it would not get stolen during the day. One electric wire ran down the ceiling the length of the house. There was one water faucet in the kitchen and a shower room had been added behind the kitchen sink on the porch. Another small room off the kitchen had a bathtub that could be filled with hot water from off the stove. The outhouse with its predictable odor was only a few feet away from the back of the house. She started a cook fire by adding sticks of wood to the glowing coals left from breakfast. The iron stove began ticking as it heated. She returned to the front room and gave Nate the envelope.

"Fourteen dollars and thirty-five cents? You making less money every week."

"The laundry be hot and it smells bad. I got to go out for air. They pay by the shirt so if all the shirts get pressed I ain't got no more work," Ida Mae waved her hand dismissively.

"Baby, I is the boss and I says you got to make twenty dollars a week. We gonna have to find you another job," Nate said as he advanced toward her.

"I ain't working no other job. You gonna have to stay home and spend less money."

Softening, Nate said, "Baby, you might be right. I'm thinking the boys and me can stay here tonight and play a little cards. We can figure how we gonna get more money."

Ida Mae prepared supper and Nate set a mason jar of chilled moonshine by his place setting.

"I am 'bout to drink up my profits. Yeah, since your pay gone down at your daytime job I been thinking you might have to find something for nights and weekends."

"Hush up, Nate. You said you wanted to stay home tonight. You got plenty to drink and we can listen to the radio,"

"Yeah, I was serious about staying here tonight. Bring out the radio,"

Ida Mae brought the clock radio into the front room and plugged the cord into the light socket above. The music of Fats Domino and Frankie Lane singing the blues soon filled the house.

Ida Mae remained standing and clapped to the beat of the music, "Nate, Saturday I want us to go dancing like we used to do,"

Before he could respond someone knocked at the door. Nate put his drink out of sight and went to the door. He looked through the top window before he opened the door for Peanut, a customer.

"Hey, Peanut, you met Ida Mae before?" Peanut was a small Negro with a wiry build and a skillet black face. He nodded politely in her direction. Nate handed him two sealed mason jars of moonshine and took his cash and a bag of sugar.

"Brick Man?"

"Yes, Peanut."

"Willie Keb's Momma got a sofa look like yours."

"Nice, ain't it?" Nate smiled. "She ain't got one like mine no more."

Peanut shrugged, "Oh, yeah, y'all have a nice night."

"Remember, Peanut, it's good to stay square with me."

"OK, OK, Brick Man, I know you's right."

Ida Mae asked, "This sofa we got came from Keb's Momma?"

"Business, Ida Mae," Nate said in a tone intended to end conversation on the matter.

By eleven o'clock Nate's gang of three had exchanged all the moonshine for cash and bags of sugar. They sat down to drink and Nate distributed the cash, calculating out loud. No one corrected his mistakes.

Nate ordered Boot Head to bring Ida Mae a chair and her own pint mason jar. She was bewildered and flattered to be included in the poker. She had not been "in" with the gang and felt like an outsider in her own home. Even more shocking, Nate gave her cash. They taught her the rules of poker. She lost money and drank moonshine. Nate did not seem to mind and he laughed at her drunkenness.

After what could have been a pleasant evening Nate's attitude changed. "Awe shit, Ida Mae, you done lost eight or ten dollars out of your pay and you lost another ten. We down at least twenty damn dollars. What you gonna do to get it back?"

"What you talking about? You gave me the money. You taught me. I guess you didn't teach me so good." Ida Mae was sloppy drunk after a pint of moonshine. She had no sense of Nate's direction.

Nate glanced around at his gang, "I can't let you leave taking all my money, but I is too tired to win it back."

Blue glanced knowingly at Boot and Willie, the wolf pack circled. "You's right, Brick Man, but I can't give it to you for nothing,"

"Blue Shoes, how much you give me for a piece of Ida Mae?" Nate asked in a matter of fact tone. Ida Mae stared back, dumfounded.

Before she could speak Blue Shoes spoke again, "No more than two dollars."

"Shut up, fool!" Ida Mae slurred at Nate. "I am your wife. We married in the church."

"You don't carry on like no married woman. You been showing me leg all night," Boot Head mocked.

"You nigger fool. I ain't paid you no never mind," Ida Mae yelled in Boot Head's face.

"Yeah, I seen it too. You been showing leg." Willie Rat added with a sinister grin.

"You ain't carrying your end, baby. It ain't like these ain't friends. Ten times and we be back to even before sun up, more money than you make all week." Nate shrugged.

"No! Fool, don't do me wrong." Ida Mae raged at Nate in horrified disbelief.

They laughed and forced her in the spare bedroom. She screamed and fought. The men beat her and stuffed clothing in her mouth. After she had been beaten into submission the drunken men joked, laughed, and hurled insults as they raped her.

"This ain't worth more than a dollar a whack, Brick Man," Blue Shoes called out.

"I ain't giving no money back. You paying twenty so y'all go on 'till you got your money worth."

"Willie Rat be so skinny we going to have to tie a board to his ass so he don't fall in," Boot Head said from the open door.

"Don't stop what you be doing, I'll go get long board and a rope. We'll tie the rope to his ass, where he don't fall in and get lost," Nate joked back.

"Better bring a candle too, case we got to find him, it be dark in there," Boot Head slurred through his laughter. In their drunken state the men laughed hysterically at any attempt at humor.

"Don't do nothing until I find it," Willie Rat called out.

"Willie don't know where to look," Boot Head called out again.

"Tell him jus' grab a leg and work on up," Nate said laughing from the kitchen where he opened the refrigerator for another pint of moonshine.

Ida Mae had been assaulted numerous times as a youth, she met her fate with tearful resignation. She thought a big strong husband would save her. He didn't, and that hurt the worst. She had tried hard, High school graduate, good job, sang in the church choir, but she didn't escape. She felt enraged, held down, beaten, her own underwear stuffed in her mouth, sold for prostitution by the man she met in church and married to protect her. Ida Mae felt nausea and pain throughout her body; she was disoriented. As the moonshine wore off, she felt the sharp stinging pain of the multiple blows to her head and body. She felt scorching rage.

After the partners received their twenty dollars' worth, they made a great show of paying Nate and left.

Nate dragged Ida Mae by her hair and arm into the kitchen. She tried to pull her torn button up dress around her. She sat on the floor leaning against the counter, her head tilted down hiding her tear-stained face. "Why you done me bad? You s'posed to help me," she said, holding a hand to her face.

"Shut up, you done to your bad self, not carrying your end. Now you get pregnant we ain't gonna know who the Daddy is."

Ida Mae screamed at the curse of her own fatherless existence, "Damn you to Hell! I hate you for that!" She came up from the floor striking with her fists, kicking, screaming, and crying. Ida Mae was strong for a woman. But Nate made his way in life fighting. He pounded her with his fists, sending her bloodied and sprawling back down to the floor.

"We ain't done yet. You been hiding money in this kitchen. Where is it?"

She said nothing. Nate pulled her by her hair to the counter and began banging her head onto the countertop. She swung wildly from her awkward position. She did not know if Nate would leave her alive.

"I ain't one of your sorry-ass brothers," he sneered.

"It's in the oatmeal," Ida Mae cried, collapsing to the floor again.

Nate emptied the Quaker Oats container including a roll of cash held by a rubber band.

"You can't do me this way and steal from me."

Adrenaline pumped into her veins. Ida Mae grabbed a heavy skillet and threw it at Nate's head. He was counting the cash but turned in time to fend off the blow. The black iron skillet broke his left hand. He groaned in pain. "Fool! Nigger! You broke my hand."

The money roll scattered to the floor as he grabbed his broken left hand in his right. Ida Mae became a screaming whirling fury of blows and punches. Nate yelled back and slugged her hard with his right fist. She went down, sliding on her blood on the floor. From the floor she screamed at Nate and threw whatever she could grab from under the counter. She felt her purse and reached for the butcher knife. Nate backed against the counter, dodging pots and pans. Ida Mae stood up griping the butcher knife in her right hand. She grabbed a plate in her left hand and threw it as she rushed toward Nate. He held his broken left hand across his stomach and deflected the plate swinging his undamaged right arm. Ida Mae plunged nine inches of knife blade into his unguarded chest. Nate fell against the counter but kept his feet under him. Instinctively, he tried to flee out the back door, but he staggered and fell backwards into the center of the kitchen floor. Ida Mae gasped for air from the exertion and fell beside Nate on the floor.

For a few seconds Nate tried to pull the knife out of the center of his chest. He groaned and a pink froth came out of his mouth, "I done been killed by a woman." Nate struggled to breathe. "After all I been through."

Ida Mae looked intently at Nate. He shook, "Mamma, Mamma..." Nate coughed blood and his body convulsed. Then he was still.

Ida Mae did not know what to do. When she realized that Nate was indeed dead her anger turned to fear and remorse. "I is sorry if I killed you, Nate." She used a dishtowel to staunch the blood.

Ida Mae limped to the neighbors, dripping blood from her wounds. They had come out on their porches having heard the screaming and crashing of pots and pans. No one had dared enter the NICs house. When Ida Mae stumbled out, neighbors called a nurse from down the street who pronounced Nate dead. A neighbor woman helped Ida Mae get cleaned up. The nurse used tape and gauze to close the wound over Ida Mae's left eye and gave her ice packs to put on her forehead and bloody mouth. Someone went to get the police, no nearby house had a phone. Ida Mae spent the short remainder of the night at a neighbor's house.

Word of a killing traveled fast. Nate's partners emptied the house of cash, sugar bags and moonshine. Other visitors took most of the furniture, kitchen utensils, and Nate's fancy clothes. Ida Mae's belongings went missing as well. Some items returned to the original owners. Keb's momma got her sofa back. Nate's body remained on the floor, the butcher knife wedged between his ribs, the handle protruding from his chest.

Chapter 3 Client

The call about Nate Reivers death came in as the night shift patrol cars returned to the station. No officers were sent until after the shift change. The report included the killer's name and the police avoided Buttermilk Bottom even during daylight. A corpse could wait.

Saturday morning two policemen assigned to the killing arrived in a new patrol car. Randy was less than forty having joined the force after high school. His red hair and a cherubic freckled face made him look years younger than he was. Randy's partner Clete was in his early twenties. He had two years of college and three months of police training. He had been on the job for three months and Randy felt obliged to remind Clete of his ignorance and junior status. Clete had brown eyes and short brown hair and was taller than Randy. He had a serious personality. Randy had been his only on the job trainer and Clete had patiently endured Randy's hazing. Randy was teaching Clete the A.P.D.'s culture of light humor as a relief to the serious and dangerous work of crime fighting.

Randy led as they approached the house. He advised Clete, "Could be a false alarm but you better pull your revolver. Southerners will fight it out and a police officer is seven times more likely to get killed in the line of duty in the South as elsewhere."

"So you have told me. I know, I know."

"I got eighteen years in and no partner of mine has been shot. You are not going to be the first. Try as you might." Randy dryly admonished. "And keep your pistol down at your side." After a perfunctory knock they walked through the open door.

"Anybody home?"

"Well Clete, that big nigger covered in blood on the kitchen floor back there could be dead," said Randy in a matter of fact tone.

"He smells dead," Clete said as he gagged for air.

"With niggers you can't always tell by the smell," Randy joked but did not laugh as he cautiously looked into the vacant bedrooms.

Clete walked ahead to the kitchen, "He is a Hell of a faker or he's dead. There's blood everywhere."

"Well don't throw up… There's no one here." Randy said. Both men holstered their pistols.

"Looks like his pals have already divided the estate. This palace has been cleaned out. They even took the light bulbs," Randy observed.

"There are a lot of empty mason jars around. Do you think it was moonshine?" Clete said thinking out loud.

Randy walked into the kitchen, "Are you joking? Of course it was moonshine. Does the Lone Ranger shoot silver bullets? Huh? Can Superman fly? Will a fat puppy poot? It was moonshine and a lot of it… I don't believe you asked that. Did you take a course in stupid at that fancy college or did you test out of it?"

"Yeah, Yeah, Yeah," Clete frowned at the lighthearted rebuke. "I took the course, I needed the credits."

"I'll give you an easy one, what do you think killed him? The cut over the eye or the butcher knife handle he's balancing on his chest?"

Clete responded in a somber tone to Randy's gallows humor. "I'm going to take a wild guess. The blood on his shirt and on the floor means we will find a blade under the handle."

"Good police work, Clete. I will make a detective out of you yet. But you're going to have to learn faster, I only have two years left to get my twenty." Randy said as the two policeman focused on the bloody mess in the kitchen

"You're too good to me,… I don't see he had a blade or gun. Poor man didn't have a chance."

"Dang it, Clete, I'm telling you for the hundredth time. Don't let the street get to you. You want to get down in the mouth? Do it when we pick up a ten year old looking the same way."

Clete continued, "There is blood on the counter and floor over here, maybe from another party to the fight. He's a big one. I bet you a coffee the knife blade didn't clear his back. Might be the big nigger-in-charge around here. Maybe a new NIC got him?"

Randy took charge, "The call-in said the wife did it. Judging by this mess, she's a bruiser. See if you can round her up and I will sketch the scene and look over the house." As Clete left Randy called out, "Go by the car and radio to Grady Hospital that we are on the scene and we need an ambulance to pick up a body. Tell them we will wait or they won't come down here."

"Sure."

Randy and Clete took Ida Mae to jail where she told her story of abuse to another police sergeant. She was recalled a few days later to the jail. A prosecutor had affidavits from three men, Nate's gang. They swore that earlier the night Nate was killed, they witnessed a fight between Ida Mae and Nate over money. The witnesses further identified Ida Mae as a prostitute who also ran a gambling house. The story was so far from the truth Ida Mae thought the prosecutor had made a mistake. The prosecutor charged Ida Mae with murder. Her neighbors confirmed they heard a great fight and three additional men had been in the house. The pro bono lawyer did not bother to muster Ida Mae's friends for comments.

Ida Mae could honestly say she had never met Alphonse Howard, Seth Thomas, or Nathan Smith. But she lost credibility in the preliminary hearing when she recognized Blue Shoes, Willie Rat, and Boot Head. She protested she never heard their given names. The three men lied as much to save their own skins as to revenge Nate. Other moonshiners ridiculed them. Since Ida Mae was nineteen years old, a joke circulated on the street that the gang was looking for a teenage girl to replace Nate as NIC.

Ida Mae's first lawyer arranged a plea bargain. Instead of life in prison or hanging for murder, Ida Mae could plead guilty to manslaughter and serve ten years in prison. Ida Mae adamantly refused to sign the plea. She declared the three witnesses lied and she defended herself against a violent man. The lawyer returned the unsigned plea bargain to the judge. The lawyer had made an X on the signature line to show Ida Mae where to sign. A courthouse clerk read the X for Ida Mae's signature. Her paperwork was processed and Ida Mae was sent to prison to serve a ten-year sentence.

***

After three and a half years in prison at her Auntie's insistence a different judge, Judge Jackson, appointed a pro bono lawyer, Dad. And the Thursday morning after the cocktail meeting with Dirk Lockhart, Dad went to the jail to interview his new client.

Several random masonry buildings across the street from the State Capital Building made up 'the jail'. The oldest buildings predated the Civil War and the hanging tower had been used since the 1800's. An experienced criminal lawyer offered to drop Dad at the new jail annex. Inside the door Dad encountered a pleasant uniformed lady who directed him to the front desk surrounded by uniformed policemen.

At the far end of the large room a tiled walkway led fearful prisoners to the loading dock to be taken to chain gang or prison. Another security detail of a half dozen policemen stood smoking and chatting by the secure doors to and from the dock. Dad caught the scent of ammonia cleanser and recalled Dirk Lockhart's comment about the reason for the tile. Jail was a desperate place.

An old policeman at the front desk looked as if he could have been at the jail when Sherman burned Atlanta but he spryly confirmed Dad's client, Ida Mae Reivers, was in a holding cell. Simple enough, Dad thought. He held in his hand Judge Jackson's order to meet his client. After signing as directed, Dad slid the large register back across the desk. The policeman noted the date and time; he shuffled papers and consulted other logbooks. "And you are Mr. Henry L. McKnight?"

"Yes."

"My log says you are to meet Ida Mae Reivers between the hours of ten o'clock and four o'clock She is in holding cell 4CW." The policeman's thin face remained expressionless as he continued looking over the books on his desk. "Are you Mrs. Reivers's legal counsel?"

"Yes, I am."

"Have you been to this facility before?"

"No, I have not."

"We do not have your name listed." He sighed as if an insurmountable hurdle had been reached. His light blue eyes roamed the room as he recited from memory a small lecture on the importance of jail security. Then he focused back on Dad, who offered numerous directories included his name as a lawyer and member of the State Bar Association.

"Well, Mr. McKnight, those directories are not proof to me. I am the one responsible for giving out passes. I mean it is my job, I will get in trouble if it is not done properly." The policeman smiled, secure in the power invested in him by the State of Georgia and the City of Atlanta. He could deny access to the jail to any lawyer not dancing to his tune.

"I don't want to cause you any trouble. How might I register?" Dad inquired humbly not wishing to offend.

"The police department requires a signed document." The old policeman said putting on his black-rimed glasses for the first time. He studied Dad's appearance. He wore his gray herringbone suit and looked like the trial lawyer he was.

Dad listed his available credentials and the policeman said he would accept Dad's signed Yale Law Diploma. This document hung on his office wall. Dad decided not to mention a law school degree did not mean he had passed the Georgia Bar Exam. The desk officer offered to have a policeman drive Dad to his nearby office a block off Peachtree Street. Dad accepted the ride to avoid the rain. He rode in the front seat so people would not think he had been arrested.

Dad explained to his police escort the need for his Yale Diploma. Patrolman Weatherford used the car radio, "Tell McConnell I am bringing in one of his New York lawyers. Then tell him I'll get back out to Ponce de Leon." And then to Dad, "You need anything at the jail, ask for Captain McConnell. He's from New York too, the second best Captain in the force."

Dad did not expend the effort to explain that New Haven, Connecticut was not New York. Weatherford corrected himself. "I know Yale is in Connecticut. We like to have fun with our Damnyankee Captain."

"I understand. When I was at Yale they had fun with my southern accent."

Back at the jail, the old policeman greeted Dad with a matter of fact acceptance of the diploma and laboriously made entries in the books on his desk. Once past the gatekeeper a policeman guided Dad to an interview room in another building. Dad felt the temperature rise and the air smelled like stagnant water as he moved further into the jail. Ida Mae Reivers expected her new lawyer at ten o'clock. Exasperated, Dad showed up an hour late. He entered the interview room and Ida Mae fixed her gaze upon him as a drowning person would upon a lifeguard.

He sat down and heard the deadbolt lock behind him. He noticed Ida Mae's large forearms and muscular hands resting on the small table and felt uncomfortable, she had killed a man. The table and two wooden chairs comprised all the furniture in the room. A large faced electric clock hung on the wall under a window covered with a heavy crosshatched wire screen. At almost five feet nine inches tall, she looked Dad in the eyes as she rose displaying her large frame. She was wide in the body and face. Her eyes held a flicker of hope and she tried to make a welcoming smile. She gave Dad an awkward handshake.

"I sure does appreciate you trying to help me," Ida Mae began in a hopeful tone. "I want you to know the prison make me dress this way," referring to her loose-fitting prison dress. "I don't go around without no foundation garment and I is innocent."

"Mrs. Reivers,…"

"Don't call me that!" Ida Mae flared disgust at the mention of her late husband's name.

"What may I call you?" Dad responded calmly.

Embarrassed, she spoke softly, "I'm sorry. I use my maiden name now, Ida Mae Norris. Just Ida Mae is OK."

"Very well, Ida Mae, I need to tell you that I am not a criminal lawyer. Judge Jackson assigned your case to me because other lawyers could not or would not take it. If your appeal is granted I will ask the judge to appoint a real criminal layer to your case."

"You ain't a real lawyer?" Ida Mae leaned back in her chair and looked at Dad with disillusioned alarm.

"I am a real lawyer but I specialize in business law. I have never tried a criminal case. I can file your appeal or you can request that Judge Jackson appoint another lawyer."

"Lordy..." she moaned, "You the only lawyer I've seen in three and a half years can you help me?"

"I would do my absolute best to help you. First you need to tell me what happened. Do you deny that you killed your husband?"

"No, I killed him. But it were self-defense. He were a bad man. I didn't know he was no NIC." Ida Mae pronounced NIC as Nick. Either way Dad did not know the word.

"Nick? Did you mean Nate?"

"No, sir." Ida Mae realized Dad was out of touch with her world. "NIC means Nigger In Charge. Nate had a territory where he sold moonshine and he was the boss of the three men that lied about me to the judge."

"Please tell me what happened from the beginning." Dad tried to sound reassuring and positive as he placed his yellow legal pad on the table. He pulled out his fountain pen and a bottle of ink, "I will make a few notes as you speak. OK?"

"Yes, sir."

Dad listened to her account of her background and the evening of the homicide.

Afterwards he faced two alarming realities. Ida Mae's desperate life with one shattered dream after another, plus three and a half years in prison, had embittered her and it showed. She adamantly claimed self-defense and wished aloud that she had not killed Nate so that he and his "no damn good" friends could be in jail instead of her. Her legal position offered no visible relief based on the evidence presented. The last three men to see Nate Reivers alive swore Ida Mae started the fight with him over ill-gotten gain from her prostitution and gambling. If she didn't deserve jail for one thing, she deserved it for another. Something extraordinary was needed, something bigger than a signature error. He sighed to even think of putting her on the witness stand. Her language and grammar were so bad no one would believe she graduated high school. She even lacked credibility on what he could prove. Nevertheless he pressed on.

An amiable policeman unlocked the door at noon and entered the interview cell unannounced. Ida Mae continued her story over a surprisingly eatable institutional lunch of Salisbury steak, gravy, mash potatoes and lima beans. The guard left four glasses of sweet tea explaining it was easier than serving seconds. After lunch was on the table he left locking the door behind him. Ida Mae had spared Dad some of the gory details part out of sheer embarrassment and part fear her flushed lawyer would throw up his lunch.

Dad had listened to her story and he thought he had a sense of her as a person. "Ida Mae, I believe you."

He looked straight into her eyes and he believed in the nineteen-year old she had been. The girl, who struggled against her heinous existence to graduate from colored high school and studied to become a nurse, the girl who more than anything wanted her own family, a vision of a home with a husband and children who all belonged to each other. Instead she was the girl who had been victimized once again in the big city by a NIC, a professional criminal. Ida Mae did not need a second chance she needed a first chance.

"I believe you." Dad repeated himself, "You feared for your life when you defended yourself. I need to ask you why you think your husband would have killed you. What reason could he have had? Maybe something you have not covered?"

Ida Mae's expression softened, she was believed. She screwed her face up in thought. "I don't know why he done me that a way. Some women in prison told me that the NICs got to kill somebody so they get respect. And the closer that person be, the better. 'Cause peoples be saying he done killed his friend, he kill anybody. But the NICs won't kill nobody's momma or some other NIC gonna kill them." Ida Mae thought some more. "The peoples say if a NIC goes to jail another NIC will kill the peoples who sent him up. Mister McKnight, I just hear that stuff. I don't know. I just knows I thought he was going to make me dead."

"Ida Mae, I agree that a reasonable person in your situation would believe their life was in danger and I will try to help you. I think I know a way to get the police and a judge to help us. Will you tell the police everything you know about Nate and his friends? I mean their moonshine activity."

"Nobody believed me before," Ida Mae shrugged.

"Ida Mae, I believe your story. If Nate's three character witnesses are moonshiners, their testimony will be discredited."

"Will the judge let me out of here?"

"I do not know what a judge will do, but it can only help. Will you talk to police?"

"Mr. McKnight, I got to ask, will the other prisoners know?"

"I don't think the police would want the word to leak out."

"It don't matter. Women in the prison say it's on the street that Blue Shoes says I'm a dead-nigger-walking. They saying they gonna kill me anyway, in prison or when I gets out. I ain't safe nowhere from them. They can't do me no worse than I am now. Ida Mae stood, "Yes, sir, I will talk to the police if they will listen and thank you very much."

They shook hands and Dad called for a policeman to lead Ida Mae back to her cell. Dad said he might ask for Ida Mae again shortly. He thanked the policeman for lunch and the extra sweet tea.

Chapter 4 Captain

After Ida Mae was led away Dad's police escort arrived, "Mr. McKnight, I'm officer Rogers, your escort, are you ready to go?"

"Not quite, I need to see Captain McConnell before I go,"

"Oh, you know Captain McConnell?"

"Not really, a mutual acquaintance referred me to him."

"Is he expecting you?"

"No, but I would like to try to see him today."

"Don't worry, your client isn't going anywhere," said Rogers.

Dad gladly walked in the drizzling rain for a breath of fresh air. After ten minutes of meandering through narrow hallways and in and out of buildings they arrived at a small foyer. Inside the too warm police offices Dad appreciated the absence of the smell of body odor that permeated the interview cells. Through an open door they saw a long narrow space, which had been a hallway. A personable and attractive lady sat behind a cluttered desk. She was tastefully made up, well dressed and accessorized. She wore her frosted hair in a bouffant hair-do with a blue ribbon that matched the blue in her print dress. She stood to greet the visitors like the hostess of a barbeque restaurant, "What can I do for you honey?"

Rogers answered, "Got a lawyer here, Mr. McKnight. He's been referred to McConnell about an old manslaughter case."

"Well howdy, Mr. McKnight. I'm Cheryl, Captain Mack's secretary, and everybody else's' up here."

"Hi, Cheryl, nice to meet you. I would like to see Captain McConnell about a current moonshine report. I neglected to tell officer Rogers. A patrolman I met earlier today named Weatherford referred me to the Captain."

"Mr. McKnight, I can take you down to the jail annex if you need to file a report." Rogers offered.

"I would prefer to talk to Captain McConnell if he's available."

Cheryl glanced over her left shoulder through a large plate glass window into the closest office, "Mr. McKnight, Captain McConnell would be glad to talk to you...Are you any relation to the McKnights from Hapeville? You could pass for Bobby McKnight's brother."

"No, there are a lot of McKnights," said Dad relieved he would get to speak to McConnell.

"Yes, Hapeville is just covered up with them."

Captain McConnell moved toward his open door. "Mr. McKnight, I'm Mack McConnell. Cheryl, would you grab us a couple of Peachtree Colas. Roy, you can have one if you got a nickel."

"It's Larry, Captain," responded Rogers.

"Sorry, I get you confused with Roy Rogers, the singing cowboy." McConnell laughed at his own joke and offered Dad a firm handshake, "Come on in."

Captain McConnell did not wear a uniform. His brown sport coat hung on a wall hook next to an empty brown leather shoulder holster. He kept his stainless steel 1911 Colt .45 pistol in a desk drawer. He sat wedged behind his desk. He had his tie loosened and his sleeves rolled up to his elbows. He had a medium build and his thinning brown hair gave way to gray. He had noticeable bags under his brown eyes, but he looked alert and on guard.

"I answer to, Mack, McConnell, Captain Mack and our Damnyankee, most people call me Mack. Patrolman Weatherford mentioned you hailed from New York. Is this a social call or a moonshine case?"

Dad appreciated Mack's directness and he responded in kind. "You can call me Hank. My client, a Negro woman, claims that she killed her husband in self-defense. His three friends filed police reports incriminating her. My client said, among other felonies, they made their living as moonshiners. She will tell what she knows in return for your help in discrediting their testimony. She wants to get out of prison."

"Hank McKnight, I like your style. She's here in the jail, right? And Rogers knows where?"

"Correct."

"Don't say another word about it until I get Parker in here. You came to the right office. In addition to my white policemen I have a colored detail. We'll use them both and Parker will coordinate the investigation."

"I prefer to use the word 'Negro.' Is Parker a Negro?"

"I use the word 'Negro' too but officially they're 'colored.' Parker is white. For their safety neither you nor your client will meet a Negro policeman. They won't last long on the street if the wrong people can identify them."

Cheryl appeared at the door. She had taken advantage of her break to apply fresh make up and she was carrying two ice cold six ounce Peachtree Colas. The thick returnable bottles sweated in the jail heat. "Here you go, gentlemen," she said, handing them the Peachtree Colas. She had wrapped them in napkins around the middle. "Anything else?"

"Thanks for the Peachtree Colas and, yes, I've got something else."

Cheryl reached for a steno pad from off her desk and turned to a clean page. "OK, I'm ready."

"First, tell Rogers I want Hank's client in this office as fast as he can make it happen. Type it up. I'll sign it." He paused for Cheryl to quit scribbling her shorthand. "Second, I want Parker in here. And third, I want you to check the duty board in case we need a deacons' meeting. Ask Parker to bring two chairs in here and damn General Sherman."

Cheryl laughed, "As always, yes, sir."

Dad was impressed. He knew a leader when he saw one and he saw one. He took a sip of his P.C. "I did not realize Patrolman Weatherford would get in touch with you so fast."

"He had to. I had him on an assignment. The guys on the street act up sometimes, it helps them deal with the stress of the job. He wanted to tell me he was taking a New York lawyer to jail since I'm from New York. You don't sound like you're from New York,"

"I'm not. I went to law school at Yale after the war. The patrolman joked that Yale was in New York."

"He knows better. I'm not from New York either. I'm from Chicago. Five men in my family were policeman. When I turned eighteen I tried to join the Chicago Police Department. The Captain told me they had limited out on McConnell's. He said if I was willing to move he could put me with a Captain in New York City that would bring me along fast. In the twenties they were looking for policeman that knew big cities but weren't known locally – "impartial" they called it."

"That makes sense."

"Yes, I was "impartial" and I got the job. I was given responsibility and rose to Captain. I put in twenty years on the New York force. The Atlanta Police lost so many men to the armed forces they offered me a great job. I am a Yankee but became family when I married a policeman's widow. It didn't hurt her father was a captain. Damnyankee stuck but it hasn't held me back. I think it helped me get the colored detail – only way to fight crime in the Negro slums. How about you?"

"I am not a Damnyankee but I married one. I am from Hampton County, Georgia and went to Georgia Tech. Some kind friends say I played football. My father did. I was on the team but my sport was fencing. I used saber. Something I picked up in Military school."

"Did you join up?"

"Navy pilot in the Pacific, my cavalry horse couldn't fly."

The captain grinned, "Yes, we have discovered our horses can't fly either. About once a month a police horse tries to fly. They usually land on a car. We can't afford them; the insurance on a police horse is more than on a patrol car. The department won't give them up. We still have some regular patrols and parade duty."

"I think people like to see them around. I know I do." Dad said.

"So they pulled Weatherford off police business to chauffer you so you wouldn't get rained on. It must be nice to be a lawyer."

"I had a slow start," Dad acknowledged. "Weatherford says you're the second best Captain, sounds like there's a story there."

"There is, and you've already heard it. I'm the best but Weatherford won't give the credit to a Damnyankee. Atlanta police hate General Sherman. Have you heard why?"

"No, I would guess burning the city down."

McConnell laughed, "Sherman is not hated for burning Atlanta, but for not burning the jail. He left our maze of dilapidated buildings as punishment to rebels. Are you Baptist?"

"No, Anglican."

"Sherman left two churches across the street unburned, one Catholic, the other Presbyterian. They say he left the jail for the Baptists. Jailors tell the prisoners that they can't have liquor in the jail because it's Baptist. We call meetings 'deacon meetings'. The Baptists on the force joke about it as much as anyone."

Detective Parker, a middle-aged man in a suit brought two straight back chairs. An athletic man, Parker wore a suit and tie. His brown hair was short but his sideburns were long for a policeman. His left sideburn partially hid a scar that ran down the left side of his face to below the ear.

"Hank McKnight, this is detective Scott Parker," McConnell introduced and the men shook hands.

"Hank, if you don't mind I will fill Parker in?"

"Sure, go ahead."

"Parker, Hank has a Negro woman in prison and she wants out. She is doing ten years for killing her husband and she claims self-defense. She says he was a moonshiner and his friends are still on the street. I told Hank if we could round them up and get a conviction I will vouch for her," Mack turned to explain to Dad. "Hank, moonshine accounts for most of the money financing the criminal crowd in the slums. We jump whenever we get a shot at a moonshiner."

The policemen were as excited as hounds with a sent of the fox; they were on the hunt. Ida Mae told Mack and Parker that her late husband's gang spent Friday afternoons gathering money and sugar bags to be exchanged for moonshine. The moonshiner operated in a dugout basement under a local house. The 'runners' delivered moonshine and brought back cash and corn and sugar in small quantities so as not to arouse suspicion. Nate's gang supplied sugar. The gas fire still ran at night under the cover of darkness. Mack listened without interruption and both he and Parker took notes. The prospect of a moonshine bust excited the two policemen. Dad and Ida Mae left Mack's office under strict instructions not to say another word about the matter.

Ida Mae returned to her cell and Dad came home to make his call to Dirk. After finding Dirk was unavailable, Dad called Dean Leyden at the Yale Law School. Dad talked to the Dean for almost an hour. They tried to evaluate Ida Mae's situation. Ida Mae was looking at life in prison or the hangman's noose based on the present set of facts. If her husband's cronies could be discredited, Ida Mae would have an improved case. It did not help that she did not come forward about the moonshine until she was in prison. The Dean suggested Dad hold the unsigned plea bargain. If things didn't improve, Dad should recommend Ida Mae sign it. She already had three and a half years invested in the plea bargain.

Chapter 5 Weekend

Friday was payday and Friday night cash laden Negros headed home. In the NIC controlled neighborhoods thieves, loan sharks, gamblers, prostitutes, moonshiners and worse lurked in the alleys, at bus stops and patrolling the sidewalks. The first crook to the prize often took all the money. Men with cash wanted moonshine, cigarettes and gambling in that order. If they were "lucky" they would have money for more mischief later in the night and if they were unlucky they would at least be drunk. Knife fights were a given and at Grady Hospital the evening shift began with stocking the treatment rooms with supplies for knife wounds. The one thing no one had to look for was trouble.

Captain McConnell's policemen were eager for action. They had the esprit de corps of a commando unit. McConnell wasted no time, he did not want the news to hit the street. He heard Ida Mae's story Thursday afternoon. That Friday his plain-clothes detectives from the colored detail found and followed Nate's old three-man gang. Fewer people walked in the rainy weather on the street making the policemen's work easier. To protect the identity of his colored policemen, Captain McConnell used white policemen to bust the still and arrested fifteen runners Saturday. The arrests included Blue Shoes, Boot Head, and Willie Rat.

Dad arrived home Monday afternoon hoping Dirk would be on time for the anticipated legal review of his progress. Mom left fresh flowers from Sunday's centerpiece on the table. A yellow legal pad, fountain pen, and a bottle of ink joined the table setting for drinks. Dirk walked through the door without knocking.

Dad jumped from his chair to greet Dirk, "Did you read about my still bust in the Sunday paper?"

"Your still bust?" said Dirk. "Hank, let me get in the door and sit down."

Dad was jubilant as if Tech beat Georgia. If there was such a thing as a moonshine bust pennant he would have waived one, "Get comfortable. I guess the bourbon you promised to bring is in the car."

"Oh, can it, Hank. You said arrive by five, and here I am, five minutes early." The two men shook hands and sat down. "Nice fragrance, flowers from your yard?"

"No, store bought. Too many gray days, Kate wanted to brighten things up."

"What's this about the busted moonshine still in the paper yesterday? Did your sixty year old moonshiner escape to brew again?" Dirk pulled off his gold wire rimmed glasses and placed them on the table. When they had settled, Dad lit a cigarette and Dirk a cigar. Dad rose and cracked the window and sat back down. As the smoke rose, Dad positioned ashtrays and Dirk twirled his ice cubes. "All right, Hank, I'm ready. What in tarnation are you into? And what makes you think I can get you out of it, if I even cared to?"

"Well, Dirk, since we last talked I have got my client out of prison and into the holding jail for colored women downtown. Judge Jackson delayed his Friday afternoon cases until today. By Saturday morning Captain McConnell arrested my client's late husband's three character witnesses. Now in jail, they face ironclad moonshine charges. They could get up two years on the chain gang. I asked the Judge to note the pending convictions both impeached them as character witnesses and confirmed the late Nate Reivers' bad character. This added credibility to my client's claims of maltreatment and that she acted in self-defense. This new evidence should be sufficient cause for him to grant a new trial."

When Dirk did not comment Dad added, "And my new best friend in the police department, Captain Mack McConnell, stood by to testify to the facts if need be. I have been on this case since Wednesday afternoon, how long do you think it would take a real criminal lawyer to get this far?"

"Don't ask me. I'm corporate now. Did McConnell say anything?"

"McConnell did not speak to the case," Dad continued. "The judge asked about the three in jail. McConnell said they had been caught red handed with plenty of evidence. McConnell mentioned they would be prosecuted alongside others arrested over the weekend. The judge congratulated McConnell and asked me to write an order for the new trial for his review. I have scribbled some notes on an order for your perusal."

"So the witnesses for the victim are impeached." Dirk muttered. He moved his thick hand to his brow as if shading his eyes from the light of the dining room chandelier and peered out. Whatever Dirk expected this wasn't it. "Are you thinking about taking this to trial?"

"No. Hell no, not in a million years. My job ends when I write this order," Dad shot back, shaking his head. "And I would not refer to Nate Reivers as the victim." Dad leaned back in his chair. He pulled his glasses from his coat pocket and put them on to study Dirk's expression. "My soon to be someone else's client suffered abuse, a life threatening fight, followed by three and a half undeserved years in jail."

"Good luck, Hank. You make sure Jackson understands you are done. You asked for my advice, you are creating work for the judge. He may want to keep you working too. He may send you and the case back to Judge Hightower. I would take any out Judge Jackson may give you to get your Negro woman out of the pokey. You make her understand her goal should be getting out first and get her record clear second. It will be a lot easier outside of prison to clear herself." Dirk took a big swallow of bourbon. He reached for his cigar propped in the ashtray. The two men sat smoking in comfortable silence. The mixed aroma of bourbon, burnt matches, cigarette and cigar smoke drifted through the house.

Dirk feared Dad was steaming full speed toward the rocky shoals of what could be a disastrous court case. He issued a warning, "I got to tell you, I don't see how much this improves things. A prosecutor will point out your client reported nothing of the gambling, abuse, or moonshining. He will try to make a jury believe she was involved. He will also have a butcher knife to wave in front of the jury. A knife used against an unarmed husband by a big black woman sitting in the dock. You told me yourself she had forearms big as ham hocks. Self-defense? She's done three and a half years. Add another one, maybe two for a new trial. By the time you are done you may be weighing four and a half to five more years minus a year or more time off for parole against a chance at life in prison or the gallows."

"The witnesses for the deceased are in jail. The church ladies and neighbors will vouch for Ida Mae."

"How many of those witnesses will show after some moonshiner's pal tells them he's going to blow their heads off? I'm trying to help you get a sense of your client's situation. It may be improved but it sure as Hell isn't good."

Mom called from the kitchen, "Little ears can hear you."

"Sorry Kate," Dirk called out. The men lightened their tone if not the language.

"Can your Negro woman do anything? How old is she and what education does she have?"

"Her name is Ida Mae Reivers. She is twenty-three years old, and she has a high school diploma. She took some nursing courses down state. I think she said at Milledgeville. She worked as a shirt presser in Atlanta. She is my client, not my Negro woman," Dad answered.

"Welcome to criminal law. Her dead husband and his 'going to jail friends' may have more friends. If you get her out; you need to get her clear back to Milledgeville or wherever she came from. They will likely try to murder her first chance they get."

"Murder her?"

"Either for killing their pal or for sending them up to prison. They'll likely find out. I learned my law on the criminal side. When I got married and had kids I moved out to the country, bought horses, and accepted my Peachtree Cola corporate job. Awful things happen in some neighborhoods. You can't fathom how bad, despicable as anything you saw in the war, maybe worse. Among the Negroes, well, it can get unspeakable. Yep, you got to get her clear." Dirk watched Dad's countenance fade from ebullient and victorious to a more somber expression.

"Well, Dirk, pour another cause I am celebrating."

"Me too. I'm going to have to tell Alice, McKnight wouldn't let me leave after one drink. Yep, I may have to file a lawsuit. I was restrained and made to imbibe spirits against my will, which was detrimental to my health."

"Detrimental to your health?"

"Yes, Alice will kick my boney backside when I come home with my lame excuse. I consider her kicking my tail detrimental to my health. And speaking of asses, you better cover yours. Let me see your notes. Include that Jackson will appoint another pro bono lawyer."

Dad slid the yellow pad across the table.

Dirk pulled his wire rim glasses on and drew the sidepieces around his ears. "Understand this document will represent the total corpus of your communication with him. No phone calls, letters, don't say boo turkey squat if you pass him in the hallway. He may have more problems than you do with this one. You may not hear back from the judge for six months to a year and that's OK. Whatever he does it will be perfect."

They continued talking, drinking, smoking, and discussing the order until Mom entered to announce dinner. Dad begged for a few minutes more. "Sweetheart, I have placed Dirk in danger by pouring a couple of new drinks."

"Yes, I am afraid so. Alice is not as sympathetic to my receiving payment in kind from Hank as you might think."

"I am on Alice's side," Mom said as she entered the dining room. "And it is time for three boys to have their dinner."

Dirk replied, "Not a problem, Kate." He swilled down his bourbon and said, "Thanks for the update, Hank. Keep me informed. Remember to accept any conditions to get her out and then work on the rest."

"Got it, Dirk," said Dad, rising to walk Dirk to the door. "Give Alice our love."

Mom called the children down for supper. I would not hear the name Ida Mae again for months.

Chapter 6 Jeb

My world began to collide more often with Dad's world in peculiar and unexpected ways. I was too young to accompany Dad but he needed a witness.

Mom, a petite blonde from "up North," caught a green light into "Polite" society through Dad, All Apostles Church, and the Daisy Garden Club. While Dad and the Almighty played a role, the ladies of the Garden Club Southernized her and taught her how to grow flowers too. In Georgia's piedmont climate flowers of all varieties bloomed from early spring to autumn. Gardening was the top hobby and activity for the ladies and garden clubs proliferated. The ladies took it seriously if it was in the yard and it didn't move it was either painted or landscaped or both. Atlanta was named 'the dogwood city' after the small flowering tree. Every home had at least one dogwood and many enthusiastic gardeners lined the road or driveway with them.

Our home on Nancy Creek Road was in gentrified northwest Atlanta. Buckhead, the closest municipality, was five miles away down West Paces Ferry Road, which was lined with some of the grandest houses in Atlanta. The juggernaut of Atlanta growth was on the way and small farms and pastureland sold for home lots. The growing numbers of homes were set amidst towering old growth pines and oaks. From any elevation or prominence the area looked so much like a forest visitors were often surprised to find the homes nestled among the trees.

The McKnight's one and a half story Early-American style home was furnished in the same style and included some heirloom furniture that dated back to the 1800's. With three boys and two dachshunds in the house it wasn't long before all the furniture looked like antiques. A large grassy side yard on the three-acre lot worked for football and baseball games. The boarder of azaleas was problematical and a base runner could not advance if the ball got lost in the bushes. The balance of the lot was too heavily wooded for sports but worked well for tag, capture the flag, and hide and seek. A child hidden under the ellie agnes bushes could not be found until a snake or hunger forced them into the open. The innumerable tall pines provided shade and in spring the yellow mantel of pollen could only be dissipated by several thunderstorms.

Not all roads were paved. Nancy Creek Road was gravel in a bed of hardened tar at the McKnight end, paved for a few blocks in the middle and gravel over red clay at the other end. Across from Colonel Carter's two hundred acre tract stood the Hamilton's authentic plantation house with stables on twenty acres and a fresh water pool continuously fed by an artesian well. Mrs. Hamilton could not have been more of a southern belle if she wore a hoop skirt. She graciously invited the neighbors swimming. It was a treat that I could hardly bear as the artesian water was so cold year round that even on the hottest summer days my teeth would chatter.

TV's and phones were available in homes but not widely used. Friends dropped in unannounced and were cheerfully received. Evening walks often lead to invitations for an immediate visit from passing neighbors. In the evening Dad often had bourbon with friends in the dining room or out on the heavily landscaped patio. He tried to keep the liquor cabinet stocked. Lively conversations about everything from the communists to parking meters in Buckhead punctuated the impromptu cocktail circuit. Being neighbors ran deep for my parents and the other children of the depression and the veterans of World War II. They faced hardships, crime and general civic responsibility with a do-it-ourselves attitude and self-reliance.

In addition to being a pair of ears and eyes on the steps I had a life out side the home as a student. Formal training for future cavalry officers began at Colonel Carter's stables, tennis courts, swimming pool, and nursery school, which was located a half-mile down Nancy Creek Road from our house. Colonel Carter was in the Georgia Militia Reserves. Old Plantation at one time covered at least a thousand acres. General Sherman's Yankees crossed the Chattahoochee River at Paces Ferry but did not burn the original plantation house, which the Hamilton's owned with their frigid pool.

Colonel Carter bought the last four hundred acres of farmland, woodland and pasture at auction. He built a stately home and donated two hundred undeveloped acres east of Nancy Creek – the wide stream not the road - to Martha Washington School for Girls and Downtown Presbyterian School. He kept the operating nursery school and stables. This was important to me because this is where I went to ride. My yet to be renowned steed, Cookie Dough, saw me once a week. Colonel Carter taught us that horses smell like transportation and that's a good thing, better than many cars and all busses. It took twenty minutes for the grown ups to mount and dismount the other four-year-old horse people. I took sugar cubes for Cookie Dough. The longer the mounting time the less likely it was Cookie Dough would get both sugar cubes.

Some Georgia Militia mounts were stabled there. Once a month the nursery school students took turns riding around the quarter mile track in a real four horse drawn stagecoach. After a few laps the Georgia Militia disguised as outlaws or Indians would attack the stagecoach only to be chased off by more Militia cavalry. After a year even the dumbest four year old had to wonder why the Indians chased the stagecoach in a circle? The heathens only needed to wait for it to come back around? They never caught on.

The cavalry always caught them. I noticed that by the time moms came to pick up the Indians were eating fried chicken and drinking firewater with their captors.

A downside to becoming school age was the two-foot long fraternity paddle my parents judged age-appropriate punishment. My neighbors' Dad down the street used a two-foot long razor strop on his boys. We commiserated. The person I feared most was Dad and the thing I feared most was the paddle. Any disobedience was punished including whining or crying. Also as the oldest I received paddling for not setting a good example, not sharing, or not taking action to help. When I left blood on the saddle I had to go to the doctor. The pediatrician also noted black bruises on my butt. He reprimanded Dad. Like a good cavalry officer I carried out orders without excuse or regard to the peril to my life – or another paddling.

The following fall, 1954, my parents took me to meet Mrs. Boyette, the principal at Hewlett Nursery School on West Wesley Road. She was a tall blonde Nordic looking woman who had worked at the school for twenty years. She wore a canary yellow dress with white patent leather belt that matched shoes. I wore a collared shirt and shorts. I crew cut brown hair and eyes and my father's lean build. We had a nice chat. Though I was small for my age and not yet five due to class size I was enrolled in the five-year-old pre-kindergarten Mrs. Boyette promised I would fit right in. There was a dress code. Boys had short hair and wore shorts or jeans. Girls had long hair and wore dresses year round with tights to stay warm in winter.

The pre-K classroom doors locked from both sides - Miss Jean and Miss Victoria, two just out of college teachers, could not escape the five-year-olds. We started the day with Prayer and a Bible story. We learned the Twenty-Third Psalm, the Golden Rule, the Ten Commandments, and some geniuses learned the books of the Bible, all sixty-six. Miss Victoria placed a gold stick-um star next to your name. Lenard cried when his first recitation of the Minor Prophets went awry. I told him not to worry – people called them Minor for a reason.

Bible stories taught us what to believe. To do right you had to believe right. "Disbelief" was what the Philistines had, it was like a lie only harder to overcome. After our Bible story we did something artistic. Finger-painting was my favorite. We stuck our fingers in bowls of paint and smeared globs of paint on paper to create art. We used the larger version of crayons for cleaner art. Crayola assured teachers that children could not break their fat crayons. We rose to the challenge.

At the appointed time for recess students cleaned their space, put away art supplies, hung up smocks, and washed hands. This process took the average girl about ten minutes and the average boy about ten seconds. I excelled in getting out the door. Miss Jean would open the door to the playground and accompany the boys and any speedy girl out. Miss Victoria would remain behind to coax the more serious artists to complete their masterpieces. The playground was fenced to protect woodland animals and slow moving adults. The mayhem was akin to letting thirty bucking broncos out of the shoots at once.

When my classmates slowed to subsonic speeds in their recess activities, we would be called in for our snack. Snack consisted of two things only a captive would consume, a liquid, orange in color but not orange juice, and shortening bread, which was not quite hard enough to break a kids tooth. At the peak of the sugar rush teachers announced naptime. The teachers needed a break.

After nap we had a story. When Miss Victoria asked the gifted young minds seated before her about the value of George Washington telling the truth, she got several answers. George did not want to break the Ten Commandments. George might never have been elected president. I offered that had George lied he might have grown up to be "no damn good." Some of the girls gasped, covering their mouths. The boys bobbed up and down in vigorous agreement. My grown up comment cost me time in the chair facing the corner and a paddling at home. One thing Mom did not ask was where I had heard it.

The advent of television turned concept of "pretend" into a daily topic. Cowboys shot on TV did not actually die they were only "pretending." Boys were asked to "pretend" to be fathers and the girls, mothers. Our Dad's worked away from the house and our Moms "kept house." "Pretend house" was popular with the girls. Boys did mimic their fathers in directing pretend children to do their chores. Most children came from families a generation or two off the farm. I fed the livestock, our two dachshunds. The dogs whined the five minutes it took me to open two tin cans of dog food with a manual can opener. My hands grew stronger than vice grip pliers.

The teachers added an eleventh commandment. If God writes another Bible, He will surely add, "Thou Shall Not Be Impolite." More children sat in the corner for impoliteness than for stealing, murdering, coveting, or committing adultery combined.

The girls played hide and seek at recess. Only a hand full of trees and bushes offered hiding spots. Then there was a large girl named Grace. Two or three girls could hide behind Grace. But according to Miss Victoria it was impolite to call her by her nickname, "Abundant Grace." When Earl was finger painting with blue paint, he unconsciously rubbed his nose leaving the telltale blue paint. After that we started calling him "Blue Boogers." This too turned out to be impolite. The one nickname that was not impolite was Joey's. His nickname was "Saint Joe." He was not named after the Saint but after the Catholic hospital where he was born. Given the rest of the kids it was good to have one saint in the bunch.

The most impolite offense was physically hurting someone else. Freddie Madison, Tall Ed, and Marvin, the three big boys, brought slingshots to school. Billy Preston, a small boy, caught a pebble in the side of the head about an inch from his eye leaving a welt. Billy was short and round so his bruise did not appear swollen. Miss Victoria told the boys to apologize to Billy and Mrs. Hewett was summoned from the big school in Buckhead. She was tall with short grey hair and clear blue eyes. She wore matching grey skirt and jacket with a white blouse and colorful scarf. She had a business like demeanor and her footfall on the porch quieted all. After she looked at Billy she met with the three boys, and the teachers in the lunchroom. Afterwards a doctor declared Billy "OK." Miss Hewett called the parents and told them not to return their boys to school.

The three big boys and their parents gathered to persuade my father to represent them to Mrs. Hewett. They claimed it was an unfortunate accident and their boys had apologized and deserved to be returned to school. This suggestion was approved by Dad, Billy and me, but, not Mr. Preston who wanted to sue everyone.

Dad presented the slingshot trio's case. He said the three boys confessed and apologized under "duress" from their teachers. Only the three shooters could say what they aimed at and they claimed it was an accident. So Dad suggested they all give thanks Billy was not seriously injured and move on without slingshots at school.

After a closed-door consultation Mrs. Hewett emerged with an icy stare that would have frosted a beer mug. She coldly pronounced that the boys would be permitted to finish school but Freddie, owner of the slingshots, would not return in the fall. Mr. Preston would not bring a lawsuit against the Madisons. But Mr. Preston's lawyer worked out an agreement with the school lawyer and Billy Preston would go to school for free.

Dad tried to be the peacemaker. Freddie could not come back to school and Billy's Dad could not sue the Madisons. Both sides of the fracas hated us. I thought "Blessed be the peacemakers" must apply to the hereafter.

***

My other learning venue was at home. We had a brand new babysitter the Philco TV. This technological breakthrough was half the size of a refrigerator. We learned all the important things in life from TV. Good cowboys did not shoot in the back, or hit from behind. Fistfights with broken furniture went with cowboys like boots and six-shooters. To save the house from destruction Dad spent $9.95 on four boxing gloves. Boys who wanted to fight grabbed the gloves and headed outside. There was no ring so trees, bushes and the stream came into play. Mom spanked us for fighting inside the house but not outside.

Guns were a serious matter even our toy cap pistols were not to be pointed at any living thing. When loaded with a roll of caps the pistols could be fire fifty times making a cracking noise and producing a blue cloud of gun smoke like a real pistol. All other guns except Poppa Lee's shotgun were locked away. His old Damascus barrel twelve gauge was a hang on the wall antique; only it leaned on the wall in a hall closet. The gun was still operational the exterior hammers could be pulled back and "fired" by pulling the double triggers. The heavy gun weighed over seven pounds but on rainy days we were allowed to drag it out, rest it across a chair and aim it at imaginary bad guys caught out in the rain in our yard. Dad seldom found time to hunt but on the fourth of July neighbors gathered and rifles, shotguns and pistols were brought out and shot. At these outings we were taught about guns and gun safety.

In addition to watching anything to do with cowboys, cavalry and knights – the McKnight's namesakes, the boys watched Lassie, Rin Tin Tin and reruns of Shirley Temple Movies. Lassie and Rin Tin Tin were adventure shows about boys and their dogs. Jeff had Lassie a Collie and Rusty owned Rin Tin Tin, a German shepherd. Neither Jeff nor Rusty had a father. Jeff lived with his mother and grandfather in a small farming community. The U.S. cavalry adopted Rusty and his dog after Indians killed his parents.

Rusty got to live at the fort and had his own uniform and horse and did not have to go to school!

Every week these two boys aided by their incredible dogs saved the day, usually after bumbling adults had failed. The boys and dogs were able to see and understand things adults just couldn't seem to grasp. When "bad men" threatened the neighbors Lassie and Jeff were the 1950's equivalent of "dial 911" they handled it. When the Indians had the cavalry surrounded. Thank goodness Rin Tin Tin could get back to the fort tell Rusty to send the other troopers to save the day. Heady stuff. If those boys could do it so could I. Though I was smaller than Jeff and Rusty I did have two dachshunds, Rascal and Biscuit, what we lacked in size we made up for in numbers.

While I preferred the boys and dogs on TV as role models I was profoundly impacted by Shirley Temple movies. The feature length films allowed much more time for character development and intrigue. In 'Heidi' she was an orphaned girl victimized by her aunt and the evil housekeeper, appropriately named Fraulein Rottenmeier. Heidi overcomes the two sinister adult women. She wins over the father of an invalid girl by teaching the girl to walk and exposing the evil women. He reunites her with her beloved grandfather and all is well. She is a girl and she doesn't even have a dog. She started in movies at age three. The year she turned five she acted as a star along side Hollywood's best actors in ten feature length movies. She repeatedly took action to save the day when adults had failed. Hollywood raised the bar for child behavior. Rather than live down to typical adult expectations I was going to live up to Hollywood standards. I asked the question, "Why not me?"

Dad unintentionally provided more motivation for my precocious behavior since he encouraged action and punished inaction so I was audacious by training. I possessed a razor sharp memory, a nearly twin brother and two dachshunds. I mused that Nancy Creek Road and the world beyond would know Jeb Lee McKnight was the equal if not better than Jeff and Rusty on TV.

The profound abilities of dogs and children portrayed on TV impressed me and I "tried it at home." After my fifth birthday, two years behind Shirley Temple, I started my climb to stardom. I took action. My first heroic deed performed for adult adulation was in the kitchen. I decided to show Mom I could make scrambled eggs for breakfast. Step one, when Mom went for the paper I locked the door behind her. With the help of two brothers, I spilled everything available to be spilled and broken numerous eggs that fell from the carton to the floor. I thought fast. I quickly ordered Rascal and Biscuit to lick up the broken eggs off the floor. They immediately understood and lapped up a dozen eggs in no time.

Absent a supply of eggs I improvised, plan B. I went to my fall back recipe PB & J on toast. I succeeded in making four pieces of toast. By standing on my bench and turning the open jars on their sides I was able to simultaneously cover the countertop and four pieces of toast with peanut butter and grape jelly. I handed two pieces down to my brothers. Billy only licked his. I saved a piece for Mom and ate my own.

My efforts to reinsert the spilled PB & J into the jars made the mess on the counter worse. Again I improvised with my dogs. Travis and I each grabbed an end of Rascal and hoisted him to the counter top. The talented dog cleaned the counter top in seconds but in his zeal to clean the outside of the peanut butter jar he pushed it into the sink and it broke. I had fixed breakfast and cleaned up.

Meanwhile Mom found our aluminum ladder and climbed in an upstairs window. Mom always looked on the bright side, she had been out of the house for an hour and the boys were still alive. Exhausted by her climb, she was too tired to spank us. She took the stranded Rascal off the counter top, wiped our faces and sent us to watch TV. I declared victory and moved on, "Well, boys, I fixed y'all a nice breakfast and now it's time for TV. Follow me." Billy remained behind for additional cleaning. He was wearing more PB & J than he ate.

Two important people came to the house after my triumphant breakfast preparation. The Lockhart's maid came to borrow sugar and stayed to help clean up. Dr. Peter Flannigan stopped by to see his favorite boys. Mom asked him to examine us to see if we had eaten any harmful thing in her unplanned absence. Doctor Flannigan explained we appeared healthy, but he had concerns about Mom. After a brief exam he pronounced her pregnant and in need of a nap. He called Alice Lockhart on our phone and explained the situation. He asked Alice if she could be spare Hattie, her maid, longer. Hattie stayed while Mom slept.

Dad reasoned, often correctly, if the younger children got into mischief it was my fault and I would be paddled. All had ended well and he got the good news of another child on the way. Mom did not understand how the door got locked behind her and neither Travis nor Billy could turn the large brass handle. I was fixing breakfast. Not only was I not paddled, the ever understanding Dr. Flannigan had praised me for fixing breakfast in my mother's absence. I would try for greater things.

Dr. Flannigan, also a neighbor and my parents' dear friend, took it upon himself to prescribe a maid for my Mom. Dad tried to dodge the prescription citing financial strain. Pete was not to be denied. A lady who lived across the street from Miss Hewett's School had offered to pay Dr. Flannigan to let her carpool with him downtown to her job. Pete's irregular schedule made it impossible for him. He said Dad could have the funds for a maid for a stop on his established route to work. It was, as they say, too good to be true.

Pete came by one evening to take Dad to meet the lady, they brought her back by the house to meet Mom. Candice, A.K.A. Candy Beerbohm, had divorced her husband. The man left town, she got the house, kids, and the money. In 1954, the divorcee siren blared louder than the six-foot tall air raid siren on top of Morris Brandon School. It wasn't done.

Candy's critics referred to her as a painted woman. "Painted" because she wore more make up than they did, and "woman" as opposed to "lady." Pete assured Mom, Candy's affections had landed on a bachelor doctor. Furthermore, she would receive, by prescription, a maid.

Candy was also introduced to the McKnight children.

I asked the obvious question, "Can you shoot a rifle?"

"Well, I have never tried."

Mom asked, "Jeb, why do you ask?"

"Dad said he has to drive fast so Indians and robbers can't catch him. I don't think she has enough room on her shoulder for the shotgun." The buxom Candy had little room for the butt of a gun. I continued, "Girls can shoot. Dale Evans, Roy Rogers' girlfriend, can shoot a rifle."

Pete recovered, "Your father will no longer be taking the route that requires a shotgun or fast driving. The cavalry has cleared Indians and robbers off the road all the way down town." It must have been true for neither Indians nor robbers attacked Dad and Mrs. Beerbohm.

In 1954 Dad owned a red convertible MG. The location of Candy's driveway at the entrance to Miss Hewett's School could not have been worse. Dad had to pick her up as cars delivering children turned into the school. The siren still blasted.

One morning, as I walked down the porch, I heard two teachers remark as Dad picked up Candy. Considering it rude to honk, he walked to the door. The teachers saw the couple coming down Candy's front walkway to the car. "Well, would you look at those two? I bet he's been there all night playing patty cake."

"No, he's married and has a child here in the Pre-K."

"What is a married man doing with a red sports car? I bet he's looking to play patty cake and she's available to play."

I chirped up. "That's my Dad's MG, they're made in England. They come on a boat because there is not a road to America from England. The top comes off."

One teacher said, "Boys don't take long to learn cars."

They asked me some forgettable questions, but the idea of Dad playing patty cake stuck. Several things happened after I repeated their comments at home. My parents had a discussion about the ramifications of what "they said." Dad moved the pickup location, hired a maid, and said he would trade the MG after the baby came.

Hattie, the Lockhart's maid, began to work for us one day a week. She was a large Negro woman, but not energetic. The Lockharts had two low maintenance teenage girls. Hattie found it difficult to adjust to the amount of work required to clean up after three boys. We played outside and we brought dirt inside. The talent required getting extremely dirty deserved some sort of an award. A small stream ran through the neighborhood, feeding many decorative ponds. Boys could catch frogs and tadpoles at the water's edge. The mud, sand, and gravel from the streambed provided an endless supply of materials for the construction of dams, bridges, and forts. The boys' ability to grind this mud into any piece of outerwear added to the process of sorting clothes for the laundry. Our laundry included three bins, whites, colors, and destroyed. Mom may have considered the option, but she never discarded a boy as too dirty.

Chapter 7 Mystery

"The Bus" arrived at four-thirty in the afternoon at the corner of Nancy Creek and Ridgewood Road. It retrieved about fifteen Negroes working as domestic servants in the area. The bus whisked them away to a mysterious other world.

Our wish to ride the bus was fulfilled one morning when we took the Buick to be serviced in Buckhead and Mom, Travis and I road the bus home. Buckhead was about eight miles due north of Atlanta on Peachtree Road. The country come to city municipality got its name from a deer buck's head that was nailed to a tree where Roswell Road forked off from Peachtree. Paces Ferry Road crossed there making five points and within blocks were a super market, fire station, combination cabstand and police station, and the Ida Williams Public Library, also, at Baggarly Park there were baseball fields and a Women's Club. If there were not ten big churches there were twenty. Buckhead was the spiritual, cultural, intellectual, and social epicenter of North Fulton County.

The bus stop was on the northbound side of Roswell Road across from the movie theater. We boarded the bus and our driver announced, "The Number 4 Ridgewood West Wesley is underway. Please stay seated and don't put objects or arms out the windows." The diesel engine strained and we pulled out, circling to the left around the block. The bus turned down Irby Street and the smell of fresh bread from Henri's bakery came through the open windows. Behind the theater on Early Street the bicycle shop displayed all sizes and colors of bikes. On the other side of the street was the blacksmith shop. A few saddled horses stood beside their owners in a line for the farrier to shoe them. As we passed the large opening in the barn-like structure we could see the blacksmith as he hammered out a horseshoe on the anvil. Further back in the shop we could see a welder, the blue flame from his torch arched over the metal.

The bus turned right on mansion-lined West Paces Ferry before turning left down humbler Moore's Mill Road. The five-mile trip lasted about twenty minutes. On Moore's mill we caught an unpleasant scent through the open windows. Buckhead was still country populated by squirrels, possums, foxes and deer, most were fast and nimble – but some were roadkill. We got off the bus at the corner of Ridgewood and made the short walk down Nancy Creek Road to our home. Our dachshund dogs ran their short little legs down the driveway to meet us. Learning the route of the 4 Ridgewood West Wesley filled an important gap in my education and would have an impact within days of my first bus ride.

Across form the bus stop grading and construction had replaced the three horses next door. After the carpenters left each day, Travis and I would inspect the house like it was our job. On Friday we heard a maid hollering at the bus driver as she emerged from a thicket of bushes. We ran up to Ridgewood Road to see the commotion. The bus driver told the Negro woman he would get fired if he stopped anywhere but a designated bus stop. She responded that she could walk home. We assured her Dad would give her a ride.

As we ran for home we saw Dad's red MG driving down Nancy Creek. We explained the situation; Dad was aggravated the bus driver left the maid. He ordered Travis and me into Mom's Green Buick sitting in the driveway. The top was down in the mild weather. We found the maid who assured Dad she could walk. Dad urged her to get in the front seat and again she protested. She did not want to ride in the front seat beside a white man. At Dad's insistence she got in the front seat of the car.

Dad, like us, assumed she was talking about walking to Buckhead, the bus's final destination, five miles away. She identified herself as Effie, the Preston's maid. She was past middle age and heavy set. She did not look like she could easily manage a walk to Buckhead. Dad stopped at the Preston's house and explained the situation. Mrs. Preston was short and round like her son, Billy, and she had gray hair with white streaks. She stated she did not drive but her maid did not live far. I could tell by Dad's expression he was getting madder by the minute. We pulled away.

"Why wouldn't the bus driver pick you up?" He asked the maid as he drove.

"He says you got to be at a bus stop or he can't stop."

"Would he stop for a white person?"

"I don't know. I ain't never seen a white person on the bus."

"He would have." Dad thought out loud.

"It don't matter I don't live far." Effie assured Dad.

"Mrs. Preston doesn't drive?"

"Not to my neighborhood."

Dad turned off West Wesley Road over to West Paces Ferry Road, which was the shortest route to the bus stop in Buckhead. The maid said she had never seen the road before. Dad explained it ended up in the same place. When he let her out in Buckhead, she said she did not recognize where she was. Dad offered to take her to a place she recognized, but she refused to get back in the car. Pedestrians stared in disbelief. Everyone felt embarrassed. The maid said to leave her and she would be fine. Travis and

I showed our puzzled father the bus route on the way home. Dad believed she could find her way. Not so.

Saturday afternoon, when her maid failed to show up for a party preparation, Mrs. Preston contacted Dad. She explained to Dad their maid indeed lived a mile away on a dirt road off Margaret Mitchell Drive. Mr. Preston sent someone who worked for him to search for her. They discovered she did not return home Friday, the day we drove her to Buckhead. The maid's children and neighbors pleaded with Mr. Preston's employee for help.

The Prestons called and Dad immediately took Mom's Buick with the top down and the two of us drove to Clarendale Drive. The afternoon sun still illuminated the unpainted clapboard houses lining the red clay dirt road. The landscape was like the poorest farm community in Georgia. Dad stared in disbelief. He had no idea a Negro neighborhood existed within a mile of our home. The fact of our good deed gone bad stared us in the face. As we started down the road a Negro man called out, "Don't go down there. Them niggers down there is bad to the bone. Turn around in my driveway or there will be trouble."

Dad was undaunted. On Poppa's farm he picked Negroes up for work or brought the doctor to similar neighborhoods without incident. Then Negro men and women filled the road and surrounded the car near the dead end.

A smiling young Negro in a collared gray shirt walked to our car and assured Dad he could get us through without trouble. He called out to another youth, "I'll be Luther, you be Popcorn."

"We be your friends," Popcorn assured us. I was young enough to hope they would be friends.

They let us move forward and Dad turned the car around at the end of the road. He rolled up his window and told me to do the same. Then he pushed the button to raise the convertible top. But our new "friends" had run along beside the car and held the top down. Some younger Negroes blocked the road and pushed some women and children into the road. Dad was forced to stop the car. Negroes of all ages formed a menacing crowd around us in front of the white clapboard Holy Apostles Church. I hoped for a moment in their Christian charity.

The mature Negroes argued among themselves. Many called to let us pass while the younger Negroes wanted the car. The arguing crowd on his side of the car distracted Dad.

Popcorn, on my side of the car, showed me a kitchen knife, "This knife be sharp as your Daddy's razor."

When I looked away Popcorn reached over the rolled up window unlocked the door and opened it. He put the knife flat against my throat with the blade side up. "Don't move white boy."

I heard a voice from the crowd say, "You done it now."

I looked up into the clear blue sky thinking I might be going to heaven. When I looked back down I felt the knife shave into my neck. It stung but I could not pull away.

They asked Dad to give them his gun. "I don't have a gun."

A Negro shouted, "Fool! Don't believe him! All white men carry guns!" The knife stayed on my throat.

Negroes searched for a gun in the glove box, trunk, and looked under the seat. Then they made Dad empty his pockets and give them his family ring and money clip both inherited from Poppa. I think his finger would have been removed to get his stuck wedding ring. Cooler heads prevailed and the wedding ring was judged too small to steal. When Dad handed over the car keys, they pulled us from the car.

Luther and Popcorn got in the car. They started it. A big boned Negro woman replaced the crowd and blocked the road. She scolded Luther and Popcorn. She claimed to have a real job and she had assisted many there. A number of women agreed. Two or three responsible looking women joined her in the middle of the road.

Dad instructed me to stay where I had been pulled from the car on the opposite side of the road from him. A Negro boy a little taller than me stood next to his mother. She was dressed in a green uniform and matching apron. They stood a few feet from me to see the commotion. I noticed the boy looking me over. He had the size advantage and began pushing me saying, "You in the wrong place."

I responded with the obvious, "We would like to leave." As I spoke I noticed Dad look over from the cacophony of the crowd and the boy pushed me again.

I knew the pushing would continue until I took action. He became a beneficiary of my boxing workouts. When he smiled and looked around for approval, I swung hard with my right fist. "Owwww," he cried as the punch landed into the front of his right shoulder. "That white boy hit me." And he began to cry.

"You pushed him first," his mother said as he went behind her, I was amazed at her evenness in the situation.

Some Negroes watched our scuffle and one called out, "That white boy hit LaVonn."

"LaVonn pushed him first. You tend to your own business," the Mom replied.

The big Negro woman took charge of the situation again. She scolded the crowd like she was their Momma. Then she fussed at the young men about the car. Everyone shouted. Before I had seen Negroes as helpful and polite, in that moment I only saw knife blades and angry faces. They screamed at each other with ferocity. The name-calling intensified.

"Get out of their car, you stupid niggers!"

"The white man getting what he deserve driving down here!"

"Shut up fool!"

"You shut up! Nigger fool. What you think they do to me if I drive through their neighborhood."

"Fool you ain't got no car to drive through nobody's neighborhood."

Luther laughing, "I got one now."

"You dumb niggers better listen to her," another Negro woman said, "She know what she talking about, the Klan gonna come down here."

Looking at Dad, "You in the Klan?"

"No, I'm here..." and Dad tried to explain his mission but was shouted down.

"You ain't got no say here, white man. You the wrong color here and we ain't got no whites only water fountain for you." Laughter followed.

The Negro woman in the road again ordered the aggressive young men to leave us alone. Dad again motioned for me to stay put and he faced the crowd gathered on his side of the dirt road.

"Take the car and let us walk out of here," Dad said.

The woman standing in the front of car scolded the men. "If you hurt them, I'll move away from here. Who you think paid the doctor when your baby girl was sick. I pay the bills around here."

"She weren't my baby," said Popcorn brandishing his knife.

"Is too your baby," another woman said. "You don't let no other man around me."

"You heard the man," Luther said from behind the wheel. "He want us to take his car. We want to take a ride, we be back."

Another Negro showing a knife called out, "That don't do nothing for me. I don't want no car ride, I want another ride."

"Come on, let's go. I'll take a swing on your tree," a woman said willing and laughing.

"Go own with your bad self," he responded disinterested. "I don't want you right this minute," he said and looking around. "I can ride her anytime." Other men snickered then looking at the woman in front of the car. He added, "I need to teach you a lesson."

"Oh Lord," she said as he advanced toward her, knife in hand. "Ain't nobody going to help me?"

Some women responded, "We can't do nothing. We ain't got no knife."

He began pushing her toward a house in the second row on my side of the street. She did not resist. He said he wanted her to scream and she began to holler but did not appear troubled at all. They covered the short distance to the house. Then I heard him tell her to open the windows so people could hear. She continued to holler but she did not sound scared.

Luther and Popcorn drove off laughing. Many in the crowd strolled away, they talked and laughed as if nothing happened.

A barefoot girl wearing a faded shirtdress looked at the house where the woman hollered. "Nobody would do me that way." Two other women ignoring the racket passed her by, "They do you that way soon enough."

"No they won't," she said in a troubled tone.

"Who your Daddy is?"

"You know I ain't got no Daddy."

"And that's why they gonna do what they want. You'll find out."

The other woman commented, "Leave that child alone. Nobody got a Daddy here. That's why we stays here."

"Nobody but the preacher's kids...And we ain't sure about them," another chuckled.

Dad crossed the dirt road to me and we began walking.

The crowd dissipated. Some older men who had stood back from the crowd asked Dad where he was trying to go. They assumed he was lost. When Dad explained he was trying to find the Preston's maid some became angry again.

The preacher appeared. He was a white haired Negro wearing a black suit. He resolutely yelled up the road at the men to leave us alone. Then he called to the still hollering woman to shut up. People obeyed because of loss interest in the fracas more than out of respect. He had been in a home no more than twenty yards away. When the anger of the crowd had subsided he made his dramatic entrance. As far as we were concerned he was offering an umbrella after the storm.

The whole situation had been like a scary TV show. And I thought some of the action was "pretend" to scare us. I quietly mentioned to Dad I thought Negro woman and the man attacking her were "pretending." He agreed. But they did use real knives, my neck seeped real blood and they stole the car and valuables. Dad took a closer look at my neck.

"Jeb, I hate the man cut you but it's just a scratch you'll be fine in no time."

"Yes, sir." This terse conversation ended speculation about serious injury.

We walked back up the hill and then toward West Wesley. I told Dad I was sorry I could not crank my window up. I asked if those people went to church. He said we could talk later. The same Negro man at the top of the hill called out in angry tones, "I told you not to go down there, fool. You going to bring trouble on us."

When we reached West Wesley Road the two Negroes in Mom's car sped by. A little bit later they came back and stopped. They argued in front of us.

"Mister, if you don't tell the Klan or the Police, we will give you back your car," Popcorn said.

"I want my ring and money clip. They belonged to my grandfather," Dad answered.

"You want a lot for a man who's walking," Luther said.

"You can keep the money."

"Mister, we can keep it all," Popcorn chuckled.

"You'll get caught."

"He's right. Give him the stuff and let's keep the money," Luther said. He got out and handed Dad the keys.

They gave Dad the ring, but Luther kept the money clip and split the money with Popcorn.

The temperature cooled as the sun set. Dad asked me if I was OK. "Yes," Dad insisted we not tell Mom. He drove in silence immersed in his own thoughts. It was dark when we arrived home and supper was on the table. Dad licked his handkerchief and wiped blood off my neck.

"Try to hold your head still, Jebby, and your neck won't bleed." When he was satisfied it was not seeping blood, we went inside.

Mom served dinner as we walked in the door. She did not notice my cut until afterwards. When she cleared my plate from the table she gasped. "Jeb, whatever happened to you?"

"Oh, nothing,"

"Your neck is cut," Mom insisted.

"It is?"

"Go look in the mirror."

The Negro didn't exaggerate the sharpness of his knife. A three-inch long thin flap of skin covered a red line of blood. The cut ran diagonally downward from my jugular toward my Adams apple.

"Jeb Lee McKnight, come back in here." Being called by my whole name was not a good thing. "Now tell me what happened."

"Ask Dad."

"I want you to tell me."

"Tell Mom," Dad said.

"A Negro held a knife to my throat and took the car and Dad's money but he brought the car and Poppa's ring back."

"Where on earth were you?"

"I don't know. Ask Dad."

A free and frank exchange followed between my parents. I knew my parents argued but I had never been in the room. Dad maintained he intended to call the police after dinner. First, he had to call Dr. Flannigan.

Unlucky for Dad, he caught the Flannigans walking out the door for a delayed dinner engagement. Pete agreed to stop by and found me sitting on the bottom stair.

"Jeb, this looks like a razor cut. What happened?"

Dad walked into the hall, "Pete, I know you're in a hurry. I'll tell you on the way out."

"Hank, I need to talk to my patient and I need you to be quiet," Pete uncharacteristically demanded as he tilted my head into the light. He felt the cut with his finger, lifting the flap of skin and fresh blood began to trickle down my neck. The wound began to sting again.

"Well?" Mom asked.

Pete observed, "It's too shallow to hurt anything but I hate the cut reached the jugular… Jeb, I have to ask you a question as part of my job even though I am certain of the answer. But you have to tell me and be honest. Did this happen in your home or did anyone in your family do this to you?"

"No, sir. It was a Negro."

"Your Dad will best understand how to handle that. I had to ask. I'll stop by on the way home, ten or ten-thirty."

"We'll be up," Mom said.

"I'll walk you to the car." Dad said.

When Dad walked back inside, he paced back and forth, lit a cigarette.

"What's the matter, Hank?" Mom asked. "Jeb's OK."

"I'm not! I tried to give Pete the short story. He said he had time because the Preston's maid didn't show today. They had to call their cocktail guests and ask them to come late. I told him Jeb and I ran into trouble when we went to look for the Preston's maid. Hell, anybody but Preston."

Dad paced for a while in silence, "Damn it, I was trying to help. God only knows where their maid is or what Preston will say. God knows it will not be charitable."

"Don't worry, Hank, we've never met their friends and the Flannigans will be there to defend you."

"It's a party for their neighbors one block in every direction, the Lockharts, Flannigans, Madisons and I don't know who else." Dad paced up and down the hallway. "Well, sweetheart, some of the Preston's neighbors may not know us, but I predict after tonight they will have heard of us," Dad said in exasperated laughter.

I had made it through the day without tears. I had been scared. I thought I might get my throat slit and go to heaven but I wasn't going to cry in front of a bunch of strangers and get paddled for it later. In my room, in the dark, with the door shut, I laid down on my bed, tears rolled down the side of my face and into my ears.

Chapter 8 Hearsay

The Prestons' maid's predicament and the following uproar would have moved an attack by the Russian's off the front page of the Buckhead paper. Fortunately, by long standing convention, the paper did not report on anything more negative than a lost dog or runaway horse. If it was negative it didn't happen in Buckhead.

Our only priority Monday morning was to find Effie. I did not have to go to school. I went downtown with Dad where I met Captain Mack McConnell. When Dad told the Captain about our mission to recover a lost maid, Mack surprised us by saying he thought he could find her in short order. Dad left me with Cheryl, the secretary, while he and Captain McConnell went to a holding area for lost people.

Cheryl did not have to sit with young boys often. She looked like she had just been handed a box of puppies, cute for a minute then what?

"You can call me Miss Cheryl. What should I call you?"

"Jeb."

"Jeb, that's a nice name."

"Yes Ma'am. I have a cousin named Jeb."

"Oh so it's a family name."

"Yes Ma'am. We're named for the same Great Granddaddy. He lives in Texas and I live in Atlanta so the family calls him "Texas Jeb" and me, "Atlanta Jeb." Everybody else just calls me "Jeb."

"That's a clever thing to do. Do you go to Texas to see them?"

"Once for Christmas."

"Was that fun?"

"Yes. Ma'am." And so it went.

"Would you like to look at pictures of police equipment?" Miss Cheryl had exhausted her small talk to boys and offered me the police catalog. A black leather belt with a pistol hostler, handcuff pouch, and Billy stick loop caught my eye.

At the holding area Dad identified the Preston's maid, Effie Carlton. She had been lost, suspiciously wandering around Peachtree Street past dark and picked up by police. When she could not provide identification or address she was brought to the jail. She was furious at Dad until the police explained he was there to take her back to the Preston's house.

Captain McConnell explained the problem as the men walked through the maze of jail buildings to Mack's office. "Thank you for identifying her. We have to keep lost folks in protective custody until somebody claims them. It's a big expense for the department; we can get as many as twenty a week. The schools are supposed to be helping us out by teaching kids their name and address in grammar school. From this side of the fence you see how disadvantaged the illiterate are. They are involved in crime more, both as victims and perpetrators, than people who can read."

"Jeb and I will take her back to the Preston's house. They are anxious for her safety."

"Thanks, we'll call ahead. The Prestons can give us the information for the paperwork. We have discovered that the same people often get lost more than once."

Mack returned after the maid issue was settled. "How's Jeb doing?"

"He's been a perfect gentleman. He's been looking through our catalogue. I think he deserves a Peachtree Cola."

"Good idea, Miss Cheryl. Please bring us three colas."

"Yes, sir, coming right up."

"Dad, look at this picture," I said pointing to the police belt. "I want one of these."

Dad, studied the picture, "Jeb, the smallest one they offer would be much too large for you."

"Your Dad is right, and only policeman are allowed to order from that catalog," Mack explained. "If you become a policeman when you grow up, you can order whatever you want from there."

Changing the subject Dad said, "Well, thank God you found the maid."

Both men removed their suit coats in the forever too warm jail building and hung them on a coat rack in McConnell's office. The Captain was wearing his underarm holster containing a 1911 style .45 stainless steel pistol. He removed his gun from its holster.

"Jeb, you're not afraid of guns are you?"

"No, sir. I'd like to see it," Mack looked at Dad who nodded. I was surprised at the stainless steel.

"Is it silver?"

"No, stainless steel."

"I thought policemen carried black guns so the bad men can't see them."

"Not this policeman. I carry stainless steel because I don't have to clean it. And if I pull my gun I want the bad man to see it."

"Why did you take it off? What if a bad man comes here?"

McConnell laughed. "I keep it in the drawer because it is heavy. As for bad men coming to the jail," he laughed again, "It's not a problem. They won't come here on their own so the city gave me a job to find them and bring them in."

Dad laughed too. "I never thought of it, but it's job security."

"Could I see one of the bullets?" I asked.

"If it's OK with your Dad?" Dad approved and Mack emptied the chamber handing me the bullet.

"How big is the lead part?"

"Well let's see. I can tell you exactly Mack opened his drawer and examined the fifty round box. "The lead is 230 grains, that's a half ounce of lead. And the muzzle velocity is 897 feet per second and it lands with 410 foot-pounds of force. It will stop a bad man in his tracks."

Mack did not talk to five year olds. I cut to the chase, "How many men have you shot?"

"None. Thankfully, I have only had to pull my gun a few times for back up."

When Mack thought I was comfortable he moved on to the business at hand.

"Jeb, why don't you call me Captain Mack? Your Dad has said I could ask you some questions and I'd like to take a closer look at your neck."

Cheryl returned with the Peachtree Colas and I said, "Thanks Miss Cheryl."

"So you like Peachtree Colas?"

"Yes, ma'am. Miss Victoria says it's the wine of Buckhead."

Cheryl chuckled, "I'm sure that's right."

"She calls them P.C.'s sometimes for short."

"We do too."

Dad's ecstasy over discovering the maid turned to mortification as I related our car theft. If anything my clarifications added to his embarrassment.

Thanks to the favorable presentation of the police on TV, I felt at ease with the policemen in the jail. Unlike the TV, the police assured Dad there was little they could do to recover his money clip and cash or bring the perpetrators to justice.

An unquantifiable thing attributed in part to the TV, I had not acted then or the day before in an expected hysterical manner. TV only had value as a babysitter if we would stay in front of it. TV westerns and dramas like Hopalong Cassidy, Roy Rogers, etc. lasted thirty minutes. The first fifteen troubles hit the fan and the last fifteen it got worse. But at the surprise ending, all was made right. We would run to Mom telling her to come watch the crisis on TV. She disciplined us to watch until God and Roy Rogers had worked out the happy ending. In the midst of the trouble I could do nothing, so I waited for God and Dad to work things out. During my trials I felt fear but not immobilizing hysteria, I acted believing God was indeed as Miss Victoria taught "a present help in times of trouble."

Mack advised Dad to sell his car.

"Not the MG," I moaned. "Dad said I could drive it when I grow up."

Mack was confused, "I thought you said you had a Buick?"

"My wife drives the Buick. Why sell them?" Dad asked.

"They will be able to spot you now. Unless you want to carry a gun, and, you are willing to use it, they may try to rob you again. They can find your car. They may drive around your neighborhood to see where you live. People who don't have anything to do and all day to do it can cause a lot of trouble."

Dad offered, "Thanks, I want to replace the MG, but two new cars would be a stretch."

"My advice is purchase two different cars, the more people in your neighborhood who own ones like them the better."

"Well, thanks again for your help, I need to get Jeb to school."

"I don't want to go to school, I want to go home," I said, and the men laughed and extoled the benefits of education. We shook hands and left to pick up the maid.

Effie rode in the back seat without comment from Dad. He was so glad to see her he would have let her drive if she wanted. When she told us she did not feel well Dad offered to take her to the hospital or his physician, Dr. Flannigan. She declined. We went straight to the Prestons. When Mrs. Preston opened the door she embraced Effie and they cried and hugged for some time. Their genuine affection for each other made quite an impression on me. We quietly withdrew without comment.

I told Dad I did not want to go to jail if I got lost. On the short ride home from the Prestons Dad assured me that all I needed to know was his name, Henry Lee McKnight, and our road was Nancy Creek. Any policeman could bring me home with that information.

***

Tuesday I returned to school. My neck cut escaped adult attention until the after recess check for bumps and bruises. The teachers beamed with relief to find I had been wounded away from school.

"How did it happen, Jeb?"

"My father said not to talk about it." I might as well have said Dad tried to slash my throat in a fit of drunken rage. For the next thirty minutes my teachers, Mrs. Boyette, the principal, and the nurse passed me around examining my neck. They turned me around and lifted my shirt looking for other slash marks. One pulled back my shorts and underwear to look at my rear end. They asked me questions designed to pry out my deep dark secret of abuse. Utilizing a child's gift for making things worse, I agreed I would talk to the priest.

Mrs. Boyette walked with me out to car pool line where Mom sat in Dad's red MG.

"Jeb has a nasty cut down his neck and I wanted to assure you it did not happen here."

"Oh thank you, no, it happened over the weekend," said Mom. Travis and two-year-old Billy jostled in the boot as I slid in the passenger seat.

"Jeb said his father did not want him to talk about it."

"No, he doesn't. It was an accident. I have a car full of children and I don't want to talk about it either," said Mom, and she drove off.

I was the only five-year-old at the big kids' chapel on Wednesday. The priest wore his black suit and collar. His glasses made his eyes look bigger and his Adams apple bobbed in his skinny neck as he talked. During the service he pulled off his loafer and wiggled his big toe through a hole in his sock to the great amusement of the big kids. The disconnection from my awe-inspiring church and the chapel service could not have been greater. I was underwhelmed. I was told the priest would "console" me.

The interview could have been worse, but I'm not sure how. I told him Mrs. Boyette wanted me to tell him about the cut on my neck. I pointed, unconcerned, at my neck. The priest had been told I had an issue with my father. When the priest saw the cut he exclaimed, "I am not getting involved in this!" He left to see Mrs. Boyette. I returned to class thinking "console" meant confuse.

Dad had to straighten the situation out. He told Mrs. Boyette we had been robbed at knifepoint. In Buckhead? Dad was suspect. He defended the slingshot trio, he escorted the painted Candy Beerbohm around in a red sports car and had admitted to administering spankings using a fraternity paddle. Dad had secured the top spot on Mrs. Boyette's bad Dad list.

Mrs. Boyette would not be intimidated; she wanted proof of this story. At Dad's request, Captain McConnell made a phone call to Mrs. Boyette. She informed the Captain that he could be anyone on the phone and she considered this a serious matter. He would have to prove himself to her and prove the alleged robbery. Captain McConnell said he would give her a personal interview Thursday morning. He sent one of his patrolmen to bring her downtown. I think the appearance of the patrol car at school convinced her. The patrolman explained he did not have the authority to let her decline the Captain's offer for a personal interview. Mrs.

Boyette got to ride all the way downtown and back in a police car.

That evening Dirk Lockhart invited himself by for a drink. The unnecessary self-invitation served notice he associated some importance to the visit. He also asked for me to be available. Dirk's opinion mattered to Dad and to lawyers around town.

Mr. Preston had called Dad and fussed about the maid and hung up the phone. Preston also called his lawyer who unknown to us had called Dirk Lockhart. Dad looked forward to Dirk's visits. When Dirk arrived, his demeanor communicated his seriousness. His lean face, high cheekbones and prominent nose accented his seriousness.

The Lockharts did not attend the Prestons' block party. Dirk assumed Preston magnified the situation out of proportion. He came over to have a drink and clear matters up. In preparation Dad placed the bourbon decanter, ice bucket, glasses, ashtrays, coasters, and napkins in their places on the table. Dad called me to the table and I shook Dirk's large hand and sat down across from him. They poured their drinks and I asked for one. This brought a smile to Dirk's face.

"Jeb, I believe you are a little young for bourbon." He looked at me and asked in mock seriousness, "Say, Jeb, you don't drink bourbon when your parents aren't around, do you?"

"No, sir."

"Probably don't smoke either, those things can wait."

"Kate, please bring Jeb a Peachtree Cola or something," Dad called into the kitchen.

Mom brought a half of a Peachtree Cola poured over ice in a small glass. Then Dirk said, "I have spoken to your

Dad about the incident a few days ago and I wanted to ask you a few questions. OK?"

I looked at Dad and he signaled OK. "Yes, sir," I said.

I recounted the story in detail. Dad was embarrassed. Mr. Lockhart knew next to nothing about the incident on Clarendale Drive. He thought Dad had gone straight to the police in search of the Preston's maid. After I finished he looked at the scab on my neck and asked me what kind of knife it was.

I answered, "It looked like a kitchen knife but the Negro told me it was so sharp Dad could shave with it."

Dirk shook his head. He lifted his glass draining its contents and sat looking into his glass for a few seconds before speaking.

"Hank, let me summarize what I think I have heard." I thought all lawyers must use that phrase. "You tried to help Preston's maid because she missed the bus. You good as kidnapped the woman, you created a scene driving down Paces Ferry in a convertible with a colored woman in the front seat. People thought Jeb and Travis belonged to the couple in the front seat. She got out of the car the first chance she had not knowing where she was. She did not get home for three days. You took Jeb in a neighborhood where you did not belong and got robbed at knifepoint. By some miracle you escaped and got your car back. In another Negro area downtown you would have been murdered and your bodies not found for days, if at all."

Dad lowered his head and I thought he might cry. "I was trying to help. None of this would have happened if the goddamn bus driver had picked her up. It was the last bus."

"Does your Dad cuss in front of you?"

"I don't know what cuss is."

"Saying damn and some other words."

After the explanation I realized Dirk had not been cussing during our present meeting. In previous meetings, I had been out of view. "Yes, sir, sometimes."

"Dirk, I shouldn't…"

"Hank, you shouldn't have done a bunch of things that you have done lately.

"The bus driver would have picked up a white woman. No one would have noticed me driving a white woman to Buckhead. The Negroes reacted to me because they feel mistreated by whites. I grew up around Negroes and never had any incidents like yesterday in my life."

"Well, you have now. You can't buck the whole city of Atlanta."

"I fought the war for the whole city of Atlanta. I fought the goddamn Japanese for three years in their back yard. The Japs tried to kill me and I damn near died of pneumonia. I have seen Japan from the air and lived to tell about it. A lot of good men didn't. They were great men, better than me. But I'm the one left, I made it back alive. And I didn't fight so Americans could abuse each other."

Dirk sat quietly while Dad calmed down. Dad lit a cigarette and took a long puff. I had never heard Dad raise his voice to Dirk or mention the war to him. During the uncomfortable pause in the conversation Dirk freshened his drink.

"Hank, don't talk to me that way."

"It's wrong to treat Negroes that way."

"It's wrong to speak to me that way. Let's settle that, and then talk about the other."

"I was rude and I apologize. But please, recognize my points."

"Hank, I'm in agreement. I don't know if I've told you but I'm part Creek Indian. Red is colored too. I have seen my uncle barred from stores because he was Indian. You aren't going to influence people if they think you're a nut case or some kind of pariah. Yes, being a combat veteran carries some weight as it should, but you must work in the system. It has been hard enough defending your pro bono work for a Negro woman, who many think murdered her husband. Lawyers who know the case tell me that they think she belongs in jail or at the end of a rope."

"It was self-defense. Dirk, I have the facts of the case."

"You think," said Dirk. "My question stands, do you want my help, yes or no?"

I continued to sit in silence as the two men stared at each other.

"Yes, Dirk I do," Dad said looking down then back at Dirk.

"OK, then. Let me think a minute," Dirk asked. Dad followed Dirk's lead fixing a fresh drink and lighting another cigarette.

"Jeb, thank you for joining us and don't worry about your Dad and me. This has been serious business and I'm glad you're OK. You can be excused." Dirk smiled to ease the tension created when he called Dad down in front of me.

"Yes, sir." I went up to my spot midway up the stairs. I had a clear view of the men in the dining room through the bannisters. Travis sat further up the stairs. We were hungry and it was past time for supper but Mom would not interrupt the men tonight.

"Hank, I have thought of this and I'm on your side, more than you think," Dirk paused to light his cigar. "I will support you as best I can around the courthouse but you must not interfere with anyone else's Negroes. If Preston's maid misses a bus it's their problem not yours. No more pro bono cases. Don't worry after this manslaughter thing, you won't be asked. From now on you work in your legitimate sphere of influence or in the political process. If you have any questions going forward ask me. Let's settle this tonight."

Dad sat thinking, Dirk offered, "Do you want time to think about it?"

"No," Dad said shaking his head, "I appreciate your help and advice. Will you help me move into positions of influence?"

"Hank, you worked for the Governor. You have more political pull than me. Ask him to put you on a board and then persuade those people. Decisions are easier from the top down and you'll live longer. Put Preston and this manslaughter case behind you. Work where you fit in and you'll accomplish much more."

Dirk held his hand under his chin thinking. "I want you to consider your own attitude toward the facts. I am not saying this is true of you, but I have seen it in others who move here from up north or go north and return. They see events and interpret them through their preconceived notions about race relations. I wouldn't want to be a Negro or a full-blooded Indian, but they get a fairer shake than most seem to think. That's my observation from both sides of the fence. In shear numbers there are more poor whites than poor Negroes. Trust me, a white woman would fair no better with the facts you have on your Negro woman. Just think about it."

Then Dirk glanced at his watch, "Alice is going to skin me alive, I've got to scoot on out of here. Let things quiet down."

Dad did want things to quiet down but Mr. Preston lived down to his reputation for suing people. Dad had to hire Stan Wallace to defend him in a criminal investigation initiated by the Prestons on behalf of their maid. The charge was kidnapping. Stan handled it and I had to give a statement about the ride to Buckhead and that Dad offered to take Effie to a doctor on the ride home from the jail. I was not told the details but the matter was either dropped or decided in Dad's favor.

Chapter 9 White

Our family worshiped at All Apostles Anglican Church downtown. The church was a few blocks from the Georgia Tech campus and one block from the Varsity drive-in restaurant. The green patina on the copper roof of the steeple complemented the brownstone. Inside stained wood paneling and pews offset brass railings and deep red carpet. All the big name Saints, John, Peter, Matthew, Mary and more had spots in the stained glass windows that punctuated the beige plaster walls. Every third or fourth pew provided a hearing aid, no one needed them to hear the organ. The instrument filled the sanctuary with a range of notes and tones from tall brass pipes along both sides of the choir.

Inside the brass alter railings, the sculpted limestone altar stood against the wall. A stained glass window above the altar depicted the angel at the empty tomb, the stone rolled away to show Jesus was raised from the dead. The ceiling peaked seventy or more feet above two rows of double width pews. The plaster walls in the choir and apse around the altar were azure blue. I thought if God didn't live in Atlanta this is where He stayed on visits.

My family took up a full pew. The lectern was formed by the spread wings of a chest tall brass angel and supported the large Bible. The church was a visual feast for a child's eyes. The service in King James English and punctuated by the calisthenics of worship, kneel to pray, stand to praise and sit to be taught, challenged my attention span. The building itself taught me the awe, majesty, and holiness of God. No one had a house like God's house.

The Sunday following the car theft I felt secure again in the splendid and familiar surroundings of God's own house. I thanked God that we survived without severe injuries and for the return of the car and Poppa's ring. I prayed for the recovery the money clip too. I told God I had been ready to go to heaven but I was glad to stay. Once I got into praying I asked for lunch at the Varsity, a real leap of faith. Hope, for a chilidog and frosted orange, springs eternal.

The acolytes, choir, and ministers, dressed in robes and white surplices, marched out to a rousing hymn. In the large church foyer, we ran into my youngest brother's godfather. He would do tricks and guessing games and give good kids like us a half stick of gum. After a stressful week our time in Church felt like a return to normalcy and security. I knew God was in heaven and all was well on earth.

***

Lunch at the Varsity was not predestined to be. We headed home, the top down, for a lunch that would no doubt include vegetables. We drove in the mild Atlanta sunshine north on Peachtree Road and out West Wesley.

As we drove toward the intersection of Margaret Mitchell Drive, a large group of white men blocked the street. A few had axe handles, some held longer poles. Dad stopped well short of the crowd. A black pickup truck behind us prevented us from backing up or turning around. I heard him mutter "Not again." He tried driving up the curb to make a wide turn by the truck. A second car pulled up alongside the truck blocking both lanes. Dad had a pregnant wife and three small boys in the back. I was tall enough to see what was happening. Dad stepped from the car throwing his suit coat back in the car and pulling off his tie.

"What's this about?" Dad demanded.

"Calm down, Mr. McKnight. We need your help in teaching some niggers a lesson," said a black-haired man wearing a white pressed shirt and dark pants.

Another beefy man, bald on top of his head, identified Dad as "the right one."

"Do I know you?"

"I hope not," the man chuckled.

"You can't block the road like this, it's a Federal offense."

"Well, boys, that'd be terrible offending the Feds," the men laughed. The atmosphere felt like a pre-game tailgate party. Parked cars and pickups lined Margaret Mitchell Drive. About forty men dressed in hats, collared shirts, and pressed pants, chatted and drank from cups. Most looked as if they could have come from church, a few had jackets. Now they had Dad and it was kickoff time.

The black-haired man gave the orders, "You might say I'm your new best friend. If you agree to join our little party your family can go. I'll have someone drive them home." Another man moved toward the car.

"No, I can drive," said Mom sliding behind the wheel.

"Mrs. McKnight, if you want to see Mr. McKnight again don't do anything stupid like calling the police," said the black-haired man. He made his menacing verbal threats in calming tones holding his hands palms out.

"You could talk to a policeman here," a voice called out followed by general laughter.

Dad said, "Get out of here. I'll be OK." Mom drove and the crowd parted. I stood in the back seat and looked back to see men forcing Dad to drink out of a pint bottle of bourbon. On Margaret Mitchell Drive I saw a man in a Klu Klux Klan robe. He pulled the white pointed hood back over his face as we passed.

We drove home. Mom was too worried to prepare food. Rather than Sunday dinner we had peanut butter and jelly sandwiches, no vegetables. We washed our sandwiches down with milk. Mom tried to keep us on our schedule. Naptime followed Sunday dinner. Before I could get up the stairs two cars drove in the driveway, one had Dad in the back seat.

A man in a tan suit and tie and a portly man in Khaki pants and a short-sleeve shirt got out. Both men came to the front door.

The man in short-sleeves spoke first. He had graying crew hair and a drill sergeant's bearing, a lit cigarette hung from his mouth. A tattoo of a straight dagger through a heart adorned his left forearm. "Which one is Jeb?"

"I am," I said.

"Were you the one with your Daddy when the niggers stole your car?"

"Yes, sir."

"But you said the family could go!" Mom protested.

The man in the suit interjected. He was older, of average size and weight, but instantly unlikeable. "Mrs. McKnight, what is your first name?"

Mom hesitated, "Kate. You said my children could go with me."

"Kate, I'm your friend and I did say that you could go. But we need your cooperation if you want to see your husband alive again. You do don't you?"

"Yes, I do."

"Thank goodness," he said looking at the other man. "Some women don't."

They guffawed and the man in the suit went on, "You haven't called the police have you?"

"No."

"Good then I can help you."

"But if I save your husband and your boy you will owe me. You understand?"

Mom did not answer.

"You want your husband back?"

"Yes, I do."

"No police, or I'll be back for what you owe." He turned to the other man and nodded to him to get me, "She understands."

The portly man with his dangling cigarette looked like a one tusked boar hog. Threatening as he looked he tried to assure Mom, "Mam he ain't with me; I ain't got nothing to do with nothing except getting Jeb." He turned his gaze to me, "Jeb, you know how to read?"

"No, sir."

"Mr. McKnight needs some help remembering. He wants Jeb to join him for a short while. See, he's in the back of that black car." Dad's face was shoved into the rear window at an awkward angle from across the seat.

The man's cigarette continued to hang on his lip as he talked out of the side of his mouth. "Besides, ain't nobody going to get hurt. He took my hand and walked me to the car. See, there's your Daddy, he wants you to jump in the car." Dad looked sick in the far corner of the back seat. Voluntarily or not, Dad called for me to get in the car.

I had never seen Dad drunk; he assured me his malady would pass. The men cheered when we arrived back at the dirt road. I got out of the car.

"Did the boy cry or fuss?" The same black-haired man who first stopped us asked.

"Not at all. Spoke right up. Said he was there when the niggers stole the car. Got in the car on his own." The man with the tattoo did not get out of the car.

"Now that you men talked to the wife, and been to the house, it's better if you leave now," The black-haired man said.

The men who brought us from the house left in the two cars. The tattooed man called out, "We done our part. Do your duty!"

"Now we gonna get somewhere."

Dad could not walk unassisted. I felt more curious than afraid as we walked toward the dirt road. The men asked me, "Where did them niggers rob you and your Dad?"

"Not this road it's the next one, down by the church," I said.

"Now we're on the right track," one said. They had gone down the first dirt road, Clarendale was the second on the left.

As the white men started down the road, some walked behind the houses, Negro children flushed out of back doors and ran for the woods behind. Some larger children shepherded the smaller ones toward the preacher's house at the bottom of the hill. The whites called for the adults to come into the road and they obeyed. After a sharp bend in the red clay road, unpainted clapboard houses lined the road. The postage stamp sized yards bore little grass and fewer ornamental bushes. A few houses sported tarpaper coverings made to look like bricks and mortar. Empty lots and a caved in house gave the neighborhood a snaggletooth appearance.

I recognized the Negro man who had pushed the Negro woman from in front of the Buick. He pushed another younger Negro woman out of the house as she hurried to button up her dress. A white man, seeing her bra was showing said, "If you selling something, we ain't interested. Button up before you come out here."

"I am being pushed," she said.

"I see what's happening. Cover up, nigger, and get out here."

"What's the trouble over there?" the black-haired man called out as he took in the situation, "You got a Negro woman trying to sell something?"

"I told her we ain't interested."

"You ain't got nothing big enough to interest her," the Negro who pushed her muttered loud enough to be heard.

"Oh, you think so," the black-haired man answered, "We'll see about that, won't we, men?"

"I ain't said nothing," the Negro protested.

"Don't lie. We got plenty of time to teach a nigger not to lie don't we boys?"

Seeing the menacing whites the Negro quickly admitted, "Yeah I said something wrong."

"Yeah you did and we'll show you."

"Get them all together first," the black-haired man ordered.

Two-dozen Negro adults and older teens walked ahead of the white men down the hill. They stopped in a dirt yard across from the church. The Negroes expressed aggravation but not fear. Some covered their mouths as they snickered at my liquor impaired Dad, who walked supported by two joking white men.

The black-haired man directed the men to turn Dad and me away from the Negro crowd. Other whites stood behind us shielding us.

The black-haired man directed the whites, "Some of you men show them nigger women what they are missing."

A man carrying a rifle handed it to someone else. He and several others pulled their peckers out and judged between them a half dozen or so that would be shown to the Negroes. The white men laughed and caterwauled the whole time. The whites demanded the Negro woman judge the size difference between several white exposed penises and the Negro's. I could hear both the Negro man and the Negro woman admitting that the Negro man finished last in size.

"Bet those Nigger men been telling you we got little peckers, hadn't they? Feast your eyes on these." The whites laughed and made obscene catcalls.

"Go on look at what you missing!"

"Tell them Nigger women in the back to move up front."

"These is just for white ladies!"

"Yea, we don't want your Nigger to rub off on us."

"Any of you Nigger boys got something you want to show? ...Didn't think so."

I was mystified, there would be a "birds and the bees" lecture in my future but it hadn't hit yet. I had it on good authority that God had provided boys with peckers so they could pee standing up in the woods. After more derogatory remarks directed at the Negroes attention turned to me.

"Jeb show us the men who took your car." The black haired man said.

I was scared, "They all look the same to me," The whole crowd of white men inhaled for a split second and a roar of simultaneous laughter followed. No standup comedian ever got a better response to a joke. The white men laughed and howled until tears rolled. Many Negroes laughed too.

"Damn, if they don't look the same, Lukey."

"No names!"

"They surely do look alike, all ugly."

"They all got the same size asses, large."

"No, it's them pants got high pockets." Laughter and joking continued for some time.

Lukey, I had learned the black haired man's name, raised his arms for quiet. He acted like the ringmaster at the circus and it was time to call off the clowns. The laughter died down he put his hand on my shoulder and squatted down to my eye level. I studied his face. He had brown eyes with a small scar near his right eye along the cheekbone. He spoke in an easygoing assuring tone, "You're not scared of me are you, Jeb?"

"No, sir." I said, speaking loud and clear, standing straight, shoulders square, looking him dead in the eyes. Dad told me animals and cowards will look away from you if you stand square and look them in the eye. Travis and I had tried this strategy several times on our dachshunds with good effect.

"Men, I do believe him. Little Jeb has some sand," He laughed and looked around, "Jeb, you are going to do what I tell you, aren't you? I'm the man in charge here, not your Dad."

"My Dad knows the Governor, played football at Georgia Tech, he fought the Japs in an airplane and he's a lawyer." Dirk Lockhart called these facts Dad's four aces; I played them as best I could. I looked Lukey square in the eyes; he blinked.

Lukey stood up and turned to look at four older white men in the center of the road. He didn't repeat my words - all had heard.

"We know all that," said a short white-haired man. The corners of his mouth turned down and his face scrunched up like he took a bite of a lemon. "He'll thank us, he should join us when he sees the good we do. Do your duty."

Men shouted out, "Yea, let's get on with it!"

"We can't stay here all day."

Steeled by senior management, Lukey looked down at me. "You got a close look, Jeb. Which one took your car?"

"I couldn't see. When the man put the knife on me he held my head where I couldn't see his face."

"A nigger put a knife on you! Where?" Lukey bellowed back to the whites.

"On my throat, right here," I said pointing to the visible scab. Silence fell as the whites glared at the Negroes.

"You hearing this, boys? Anybody think we shouldn't be here now? A sorry, low life, piece of shit, Nigger put a knife on Jeb!"

"That ain't right!"

"We gonna teach 'em!"

"Ask that lawyer if he still loves niggers."

"Yeah, nigger-lover, look what they done back to you!"

"Maybe you wont do nothing, we'll teach them niggers not to put a blade on a white boy."

"Teach 'em with fire!"

"We are with you, Jeb," voices called out.

"That wasn't a man that cut you, Jeb, it was a sorry nigger!" said Lukey stooping back down to me. Anger covered his face, his nostrils flared, his jaw set. He turned his head back to the white men, "Check them niggers for knives."

The party atmosphere vanished and the angry men steeled themselves for action. A single thin white stepped forward. He was dressed in a round neck white shirt and suspenders buttoned to the inside of his pants. As he walked alone and unafraid through the fearful Negroes, butcher knives began to hit the ground. I watched wondering how they hid such long knives in their clothes. He joked, "Look at all these knives a lying on the ground. These knives belong to any of you niggers?" No one spoke, he picked up about ten knives lifting them up to show to the approving whites. "What y'all think? I found me all these knives and don't nobody claim them." He got a few laughs, "They's mine now."

I heard some Negroes muttering, "They gonna kill us."

"No they ain't."

"I is scared."

"Shut up, fool."

A few men gathered around to examine my throat.

"Lordy, Jeb's lucky that nigger didn't cut through to his little jugular vein. He'd a bled out for sure."

"Easy, don't scare the boy. He's done fine so far." Lukey warned.

"You're safe with us, Jeb. You and your Daddy, we'll have you back home in no time," said one of the men who had stepped up for a closer look at my neck.

"Stupid nigger, don't know no better."

"Niggers could have killed them both if they wanted," a voice of moderation called out.

When I lifted and turned my head to show my neck, I noticed a white man standing on a small elevation above the two groups. It was the man with the rifle. His attentive dark eyes peered from under the turned down brim of his black felt hat. He focused on the Negroes bunched below him. His left leg was further up the incline and his black leather boot dug into the red clay. He said nothing but held a western style lever action Winchester rifle. Everything about his demeanor communicated his fearless willingness to use it then and there. I felt satisfaction seeing the state of our former tormentors. The frightened Negroes felt the hate and huddled closer together. Some clung to one other and I noticed a Negro had wet his pants.

A few men viewed my neck. I moved closer to Dad as Lukey addressed the crowd again, "We will have to teach these niggers a lesson." The whites shouted their approval.

"Jeb, which house did they come out of?" Lukey squatted to look me in the eye.

Dad roused himself to speak. He managed to slur, "Leave him out of this."

"Let him say," the whites called out.

On our ill-fated drive down the dirt road a young man ran into a house and came back out leading several other youths. I pointed at the unpainted clapboard house close to the road. I had no clue what was about to happen. Lukey looked back at the older white men in the center of the road. The prune faced one said, "Go ahead, do your duty."

Lukey pointed at the house behind the church. I heard a Negro woman gasp, "The preacher's house."

I corrected them, "No, sir, it is this one close to the road."

A young Negro cried out, "There's a baby in there!"

Another Negro answered, "No they ain't."

Now addressing the Negroes, Lukey said, "Hold that boy." And a few Negroes grabbed the one who had spoken. Whites then searched the unpainted clapboard house.

"Ain't no baby.

"Ain't no baby nothing in there."

"All right," Lukey said turning with his hands on his hips. "Teach that nigger not to lie to a white man." The Negroes holding him punched him in the face until he bled.

Another Negro told the whites something, "He said the house is vacant, don't nobody live there."

Lukey called out, "Men, we got our house, everybody agree?" The men shouted their approval.

The black minister who had not been rousted came out as if to intervene. Whites close to him said something to him. He knew the details of the car theft. He spoke to the Negroes, "I can't do anything for you." A Negro woman asked about her children, "They are safe in my house. You should have thought about the white man's child. That's why this trouble is here," He turned to go back in his house.

The bleeding Negro called out to the preacher to ask the white men to let him go in his grandmother's house, the closest house to where he stood.

Lukey asked, "Is that nigger lying again?"

"He don't know for sure, but he thinks the woman what lives there is his grandmother."

The laughter by Negroes and whites was predictable and eased the tension a little. The Negro holding him said, "He's a fool nigger, he ain't no-count, he can't hurt nobody." They released the bleeding man to an older Negro woman. She helped him on to the nearby porch and dabbed his bloody face with a dishtowel. The preacher went back to his house.

Lukey stood a few feet away. Dad seemed oblivious to his surroundings. His glazed eyes looked far away and the two men on either side held his full weight. I asked if he was OK and they shook him until his eyes focused. I asked Lukey if Dad could have some water.

Lukey said, "Do it. Bring Mr. McKnight a glass of water." A minute later a Negro appeared from nowhere carrying a glass of water, which Dad drank.

Lukey ordered the Negroes to remove the furniture from the house I had pointed out. They brought out tables, and chairs, but no beds were found. An angry Negro woman called out, "That table be mine. You can carry it on back up to my house where you stole it from." The Negroes looked at Lukey for approval.

"Put it down, you can move it later." Lukey looked at the Negro woman who had spoken. "You sure it's your table?"

"Yes, I am!" she shouted.

"Ask her where she stole it from," a white called out, laughter followed.

"I bought that table at the Nearly New Store," she said.

"OK, I believe you. You boys carry the table up to her house when we're done." Lukey called out, "Men, these niggers don't just steal from white folks, they steal from each other." The whites and a few of the Negroes laughed.

"Burn 'em all out! Save us from having to come back up here." The man with the rifle hollered. The Negroes quit laughing.

"Yeah, burn them all out. He's right. We'll have to come back later if we don't do it now."

"No, men, we came for one house today. Beside we only brought one gas can," Lukey maintained control.

"Send someone for more," A white hollered.

"Get a move on. We been here long enough," another white answered.

White men directed the Negroes to empty the can of gasoline throughout the house. The long poles I had seen earlier turned out to be unlit torches. Lukey asked me, "Jeb, can you light a match?" Another white man handed me a pack of matches.

Dad lifted his head and struggled to speak, "No, Jeb."

I handed them back. "Dad won't let me use matches."

A commotion arose behind us. The Negro with the bloody face reappeared from the home across from the church gripping a long kitchen knife. The man on the hill grasped the rifle and pumped the lever chambering a round. He stood on the alert, his finger on the trigger and thumb on the hammer, the rifle pointed up but at the ready. In a stern voice he commanded, "Tell that nigger to put the knife down and get back on the porch."

The Negroes disarmed him. They shouted and slapped him forcing him back on the porch. He yelled his unintelligible protests but he got knocked down and bloodied again. One Negro joked, "He's a hard nigger to keep on the porch."

Lukey, angered at the interruption, said, "I don't give a hoot what you do, but keep him there or we'll give somebody a tar and feather coat."

"Police, let's go!" a white man hollered from the top of hill.

"We're about done here," Lukey took the matches from the man and handed them back to me. "Do you know how to strike a match? Show me. You won't get in trouble."

I looked at Dad, his eyes did not focus. I struck a match. Lukey raised my hand holding the lit match and called out, "Jeb is with us!" The white men all cheered. He then took a torch in his free hand and touched it to the burning match and lit the torch. The whites handed the torches to Negroes to throw though the doors and windows. In minutes the house was engulfed in flames.

"Someone run on ahead and explain how it is to the police," Lukey ordered. A white man jogged up the hill.

Lukey spoke as he brushed one hand off with the other, "Mr. McKnight, it's time for you and Jeb to thank us for teaching these niggers not to steal. You do want to thank us, don't you?" he paused looking at Dad, who seemed reanimated by the flames. "You and Jeb could leave with us or stay here."

I saw the glint of anger in Dad's eyes, "Thank you for teaching the niggers a lesson."

"How about you, Jeb?"

"Yes, sir. Thank you, I did my part." I didn't want to be left in front of the burning home. I had learned the word "duress" and this was it.

"Yes, you did," Lukey smiled and other voices joined in congratulating me.

The whites stood unafraid and unhurried in their places. Lukey turned toward the Negroes and snarled, "You niggers glad we taught you a lesson? You glad we taught you not to steal, so you don't end up on the chain gang?"

"Yes, Sir, we is thankful."

"Yes, Sir, we is, sure enough."

"We is all thankful!"

"I didn't hear everybody," Lukey warned looking over the cowering Negroes.

Lukey snarled again, "We ain't going nowhere until you tell these men, who gave up their Sunday afternoon to come teach you sorry niggers not to steal, 'Thank you.' You niggers also tell them you're not going steal no more. Now do it!"

A sweating Negro stepped in front of the other Negroes. He turned, giving them instruction and then counted to three and they shouted in unison. "Thank you, we ain't gonna steal no more!!!"

Luke shouted back at them. "You damn sure better not or we'll come back and burn every nigger house on the road!" Then turning to the whites, he said in a calm voice, "Alright, men, you done your duty. It's time to go and enjoy the rest of your Sunday."

Dad continued to need assistance, and I walked behind thinking I did not ever want to see this place again. The scent of the burning pine clapboard followed us up the hill. Lukey walked up beside me, "Jeb, I want you to notice we did not hurt your Dad. He's a fine man and he will be OK."

"Yes, Sir. He told me in the car he would be OK in a few hours," I said.

"You did real well. When the boys went to get you, I was afraid you would be a squalling kid. You were a man about it and we are proud to know you. Isn't that right, men?"

"That's right, Jeb."

"He's a man-pup."

"And he can sure handle a match," followed by laughter.

I felt like telling him, squalling, even whining, earned a vigorous paddling at my house.

Lukey continued, "We know your brave father fought in the war. This apple didn't fall far from the brave tree." He patted me on the shoulder.

"That's right."

"You tell him."

"Jeb, we want you to understand we had to do what we did today. They're too many niggers for the police to keep up. So we help out. Sometimes we got to teach a bad white man. We are the backbone behind law and order."

The men spoke to me as if I would understand and remember everything they said. Whether I understood or not, I did remember.

The men showed no sense of urgency as they ambled up the dirt road. The fire crackled while flames and smoke shot upward into the clear blue sky.

"You going over to Lukey's?"

"No, names!" Lukey called out in an exasperated tone.

"OK. OK. Sorry. I'm sure they're plenty of them in Atlanta."

"Yep, mostly niggers." Many laughed and snickered at the good-natured jab at their leader.

"Some men are thinking they will get a wee swalley of shine at my house better pick something up else on the way back," Lukey announced. As he turned his head backwards to speak he saw the table sitting in front of the burning house. "I know I told some niggers to carry the table up to that nigger woman's house. Get moving." He took a few more steps and turned around to see his orders being carried out. The Negro woman walked in front of two Negroes as they carried her table. He stood and watched. "The table better stay in her house or we will be back."

One of the two Negroes asked, "You coming back to check?"

"Shut up, fool," the Negro woman said.

"I don't have to check. We will find out the same way we found out you stole the car." He left the impression someone in the community had told them. He smiled and turned back up the hill.

The whites continued to talk among themselves. They laughed and joked without a care for the policemen up on the paved road. I heard random voices in the crowd.

"You going for some shine?"

"No, my kid's singing in church tonight, the wife says I will be there."

"Your wife tells you what to do?"

"Aw, shut up. Like yours don't tell you."

"Tell her you been doing your duty."

"That's right."

The man with the rifle passed us by, "Yeah, it's a .45-70, it will kill the biggest buck nigger you ever saw with one shot. Yankees use them to hunt grizzlies and moose."

He passed a bullet to the man beside him. "Dang that's the biggest bullet I ever saw."

"It will cut a little pick-a-ninny in half," the rifleman said taking the bullet back.

They passed us by and the next group talked about post fire refreshments. "I ain't drinking no junk shine, no how. Any bourbon left we give the lawyer?"

"No, you-know-who said make sure he drinks the whole bottle. Anyway, you-know-who has some mighty fine shine, it's real smooth, better than store bought."

"The lawyer drank it all?"

"He's wearing what didn't go down his throat."

"No wonder he couldn't find the right road."

I felt relief as I saw the paved surface of Margaret Mitchell Drive come into view. The whites had parked their cars pointing toward West Wesley. I noticed the tag numbers did not begin with the number one signifying Fulton County - Atlanta.

Lukey listened to the older men. "We got the police OK. They ain't got no radio and they don't know about the nigger neighborhood. We told them we built a bonfire." They discussed the police and the fastest routes out of the county.

"Sounds good to me," Lukey gestured for a man to come over to him. "Mr. McKnight, this man will take you and Jeb home. The police will talk to you sooner or later. I think you should remember, we did not hurt you or your son. Like it or not, we kept you safe with us." Dad, still walked assisted by two men, said nothing.

"Get them straight home. Don't let them talk to the police. You know the close bridges. Take the men you brought and we'll stall the police. Get going."

When we reached West Wesley Road we saw two young policemen and one patrol car. The policeman looked as nervous as the two new boys at the high school dance. One policeman pointed to the smoke rising above the trees and asked about the fire.

"Remember, we told you it's a bonfire," a smiling Klansman said.

Pointing at Dad, the same policemen asked, "What's the matter with him?"

"Too much to drink, don't worry we will take him home," Lukey answered as he walked up. A sedan pulled up and men pushed Dad and me in the back seat. When we arrived home Dad threw up in the front yard.

The men laughed and called out the open car windows as they drove away. "Mr. McKnight you shouldn't drink so much cheap whiskey."

Chapter 10 Trying

The same two policemen we saw at Clarendale came to the house an hour after we arrived back. Dad talked to them. He drank black coffee to sober up. When the police questioned me I recalled Dad's embarrassment at my detailed account of the car theft so I gave a short version of events. The police asked if I could identify the men. I said, "Maybe if they wore the same clothes, I could identify the man in the white suit."

As I described the Klan outfit, the police shook their heads. One said to the other, "I'm not doing a thing on this."

"Me neither." The other responded.

Dad looked up in disbelief, "A mob burned someone's home down, you have to do something."

The policemen looked young and competent, like men who would accept a challenge. But, the first policeman, tall with short blond hair, explained, "Mr. McKnight, you got nothing for us to go on. And if you could identify a man, he would have ten church going saints to say he was somewhere else. We work Sunday's because we don't have seniority. Somebody up the line would have to get on this but it won't help. No, sir, you can raise Hell and get fifty policeman on this or do nothing; the outcome will be the same. Nobody talks."

"Well, not exactly," his wiry partner with close cut light brown hair said. "They're laughing and drinking and talking about it now, but if anyone speaks to us, he is a dead man."

"I don't believe this is America," said Dad shaking his head. The tall policeman sat with Dad in silence for a while then said, "Mr. McKnight, we need to get back downtown, the next shift needs our patrol car."

"What are you going to tell them about this?" Dad asked.

The tall policeman spoke again, "Mr. McKnight, you won't like it, but it will be the truth. My notes say that Mr. McKnight described being robbed by Negroes a week earlier. Today, at the same location, Mr. McKnight was removed from his car and forced to drink liquor to intoxication. He and his five-year-old son witnessed a mob of twenty to thirty white men enter a Negro neighborhood. They did not see any whites touch any Negro. They claim the whites intimidated the Negroes to fight each other and burn down a house. The white men supplied torches and gas. The boy said he saw a rifle but never saw it pointed at anyone. Neither Mr. McKnight nor his son knew their assailants."

The wiry policeman concluded studying Dad's face for a response. "Mr. McKnight, somebody downtown is going say 'street justice' and close it up. If they don't, your boy saw more than you and he wasn't drunk. It will come down on him."

I sat in silence and sensing Dad's frustration I spoke up, "I would know the one with tattoo on his arm. He left after dropping us off. And they weren't from Buckhead."

The second policeman asked, "How do you know they weren't from Buckhead?"

I said, "Their license plates did not begin with number one. The tags I saw began six and eight, I think maybe nine too. Anyway, no tag started with a one. I don't think they were from Cobb County because I heard them asking what was the quickest way out of Fulton County. If they were from Cobb they would have known it's just a mile away."

"If we could find a car, I bet dollars to doughnuts the owner will say he wasn't driving it today," the tall policeman concluded.

The police possessed little in the way of evidence, my recollection of a tattoo and two tag prefixes. We couldn't even identify the make or model of the cars. Dad asked the policeman to give the information to Captain McConnell.

Monday after the house burning, Dad began driving the Buick to work and parked it at night in a neighbor's closed garage. Wednesday we had a new Ford station wagon. Mom liked the two-tone paint, turquoise blue body and white trim with white wall tires. The radio had push buttons to change the stations. At least one of the neighbors on Ridgewood had one like it. The Ford came equipped with three rows of bench seats. When I asked Mom if the extra seats meant she was having more babies she almost turned the car over. "No! No more babies." She was under a little stress.

In addition to purchasing the new car he contacted GBI and FBI agents from his moonshine case. The Atlanta Police offered little beyond sympathy for the theft of a money clip and shack burning with no one seriously hurt. Dad wanted to find a violation of Federal Law so he could involve the FBI to go after the Klan. He suggested making the case that the Klan blocked a public road – interfering with interstate commerce – the most commonly used constitutional law for involving Federal agencies at the state level. The GBI agents referred him to a former state prosecutor named Stan Wallace to see if he could build a case.

Stan came over for cocktail hour the week after the house burning. I saw him through the front door side light windows as he strode up the front walk wearing a blue suit and narrow tie. Stan was tall and athletic. I knew the drill if Stan didn't. I sat, while the men drank until called upon to answer questions. Cocktail hour of late had been more serious than social.

Dad placed the drink fixings on the table. Mom quietly brought out demitasse spoons. "Hi Stan, I thought you gentlemen might like something to stir your drinks with." Mom thought it bad manners for Dad to stir by pushing the top ice cubes around with his finger. The spoons made just one uninvited appearance. The manly art of cooling bourbon by ice twirling would continue uninterrupted.

"Hank, let's get down to business. I don't know what agent Todd told you apparently it was good enough for you to invite me over. He gave me quite a resume on you. I assume you would like to know my qualifications?"

Dad sat back in his chair, "Yes. Though I am a lawyer I have never hired a criminal lawyer."

"Education first, I attended Boys High in Atlanta, before prepping a year at Bolles Military, in Jacksonville, Florida for The University of Virginia. I graduated from Virginia in June of 1943 and joined my destroyer at Pearl Harbor in August. At my grandfather's insistence I followed him and my father to Georgia law school after the war and served as a state prosecutor for the first seven years of my law practice. I don't want to alarm anyone but on police advice I carry a small pistol for self-preservation." Stan opened his coat to show Dad the handle of a small revolver barely visible above his belt.

"I'd prefer you did not bring that in my house."

"Very well, I'm certain I am safe here. I did not want you to be startled if you noticed it. There's not much else to say. I am a third generation lawyer and my son Stan will be the fourth. I know you went to Yale Law and you served as a Navy pilot," Stan concluded.

"So you had sea duty in the Pacific?" Dad inquired.

"Yes. Don't talk about it much but since you asked - gunnery officer on the Ibbotson, a Fletcher class destroyer. In our first action we put five torpedoes on a Jap Cruiser, three of which exploded. Then we put fourteen five-inch shells in her. I marveled at the Japs' damage control, still do. We did everything but sink her. Twenty-three years old, the captain was incapacitated so I asked for the helm and he gave it to me. Every eighteen to twenty seconds I made a sharp turn to avoid the incoming Jap rounds. After we loaded our guns I held course and gave them eighteen seconds to find the target and fire before I turned again. The Jap's kept up their fire. They took out our bridge, would have killed us, but we had already moved command of the ship. We had plenty more of the war. I know you did too."

"Yes, I got my share of war." Dad returned to the subject at hand, "On the legal side, had any run-ins with the Klan?"

"No, as a prosecutor and not to my knowledge as a defense attorney, though I could not tell you if I had, you understand.

"Yes of course. I understand you have read my statement and you are here for Jeb's side of things."

"Correct," Stan started right in, "So you're Jeb."

"Yes, sir."

"This is Jeb?" Stan looked at Dad with a puzzled expression.

"Yes, Jeb is our oldest. He was the one with me both times.

"After what I have heard and read of the incidents the last two weekends I expected a bigger boy..." Stan paused to take out his pen. "Your Dad invited me to your home so I could ask you some questions about the men who stole your car and the men that burned the house. You do think these things are wrong, don't you?"

"Yes, sir."

"I guess you hate those bad niggers that held a knife on you and stole your Daddy's car."

"No, sir. Dad says to call them Negroes.

"I agree with your Dad. How about those murderous white men that made your Dad sick and had the rifle and burned the house. You hate them don't you?"

"No, sir. I don't think so. I'm glad they're gone."

"Me too. Sorry, Hank, I had to get through that - anger affects the testimony. Jeb seems pretty well adjusted. Congratulations to you and Mrs. McKnight.

Stan pressed on, "Jeb, I want you to try to answer the questions I ask and say no more. I may ask you some things different than your father would to see what you think. This is about what you think. Do you understand?"

"Yes, sir."

"I told your Dad I wanted to meet you. I think you are a brave boy," Stan continued asking questions until he had heard every detail about both trips down Clarendale Drive. He asked me several qualifying questions.

"Hank, I am impressed with Jeb's memory and the details...quite impressed."

"Me too, I think he remembers more and his recall of details makes me think he may have photographic memory. My Dad was an aeronautic designer. People said he had it.

He could look at a set of plans and reproduce them from memory."

"Jeb is recalling pictures of what he has seen, more on that later." Stan turned his attention back to me, "Jeb, I want to make sure I heard you correctly. So I will summarize. I will leave several things out but I will be repeat the parts I think are important."

Stan paused and looked at some notes he had made on a pad. He added some bourbon and an ice cube to his drink. He lit a cigarette. I noticed one smoldered in his ashtray.

"Two cigarettes, that looks stupid," Then taking a sip of bourbon he charged on. "Jeb, I will ask you not to interrupt. I don't think you would, but let me finish what I am about to say. Same for you, Hank, but listen with your lawyer hat on for what might be actionable."

"Your whole family was in the car when white men blocked the road. Your father got out voluntarily and threw off his coat and tie. Then your mother voluntarily left and you saw men hold a bottle to your father's mouth. As she drove through the other men, you saw a man in a white outfit with a tall pointy hat like a witches hat. After you had lunch at home, two cars came back. Your Dad was in the back of one of the cars. At his request you got in the car. The men drove y'all back to the dirt road where your car had been stolen. The men in the two cars including the tattooed man, left. The other men took you down the correct dirt road, which you showed them." Stan looked up from his notes to see us paying rapt attention, and then he continued.

"The whites told the Negroes to come out of their houses, which they did voluntarily. It was rude, but you did not see any physical pushing or pulling. The whites told the Negroes they had come to teach them not to steal. The whites told the Negroes to teach one Negro not to lie and they held him and beat him bloody. But the whites said teach him a lesson, they did not say to beat him. So far, the instructions you and your Dad heard the white man give were to teach them not to lie to white men and not to steal." Stan paused to take a long drink.

"Lukey told the Negroes to take out the furniture, to pour gasoline in the house that you pointed out and asked you to light a match. He took your arm and touched the match you lit to a torch. They told the Negroes to throw the burning torches in the house and it caught fire and burned. During some of the time your Dad had his eyes closed. Two men held him up and you thought he might be dead, so you asked them to give him some water and they did. You went back up to the paved road. You saw, but did not talk to two policemen. They brought you and your Dad home and your Dad threw up. And then the two policemen came and asked questions." Stan drained his bourbon and raised his gaze to look across the table at me, "But the whites never touched a Negro man or woman. Is that right?"

"Yes, sir," I said to Stan but noticed Dad shaking his head.

"Don't shake your head, Hank, or Jeb will think it's something he said. It's frustrating I know, but I have a few more qualifying questions.

"Was Lukey the one in the white suit? The one who told you to light the match?"

"I don't know."

"Perhaps," Said Stan, then rubbing his chin and grimacing, "But we could never prove it with what we have."

"Jeb, has your Dad talked to you and helped you remember at all or helped you on what to say?"

"No, Sir."

"I believe you." Then he glanced at Dad, "Jeb's got such a good memory for a boy his age it could sound like we schooled him, the problem is we still don't have a case."

"You're joking?" Dad said.

"I wish I was. I left out the other about giving someone a feather coat and the pecker comparison. These would distract in a trial and not prove anything. Neither of you said you saw tar or feathers – an empty threat. The other matter is risible, laughable – criminal perhaps but neither of you saw. I've never heard of it."

"Me neither," Dad said.

"But I do believe Jeb, every word from his five-year-old mouth. I believe it all and I believe he is five. Though we should have his birth certificate. If I held things up a couple of years the jury would be looking at a seven year old and his story might be more believable. I have pictures to prove the house was burnt. The other lawyer would go after Jeb's credibility on every issue."

"How? He would not want to put his clients on the stand." Dad asked.

"No. He would attack Jeb try and confuse him and make his age a question. Believing that truth can be stranger than fiction and proving it are two different things. Someone testifying to a stranger than fiction truth has immediate credibility issues. After all a jury is trying to decide what to believe – what's believable? I have seen it – "unbelievable but true" by definition cannot fly with a jury. They have to believe that it is true."

"But you said you believe Jeb."

"And you too," Stan replied. "This would be a real feather in my cap. I think the youngest child to appear in a Georgia court was twelve. I could beat that by years. I'd could write articles and speak on it the rest of my life. I have already talked to a child psychologist who is willing to testify. He said preliterate children remember a picture of what they see better than adults do. Jeb I believe is more gifted in that respect than any child of any age that I have talked to – including my own and I consider them smart. The psychologist said he would help me write a book on it, he had other examples of children acting beyond their years."

Stan reloaded his drink; "I began my conversation with the psychologist by saying you're not going to believe this boy is five years old. Now that I have heard it from Jeb it's more amazing. Jeb, you behaved and remembered very well. The psychologist said it's unusual but boys' maturity up to age twelve is all over the place. He said there's not a straight line for development. The first child is the most likely to step up in a crisis and act years above his age. They are the first to be given responsibility even if it's a household chore."

Stan noticed I looked confused, "Jeb, a psychologist is a doctor who helps us understand how people act and think. When your Dad told me about your experience, I thought he described the behavior of an older boy. So I went to the psychologist and he said you just acted older – like an older boy."

Looking back to Dad he added, "He could testify."

Dad put his cigarette out, "I was with Jeb and I have difficulty believing how well he behaved under the circumstances. And his memory for details is extraordinary. I have not told people because I thought they would not believe it."

Stan laughed, " I thought you weren't talking for other reasons."

Dad smiled as he lit another cigarette, "I have had better days. It's still incredible."

"If your talking Jeb's behavior beyond his years the psychologist gave me several examples."

Stan noticed it troubled me to be the subject of the conversation.

"Jeb, your Dad and I think you acted like a boy several years older than you are, you acted like a big kid. People who did not see it may have difficulty believing what your Dad and I know you did."

Stan lit another cigarette and fanned the smoky air. Dad got up and cracked a window to allow some smoke to escape. Stan continued, "OK Hank listen to this because it could come up again. I have examples, a five year old that plays sports with eleven and twelve year olds has impressive athletic ability but he also rises to their maturity level, or closer to it. When I was a senior at Boys High we had a freshman quarterback. He was our team leader and a fine quarterback. He didn't act like a freshman and we didn't treat him like one. You will be familiar with this one- the war. Under fire, men acted all different ways. A lot of nineteen year olds stepped up and took action and responsibilities far beyond their years. This is why I believe Jeb's story."

Dad began to speak but Stan continued pointing at Dad with his cigarette in hand, "Not just because you were their but because I have seen it. I saw it in me!" Stan laughed. "I just told you about it not five minutes ago in the Pacific. Twenty-three-years old, on my first ship larger than a motorboat for six months, essentially I asked for command and the captain gave it to me. I thought I deserved a medal. But in light of Jeb's experience, I think the captain thought no one would believe a twenty-three year old novice could do as well as I did. Not only did I command an effective attack on a Jap Cruiser, but also, I saved our ship from getting sunk. And three hundred and twenty nine men, including me, were thankful for that – we had some casualties. Anyway, we started with a crew of three-twenty-nine."

Tears formed in Stan's eyes as he recalled the war and mentioned the casualties. We sat in silence for a while and he returned to the matter at hand.

"You don't know how to read yet do you, Jeb?"

"No, sir. The tattooed man asked me that too."

"I bet he did. When do they teach reading these days?" Stan asked Dad.

"First grade. They may learn their letters and how to spell their name earlier."

"And Jeb's two years out. I could keep this out of court two years if we had something," said Stan, half talking to Dad, and half thinking out loud. Stan frustration showed.

Stan continued on a somber note, "It's a shame, Hank, you don't have a thing. If I go in to court with what we have now they're liable to charge Jeb for starting the fire." I looked dismayed and Stan reassured me. "No, Jeb, I'm kidding. I guess this isn't something to kid about. The GBI checked on the Negro preacher. He moved out the Monday morning after the Klan visit. If you raise too much Hell, the Klan may be back to see you."

"This is a heinous crime, several crimes, and all felonies. I don't believe they got that much pull in Atlanta," Dad said.

"Well, maybe they don't. You saw one in uniform and there are at least two Klan organizations. I didn't think about it until now but we would have to start by trying to prove which one, there may be several Klan organizations. I am sure he didn't tell you which one he was in."

"My Granddad, old Stan II, used to say the Klan took a lot of credit for stuff they didn't do. One Grand Dragon lives a few streets over from me in a nicer house than mine. The Klan had enough influence to get a parade permit not long ago. I didn't go. The paper said more than a hundred Klansmen dressed in sheets rode horses down Peachtree Street."

"You're kidding?" Dad said.

"No, I'm not." Stan said as Dad sat in silent disbelief. Then Stan added, "It's obvious to in me they have good legal advice from somebody. This incident didn't happen this way by accident." Stan paused to light another cigarette.

"And if they did, it's another felony. The bastard ought to be disbarred," Dad said as he finished his drink.

"Hank, you can't tell me you were born in Georgia and never heard about the Klan." Stan raised his voice, "Hellfire, the policeman said it was 'street justice,' you're a lawyer you want justice don't you? Fear of the Klan got your car back and you and your son weren't killed in the first place. I might take their case. If I had to take part in a trial I'd rather be counsel for the defense. None of my clients would testify, if they could ever be identified. The prosecution would have just two witnesses, a man, who was so drunk he was throwing up sick, and a five year old, who can't read. And they saw different things."

"I don't believe it." Dad lit a cigarette in the wearisome quiet, "Stan, it's no way to run a city in America. Someone's home was burned down."

"Sorry, Hank, I didn't mention it before. I know you saw furniture moved out but the GBI investigated and it was a vacant house. The property does not have a current title or insurance. One Negro said he was glad they burned it down because bad kids hung out there. Jeb commented a lot of young Negroes came out of the house. He picked the right house." Stan mocked raising his right index finger, "Another point for the defense destroying a vacant building that had become a nuisance."

Dad shook his head. "Damn, damn, damn…it's just not right."

Stan, lifting his head out of his hand and putting on his black-rimmed glasses and looking at Dad said, "Well I hope you are not talking to me and certainly not to Jeb. You're a lawyer. What do you suggest?"

Dad remained silent. He drained his bourbon glass and gave the ice cubes an idle twirl.

"Hank, no prosecutor or law enforcement officer will waste his time on what we have. You didn't see the rifle and Jeb didn't see it pointed. Neither of you saw a white strike a Negro. Jeb did I ask if you saw anyone shake their fist like they would hit someone?"

"No, sir."

"So you only saw Negroes hit the other Negro man."

"Yes, sir." I added, "The time when the Negroes took the car a Negro boy pushed me a few times and I slugged him in the shoulder."

"Wow, Hank, I love this kid." Then looking back and holding his fists up in a boxing pose Stan asked, "Did you cry then?"

"No, sir. But the Negro boy did and he stood behind his Mom."

Stan clapped his hands, "Did you see this, Hank?" Dad nodded his head. "Hank, I would be so proud of young Stan if he stood up to a bully, I would buy him a steak dinner. Would you like a steak, Jeb?"

"I like the Varsity."

Stan laughed, "Hank, take that boy, no, take that young man to the Varsity." I smiled and was glad for the levity and proud someone thought I had behaved well. I felt we had reached the happy conclusion like on TV.

"Have a drink, Hank," Stan said, lighting a cigarette and pouring another for himself.

"No thanks, I don't want one."

"Don't thank me. It's your whiskey I'm offering," said Stan trying to cheer Dad up. "Come on, Hank, be a good host. I don't want to drink alone."

Dad's face showed his complete discouragement.

"Jeb, you can finish your Peachtree Cola," said Stan pouring the rest of the Peachtree Cola from the bottle over the remaining ice in my glass. Then continuing to try to raise our spirits, "Jeb, I was serious about how well and brave you acted through all this. I am proud to know you. I hope my son would do as you have done. I'd buy him a steak or take him to the Varsity, whatever he wanted. Your Dad feels proud too. Don't you, Hank?"

"Yes, I do," said Dad.

"Well, tell him, Hank," said Stan. "You boy stood on the firing line. He kept ranks. He did his duty. I learned about duty at Boy's High. Did they teach that up at your fancy law school?"

He smiled at his jab at Dad's alma mater and continued looking at me, "Jeb, I am proud to know you, you and your Dad."

Neither Dad nor I understood what Stan was trying to do. "Let me pour you a drink, Hank."

"No, thanks," said Dad as Stan poured anyway.

"This isn't the brand they made you drink is it?"

"No, I don't care for another drink."

"Hank, I have sat in this chair before." Dad looked and I lifted my head. Stan had never been in our home. "Well, I got your attention," he said smiling and patting the side of the chair. "Yes, not this chair but too many like it alongside good people like you, maybe not a boy as young and brave as Jeb. Sometimes things happen, bad things, and you try, but there is nothing you can do about them because the system we have requires evidence we cannot provide, not now anyway. We all feel bad we can't do anything and we should but we have to put this behind us and go on. These people may get caught the next time or they may end up in jail for something else. Those who choose to live outside the law end up in jail, on the end of a rope, or face down dead in the street. I have seen it numerous times."

Dad sipped his drink, "Well I guess I haven't seen it."

"What's troubling you so much? Scary – yes, ugly – yes, against the law – yes, but at the end of the day, both days, you and Jeb walked free and a vacant house got burned?"

"Stan, in the war we often had a lot of time to chew the fat between missions. Heck we would chat in the cockpit. We talked about what we were fighting for and dying for and this wasn't it."

Stan put his hand to his brow, "I am curious because it isn't much different than when you left. In the war we both lost friends and comrades, but I have to say, in Georgia, aside from the killing overseas, the goddamn war has been the best thing to hit our economy in a hundred years. Things are better for whites and Negroes. We have a large number of non-farm jobs we never had and we keep getting more. Poor farmers and their families used to work ten to twelve hours a day and pray a crop came in. Then they died of malnutrition and pellagra before they turned fifty. The Hell of it is every poor cracker that could pass the physical volunteered to fight the war for this nation. Now they have eight hour a day jobs. They get paid in cash no matter what and the kids go to school instead of work on the farm. If they get sick they can see a doctor. The big farmers have to pay better wages to compete for labor. I could go on. Yes, aside from the shameful loss of life, if I had known all the good the war was going to do for Georgia I'd attacked the Japs myself."

"Yes, I must agree Atlanta is more prosperous. But the vigilantes, the violence, the Klan, anti-Negro prejudice, it's not the way America is supposed to be."

"Hank, it's never been the way it's supposed to be, number one, and number two, you'll never get rid of prejudice. I'm prejudiced against some people and things. You went to Tech and I went to Georgia. There is prejudice right there and you're prejudiced against the Klan."

"They burned a house down!"

"And that's against the law! If you catch them I'll try them. Right now all I got is burning a vacant house without a permit. And I'm not even sure they need a permit. But the same group may go out and take up a collection for the March of Dimes to stop Polio next Sunday. We can't try a case on your prejudice or mine. You can't legislate against prejudice or we'll all go to jail."

"Oh come on, you have more than that," Dad said.

"I'd have something if someone owned the goddamn house! If a bank had a loan on it, or if there was insurance but there's nothing. No current record, or claim of ownership that I can find. Someone trying to collect on the fire would have more legal problems getting a hearing than you do." Stan guffawed as he spoke again, "If we ever find the malefactors I could claim the house was mine and ask for damages. They have nothing to prove it wasn't my house. I could say I wasn't home. I might claim what's left for a rental property."

Dad thought out loud, "There are so many people involved, so many felonies, you'd think we would have more to go on."

"Yes, I would have more if we had a defendant you and Jeb could identify, but I don't. For the time being you do not have anything more you can do. You gave it your best shot now drop it and move on."

We sat again in frustrating silence, Stan added, "You're a lawyer sometimes there is a wrong but you lack proof or the defendant has no resources you move on. I mentioned "crackers" you know too poor to fence their livestock so they crack whips to drive them. I had a man want to sue the cracker who owned the cow he hit on the highway and totaled his car. The poor farmer came to the scene. Most don't. He offered the man the road kill. I looked into it. The poor farmer owed everyone and it was his only cow. I told my client that he should have taken the beef. Here's my point, my client was one hundred per cent right but there was nothing to do, at least to the farmer. And you were one hundred per cent right and the Klan and the car thieves were one hundred per cent wrong but we don't have evidence for the police or for a case I can pursue. I'm sorry but that's it."

Stan's frustration showed and he tried to lighten up as he rose to leave. "Call me the next time something comes up. I will accept your bourbon as my retainer this time. If there is a next time I will ask for twelve year old Scotch, I'm worth it, and you may like it too."

We stood up as Stan rose to leave he addressed me, "I'll repeat myself, Jeb I'm proud to know you. You got more sand than boys twice your age. Heck you got more sand than a lot of adults." We exchanged a firm handshake.

"Thank you, sir, Lukey said I had sand too, but I don't know what it means."

"Lukey was right about one thing." Lowering his voice and leaning toward me he continued, "It means you can keep your head when the shit hits the fan. Your Dad can explain it." Dad walked him out to his car. After Stan left Dad gave me a quick talk on "sand" giving ballast to a ship so it could sail straight in rough water. I better understood shit hitting the fan.

Chapter 11 Shopping

Mom invited her friend Jan Biden, married to one of Dad's fraternity brothers to ride to the huge Gold's department store downtown. Mom thought I would forget about the house burning excitement with some early Christmas shopping. She was right, I wanted toys, balsa wood airplanes powered by rubber band driven propellers, electric trains, soldiers, Indians, cowboys, knights and forts Dad had to assemble. As a bonus, we might see Santa Claus and the giant Christmas tree.

Everybody went downtown to shop, see, and be seen. The ladies dressed for the occasion. Mom cleaned us boys up and she wore a Sunday dress. Ladies went to luncheons and fashion shows at the larger stores. Uniformed drivers in a fleet of trucks painted in the store's signature green color and logo delivered packages to the home. The multi-storied stores and parking garages sprawled for blocks.

Billy was left in the care of a maid and the two ladies felt sufficient to handle Travis and me. The ladies congratulated themselves on finding a parking spot in the closest garage. They decided to take us boys to the street level and outside to see the Christmas decorations.

The plan called for us to exit the garage on to the street. We came out at the extra wide sidewalk built for the bus drop off as a city bus pulled to the curb. A number of Negroes stepped back to allow people off the bus. A young Negro man caught my eye as he walked up the street. He had a strange look in his eye, he held his right arm under a dirty brown sports jacket. As he approached the open bus door he pulled out a large hunting knife that would have made Jim Bowie proud. He stepped to the open bus door brandishing the foot and a half long blade.

"Give me the money," He shouted above the screams of passengers. I watched from the width of the doublewide sidewalk as he climbed on the bus demanding the bus driver's leather cash purse. Oblivious to the commotion Jan and Mom continued to look over the façade of the store for early Christmas decorations.

"Mom! Look!"

By the time she looked the man had boarded the bus his body shielding the knife from our view. The passengers continued to scream and the terrified driver handed over his cash purse. Mom could not see what was happening but she sensed something was wrong. The ladies pushed Travis and me against the building.

A white haired man stopped in traffic heard the screams and turned his car into the bus lane. He jumped from his car in front of the bus and threw off his sports jacket. He pulled an auto-loading pistol. He left his car in neutral so it rolled out of his way as he ran the short distance toward the bus.

The crowd of Negro women at the bus stop panicked at the sight of the man with the gun. They flushed like a flock of magpies flapping and screaming en mass through the doors into the garage. Petite Jan tried valiantly to get Travis, her charge into the door but was pushed aside. Mom tried to shield me and then pulled Travis from Jan back to the wall of the store.

The Negro brandishing the knife had the money purse but was still on the bus. The white man pointing his pistol shouted to the bus driver, "Get out from behind him so I can shoot!...Boy put down that knife or I'll shoot! I mean it! I will shoot you! Boy this gun will kill you!"

The Negro youth turned back and forth threatening both men, apparently trying to make up his mind. The driver with his hands in the air got behind his seat against the side of the bus. The white man knelt by the extreme left-hand side of the open bus door. He aimed his pistol at an angle so if he missed or a bullet went through the thief it would go high and wide of the terrified driver. When the youth moved back at the driver he fired twice. The sharp report of the pistol shook the store showroom window. After two shots the Negro turned and lunged down the bus steps. He tried to use the money purse as a shield with the knife leading the way. The man fired two more shots at point blank range as he backed away from the Negro who came at him with the shiny knife blade extended. Travis and I had covered our ears but we could feel the window shake behind us. The Negro missed with the blade and collapsed on the sidewalk three steps off the bus.

The man continued to point his gun at the downed Negro, "Let me go mister. I learned my lesson. I ain't gonna steal no more."

"You ain't going nowhere boy," The white man said without animosity.

"I don't feel nothing, is I shot?" Then the Negro looked at his bloody shirt, "Is I dying?"

"Could be, I'm not a doctor."

Jan and Mom looked at each other aghast, afraid to move or speak. After a few silent moments people started to move, Negro women came out of the garage and headed for the next bus in line.

"This pavement be so cold... Tell my Momma I's sorry," the Negro said raising his voice as his eyes fixed on the sky and added in a diminishing tone, "I is so cold." His mussels relaxed. A few moments passed before a death rattle shook him.

The shaken bus driver closed the doors and the shooter banged on them to open.

"I saved your butt. You're welcome and here's your purse," and threw him his cash purse. "Ask your passengers if anyone has something to cover up the blood."

His driverless car had rolled into the intersection. A patrol car pulled to the curb and the policeman unaware of the shooting, started to write the man a ticket. Passers by pointed the policeman in the direction of the dead Negro.

"Hey! That's my car don't give me a ticket. I just busted up this robbery," the white-haired man called out. When the policeman looked up the street he added pointing downward, "This nigger's dead. Wasn't anything to do for him."

A Negro woman offered a new towel to the policeman to cover the corpse. While the policeman's back was turned a Negro youth picked up the hunting knife and walked a few steps away stashing it under his jacket. A senior policeman arrived on a motorcycle.

"I'll take care of this. Please remove that car from the intersection."

"Yes Sir," the junior patrolman replied. On the southwest side of the intersection the Atlanta rail yards began. A quarter a mile away was the main rail terminal sitting above a spaghetti network of tracks. Had the robber been successful he could have run down the tracks where no car could follow.

After a brief discussion with the parties the senior policeman declared the shooting was self-defense.

Jan was short. She cut her brown hair in a pageboy haircut and wore tortoise shell glasses. She had on a nice go-shopping dress and carried an appropriate purse. She stepped up to give her name as a witness. The policeman told her it was not necessary. She then volunteered that she thought the shooting unnecessary. The policeman, who had ruled it self-defense, did a double take. He told her he had a lot to do.

Jan said, "I'll just stand right here."

In the interim, Jan spoke to the bus driver. His money purse and cash had bullet holes. He fussed; he had been in the line of fire. Jan said he should complain that he and the passengers had been endangered and frightened. She wanted an investigation to see if the Negro was shot in the back.

Jan asked the policeman, "I am a witness and I think the bus driver has some things to say. How will this be investigated?"

"Mam it doesn't matter. The Negro was committing armed robbery," The policeman said in disappointed tones. "I don't think anybody is going to miss this one."

"His Momma gonna miss him," a large Negro woman said as she exited her hiding place in the garage.

"That's right. His mother will miss him. He could have family and the shooting may have been needless," said Jan clutching her square handbag in front of her.

The motorcycle policeman looked at Jan and pushed his white helmet back on his head. He wore boots to his knees and gold stripes ran down the outside seams of his blue jodhpurs. He called to patrolman at the car to send the shooter back up to him to clear up "some loose ends." He also asked him to make sure a Grady ambulance was on the way to get the corpse. The Negro youth, who had picked up the knife, remained to watch.

The shooter expected praise for his quick and decisive action. Not so. The sound and fury signified miscommunication and misunderstanding. Onlookers made numerous remarks and suppositions about the position of the assailant and his knife when the man fired the fatal volley of shots. The large Negro woman asserted she had seen the assailant shot in the back. Jan would not permit this. "Mam, you almost knocked me and those kids down running into the garage. How you could have seen the shooting?"

"Well did you see it or not?" the policeman said.

"No, I guess not," and she headed for the next bus in line.

Then looking at Jan, the policeman said, "Mam, niggers do lie."

"Well I agree she was mistaken," Jan said parsing the truth. "But I think he was shot in the back and I do not see any knife."

The policeman was disturbed to find the knife gone and called out "Did anyone what happened to the knife?"

"We did," I answered.

"Hush Jeb" Mom said.

"That Negro took it," I said pointing at the youth who confirmed his identity by running in the direction of the second policeman. A passerby tripped him. The youth fell headlong and the knife skittered across the pavement. The policeman put the recovered knife in a case on the motorcycle. The patrolman handcuffed the Negro youth, bloodied by his fall, and put him into the back of his car.

"Mam if those boys saw what happened, please let them speak so we can get on about our business."

"He started back up the stairs. It looked like he was trying to stab the bus driver. Then he turned and dived at the man shooting the gun. I'm not sure which way he was turned when the shooting started. My Mom moved in front of me, then in front of Travis but I saw most of it," This was not what Jan wanted to hear.

Mom was shaken. "I tried to shield my children,"

Jan seeing her angst said, "You did the right thing Kate."

Travis then chirped up. "Does it matter who the knife was pointed at? He was going to hurt someone and he got shot."

"Out of the mouth of babes," the policeman said. "Anyone who wants to file a report may do so at the police station." On advice from the policeman, the shooter had said nothing. Then turning to Travis and me the policeman asked, "Do you boys remember anything else."

"The man kicked the knife away and pointed the pistol at the Negro but he didn't get up," I said.

"Anything else?"

"Yes, sir," Travis said pointing at the corpse, "He said something about his Momma."

"They always do," the policeman said shaking his head.

Jan spoke up, "We're not going to know what he said because he is dead now. Grady hospital is not five minutes away. We have been here twenty minutes and no ambulance has arrived. They might have saved his life."

"Mam, he was shot to pieces. He could have fell off the bus into a Grady ambulance and been dead before he got five minutes from here."

Jan, returning to the subject of the shot to the back, asked if the policeman could tell the direction the shots from the wounds. The policeman pulled a royal blue towel with the store tags still attached from off of the corpse. He rolled the Negro over on his stomach showing two red holes in the right side of his back. He rolled him back over and examined the two larger bloody areas in the center of his chest. The policeman looked at the shooter, "You can say something if you want, or not. You can write out a statement at the police station."

The shooter said, "I don't believe this, I heard the screaming and jumped out of my car. The Negro already had the cash purse. When he saw me, he tried to hold the knife on the driver. I shot him twice to save the driver and twice more when he turned on me. One shot went through the cash purse. I backed up. He made it off the bus before he fell on the sidewalk."

Jan asked, "Have you ever shot someone before?"

"Yes."

"Another Negro?"

"No, Ma'am, I shot a white man holding a gun on a married couple."

"Did you kill him?"

"No, Ma'am, he's serving life in prison. He had killed two other people. People were real happy I shot him; it saved those two people's lives. It was in the newspaper." Jan's reaction bewildered the shooter.

The policeman said, "Well I want to thank you. You are a hero and deserve all our thanks and a good citizen award."

"Thank you, officer. Can you help me get my car out of here?" The shooter asked.

"Glad to."

A Grady ambulance arrived. Two Negro orderlies both dressed in white shirts and pants jumped out, rolled a gurney and loaded the corpse. Jan spoke to the orderlies, Why wasn't the siren on?"

"Mam, we don't turn it on if they dead. The police said to pick up a corpse."

"Aren't you going to check him to make sure?"

"No need to check this one, Ma'am. He's dead. And you can keep your towel," referring to the royal blue towel left where the corpse had lain.

A white janitor in a forest green uniform from the department store mopped up the blood. He did his job and emptied his bucket in a street drain basin.

Gold's welcomed middle class Negro shoppers and extended them credit. We followed two well-dressed Negro women, who had seen the shooting, into the department store snack bar. We recovered by drinking a Peachtree Cola. The whole event unnerved Mom and Jan.

"I can't believe what has happened in the last few weeks. Jebby has seen it all."

"I know. It's incredible. There should be an investigation," Jan suggested.

The two women talked at length in exasperated tones about what they had seen and what they should do. They decided to consult the husbands prior to going to the police. Mom lamented that the purpose of the trip was in large part to make me forget about the recent violence in my life and now Travis and I had seen a Negro shot to death no further away than across the sidewalk.

"What do we do now?" Jan asked.

"I don't know. If the shopping was supposed to divert the boys attention to what's happened before maybe we should let them focus on shopping now? I don't know what the proper thing to is." The impact of crazy recent events caused a pause in the lives of the two women and they could not overcome the inertia.

After a moment of reflective silence Jan smiled wryly, "I don't know. I don't recall if Emily Post addresses the question of 'Should you go shopping after seeing a Negro shot down on the street?'"

Mom noticed the two Negro women at the other end of the snack bar, "They were there let's see what they do." As if on cue the two ladies got up and headed into the store.

"The Negro ladies are going to shop, we have a good parking spot, cash in our purses, and the babysitter is paid for. I say shop 'til we drop…You boys OK?" Shopping? What choice did we have. Jan waved our band on toward the merchandise. Their high heels clicked on the linoleum hallway as ladies started for the merchandise and the shopping was on.

It was the old bait and switch, there were no Christmas displays, decorated trees or Santa Claus, Travis and I followed in their train like two prisoners condemned to hours of trying on long pants and sweaters.

I prophesied to Travis, "Dad is going to call Mr. Wallace."

Chapter 12 Review

The day after the shooting Dad invited himself to Stan Wallace's home off of Peachtree Street. The two story red brick home had dark green shutters and a large formal entrance. Sidelight windows surrounded the white front door. The pleasant fragrance of flowers filled the air. Boxwoods, azaleas, camellias, holly bushes, flowerbeds and dogwoods were decoratively placed around the house, driveway and walkway. The inside of the house was spacious and tastefully furnished. The friendly golden retriever rose to greet us and quickly reclined back on the hardwood floor. The men wore dark suits and ties and I was in blue jeans and a buttoned shirt. I wore my authentic cowboy boots from my cousins in Texas. Stan led us into the dining room where ashtrays and drink fixings were on the table. Greetings and handshakes were made around.

"Mr. Wallace, you sure do have a lot of bushes." I observed.

"Yes, Mrs. Wallace landscapes anew every fall and spring. I'm afraid to stand still in the yard for fear she'll put a flower bed around me." Stan chortled at his own joke as we sat down.

I observed portraits of five children around the dining room walls and asked, "Are those pictures of your children?"

"Yes Jeb, five of them, I am one up on your Dad." Stan laughed to himself, "I have too many to feed, but in the moment the subject of children comes up with Mrs. Wallace I feel like I can feed the world." Dad and Stan laughed and laughed more at my uncomprehending expression. "You'll understand when you are older."

Dad had purchased a fifth of scotch and had it in hand. He had given Stan a synopsis of events over the phone and was in good spirits. No one in the family was hurt and "It damn sure wasn't his fault this time."

"Good to see you again, Hank. Seems like I barely got home good before you called again, I may have to get a retainer."

"I have twelve year old Scotch for you," Dad offered.

"I allow thirty days for payment. It's been two weeks or less. I think I should follow y'all around; your lives are a heck of a lot more exciting than mine. Jeb, the white man pulled the trigger this time? It wasn't the same one was it?"

"No, sir." I smiled recognizing the joke. "He had white hair."

"And he wasn't shooting at you? You weren't scared were you?"

"No, sir."

"I didn't have to ask, I knew you wouldn't be," Stan said as he poured his scotch and Dad his bourbon and then both men lit cigarettes. The meeting lacked the urgency of the previous meeting.

I told the story and Stan asked a few questions. Stan laughed at the end when the women decided to go shopping anyway. Dad asked if he was surprised.

"Surprised?" Stan smiled, "I'm shocked they even considered not shopping. I do not think my wife and daughters would have stopped for the Peachtree Cola. Anything more to this story?"

"No, sir."

""I am must say I am encouraged to hear Negroes can shop in Gold's and be served at the snack bar. Women shopping together...Maybe we can drink from the same water fountain. Anyway, I'm mildly surprised Gold's security guard was not involved. A trend I am not sure I like among downtown businesses is to provide their own security. The police ought to be there and if we need more, hire them." Stan looked at Dad.

"We can save police manpower for another day."

"OK, I'll ask Jeb. No one shot at you and you didn't shoot anyone, did you?"

"No, sir."

"Here's my point. I do not have a client here." Raising his glass, "I have a retainer, a damn fine one, but no client."

Dad began, "We wanted to know about the shooting."

"Yes," Stan answered. "Justified or not? Do you want to know if it was justified, Jeb?"

"I don't know what justified means."

"Justified means a person is in the right to do the thing. It is a permissible thing to do under the law, or OK to do. You understand OK?"

"Yes, sir."

Raising his voice in false drama Stan continued, "Yes. It became justifiable homicide when the policeman said it was. Period."

"If his report says the shooting was justified, it stops there. Then, yes, because the citizen shot an armed man threatening another's life in the commission of a felony. A reasonable man would assume the uniformed bus driver had his life threatened. A robber holding a knife is a deadly threat. It doesn't matter whether he had been shot in the back first as he threatened the driver or not. It was also justifiable homicide when the robber turned and lunged pointing the knife at the citizen holding the gun. The citizen justifiably defended himself. The robber did the shooter the good favor of dying on the spot. We ought to be thankful for the armed citizen who acted in a reasonable and lawful manner. I would be if I was a prosecutor."

"Wouldn't it be better if he made a citizen's arrest?" Dad asked.

"Hell, Hank, it would have been better if the damn Negro didn't attempt armed robbery. He'd still be alive. Some poor man driving down the road with no police training jumped into action. Anyway, what could a policeman have done?"

"I wanted your take on it."

"You got it. And what's worse about this situation is that somewhere in Atlanta tomorrow another bus driver will be robbed at gun or knife point by a young Negro or white man, who dropped out of high school and got tired of the menial jobs he was qualified to do. He thought he would get out of a money bind by robbing one bus or one citizen. When he got away with the first one, like fox in the hen house, he will keep stealing until he's caught. The criminal life sucks him in further and the outcome is always bad."

"That's a shame. I hate to hear it's such a common occurrence. Why don't they stay in school?"

"I don't know. The truancy rate in the Negro high schools is much higher and the poor Negro fathers tend to abandon their families. I don't know that anyone has made a study of the effect of this on the children. It can't be good."

"Segregation makes life harder for Negroes and that has to be reflected in the Negro community."

"I agree with you on that. I like you and I think your heart is in the right place. You and I agree on many things. It's outrageous we can't all drink from the same water fountain and I'm talking about whites and coloreds. But we have a system and though not perfect it works pretty well. I'm not certain you or I could improve it, but I am certain it's not our job to fix it. You want to fix it then vote for a new lawmaker. I have heard about your pro bono manslaughter case. You don't need another case like it for a long while. Do your part and move on. You haven't heard back on your order have you?"

"No," Dad responded. "What do you think will happen?"

"Don't know. If I had to guess the judge is going to let her serve more time while he considers your order. He's got it and he has to do something. Don't you do anything, no letters, no calls, nothing, don't even speak to the judge. I guarantee he won't forget about this one. He's got a citizen serving time without a conviction or signed plea. The judge may have more legal problems than your client does. I can give you my word, no I won't, my word is too much, but I do guarantee whatever he does it will be letter perfect. I cannot emphasize enough whatever it is - take it and thank him! This case is more mess than an inexperienced criminal lawyer should have been asked to clean up. I'm glad to help you. I hope things calm down."

"I have other fish to fry."

"Yes, I've heard about your post as Attorney General of the Jekyll Island Authority. The paper said the beaches and two hotels would open soon. Good luck."

"Yes, the beaches will open in December. One white and one colored hotel will open when they get certificates of occupancy. There are plans for a convention center."

"One or two?" Stan asked with eyes raised.

"Can't afford two. One will have to do, two sets of bathrooms and water fountains. It's not underway yet I was hoping the 'separate is not equal' ruling by the Supreme Court would change things, not yet."

"It's coming that genie will not go back in the bottle. It's the law now. The justices have written a decision but I have not heard that they have written an order for implementation. I think we are looking at ten years of lawsuits."

"Ten years?" Dad sighed

"Sure, will make a lot of lawyers rich. I say let them argue, it leaves more work for me." Stan laughed good-naturedly and added, "We're in agreement. Let's not talk politics, it will ruin our suppers."

Dad grinned with a weary smile, "I understand you played basketball."

"Yes and you are nice to bring it up. But if you are interested, you are the only one in Atlanta. I am actually a big football fan. I played at Boy's High but no college wanted me because I was so skinny back then. Georgia is my team. My high school coach used to lament, we had a football team all we needed was football players. Bobby Dodd has the football players. He is going to take Tech to its fourth or fifth straight bowl game and he wins them all."

"He's done well."

"I'll swap you Coach Wally Butts for Coach Dodd." Smiling at his joke Stan continued, "Poor Wally gets fewer top players. Those football recruits see the bright lights of

Atlanta and Wally can't get them to Athens." The conversation ended on sports and we went home.

***

Jan tried to pursue the matter further. Dad declined. After Dad's refusal she came by the house to make an appeal to Mom.

Jan persisted, "Neither the police nor the bus company will do anything more about the shooting. There will not even be a police hearing. Without Hank nothing more will be done."

"It is the only shooting I have ever seen and I just want to forget about it. I have Thanksgiving now and Christmas around the corner and my parents are coming down from Chicago. If I see another shooting or the Klan again before they get here I'll go back with them. I will support Hank, whatever he wants to do. My Dad and brother made it clear that Hank has a place at their law firm. Hank came back to Georgia at the governor's invitation, that's how he got the Jekyll post. If it wasn't for that, we might be living on the North Shore and that sounds good to me now. That's how I feel."

Jan had no children and a pushy personality. "Kate, I appreciate your feelings but we were the only white witnesses to the shooting and if we don't do something nothing else will be done."

"Jan, I'm glad you appreciate my feelings. You will have to go this one alone. Stan said justice was done, I consider the matter closed. I am concerned about the effects on Jeb and Travis. We want to forget about it and focus on the holidays."

"Then I guess that's the end of it," Jan sighed.

"It is for me. I am busy sewing Christmas stockings ad if you want to talk turkey I just pulled ours out of the refrigerator."

Despite Dad's efforts to diffuse the situation the tension and drama were as thick as the smoke off burning pine straw.

Chapter 13 Haymaker

The Klan episode and the Negro shot to death downtown headed the list of topics NOT to be discussed. And after each crisis my parents assured the kids things would return to normal.

I became interested in self-defense. I asked Mom to tell Santa Claus I will be the best boy ever for a western style lever action Winchester .45-70 rifle. Dad said to master boxing. I could learn the manly art of fisticuffs. Travis, my not smaller younger brother, could learn too.

Travis discovered a technical loophole in the 'must take boxing gloves and fight outside'. He reasoned the gloves had to be in his possession but not necessarily on his hands. As I struggled to put on the heavy gloves, Travis, held his gloves by the laces in his left hand, and hit me square in the gut with his bare right fist. It hurt and I couldn't breathe. I had focused on hitting Travis's head, his hard head made this wasted energy. Travis taught me a blow to the soft gut hurt and stopped breathing.

Dad explained to Travis the twofold purpose of the boxing gloves, first, the necessary delay in getting the gloves, going outside, and putting the gloves on, allowed for tempers to cool. Second, the weight of the gloves insured we could not hurt one another and we would tire quickly. He who hit first was deemed to have started the fight and liable for damages and punishment. Dad vigorously punished any violation of the rules for boxing with the paddle. So many fracases began over who was starting the fight or breaking a rule.

At school Tall Ed and Marvin liked to bully the smaller boys. The playground had an artificial ravine where earth had been scooped out during construction. We often tried to run down one side of the man-made canyon fast enough for our momentum to carry us up the other side. Ed and Marvin thought they would run down behind me and push me down as I started up the other side. They had tried to do this to me for days but I ran faster than they did. They changed their tactics one ran behind me and the other got in position at the bottom of the hill to push me. The push down was part of a larger plan. When they succeeded I did not cry but I didn't laugh either. They offered to let me hit Tall Ed if I did not tell on them. No doubt Marvin came up with this plan, especially the part about Tall Ed taking the blow. Marvin had black hair in an uncombed crew cut, the hair above his forehead stuck straight out like a diving board instead of falling down in his face. This made his deep-set dark blue eyes look even further back in his head.

The bullies schemed but I was in training. I think they assumed I would swing for the shoulder. Against the possibility of retaliation I wanted to take out Tall Ed with my first swing. He had combed back brown hair and brown eyes and seldom spoke, he went along with Marvin's schemes. Tall Ed made a head shot impossible and a shoulder shot awkward. Thanks to the lesson from Travis, I decided to swing for the gut.

I had confidence in another tactic, prayer. The slingshot trio mocked Miss Victoria's faith lessons and claimed to be Philistines. They did this to aggravate Lenard, the Baptist kid. According to Miss Victoria God did not like mocking nor Philistines and He was the Person I was going to pray to. "God help me against Tall Ed as you helped David against Goliath, the tall Philistine. Amen." I did not know what "Amen" meant but it was an important part of prayer and I needed to bring the good stuff.

Tall Ed and Marvin laughed thinking I either would not hit Tall Ed or could not hurt him. Tall Ed, as promised, stood still, with his arms dangling at his sides. I asked for a moment to consider their proposition. As they laughed, I silently prayed my one sentence prayer. Then I swung using my legs to shift my weight, turning fast and leaning full into the blow like a baseball swing. I hit Tall Ed so hard in the gut I thought my fist would come out his back. Yes, all the wind went out of him and as a bonus he crapped in his pants before rolling on the ground like a dog trying to pass a chicken bone. Marvin laughed thinking Tall Ed was hamming it up for the audience. As he continued to hold his gut and gasp for air Marvin asked what happened in disbelief. The agreement not to tell on me had been a trick. Ed and Marvin would not tell, but they arranged for some girls to tell on me.

The teachers shared Marvin's disbelief. Tall Ed towered a head taller than me, but a half a dozen girls swore by all things holy they saw me strike the blow. Then there was the crap in his pants. And I could not tell a lie because of the ninth Commandment and George Washington. Plus, I didn't want to blow my chance at the presidency. Yes, I hit him, and yes, I was sorry. If he had quit rolling around I would have apologized. Not good enough, I had to be separated from the good boys and girls until Mrs. Boyette could talk to me. I prayed silently, "Oh, Jesus please don't let her use the damn phone. Sorry Jesus I didn't mean to say damn. And Amen"

Miss Victoria took me to the vacant lunchroom, the pit of despair, a large lonely holding cell for Mrs. Boyette. It was my first trip to the lunchroom, a place that smelled like food but I was not hungry. A Negro man in a white apron moved in and out of the lunchroom preparing the tables for the big kid's lunch. I had never seen the cooks up close as the five year olds went home for lunch. The elation of clobbering Tall Ed ebbed. I sat with my elbows on the table supporting my miserable head. I heard the Negro man say in the kitchen. "I knows I seen that boy before."

"Quit your yapping and get juice out on the table."

Curious, I studied the Negro the next time through; I did not recognize him.

Next, the two Negro women came in carrying food on platters. LaVonn's mother led the way in her institutional green dress and matching apron. Our eyes met and our mouths fell open. The Negro man said, "Thelma, that's the boy what hit LaVonn ain't it?"

"Hush up fool!"

The facts struck like lightning. The three Negro cooks lived on a nearby dirt road, Clarendale Drive. They walked less than two hundred yards to work. In the last few weeks there had been a car stolen and a house fire on their road. And they recognized me.

Thelma went back in the kitchen, where the knives were, and I made for the door. I tried to return to class. I encountered Mrs. Boyette who said I would be punished for leaving the lunchroom. She told me to return to class. The Negroes knew me and nothing else mattered. I did not tell anyone at school. I do not know how many cooks would have kept my identity secret but I guessed it was less than three.

I told my disbelieving Mom, driving her stylish new turquoise Ford station wagon, the cooks at Hewett recognized me from the car theft and home burning. Now the Negro cooks could identify our car. An older wiser boy would have told his Dad rather than his ready to go back to Chicago Mom.

Dad arrived home at five. He left his charcoal gray suit and tie on as he set the table with the drink fixings and his checkbook. Dad paced back and forth. On Stan's instructions he would not speak to me. Stan arrived wearing a dark navy blue suit and black leather satchel style brief case. A secretary in a dress and jacket sat beside Stan.

"Hank, how much can you write a check for tonight."

"I had to buy a new car, a thousand at most."

"Fine, write one for five hundred, I will return what I don't use. I will add twenty dollars for every time you interrupt me. Here's my engagement letter, look it over and sign it. You haven't talked to Jeb, have you?"

"No."

"Good, I have to ask. Jeb, did your Dad ask you about anything that happened at school today?"

"No, sir." Stan's unsmiling professional attitude had me worried about hitting Tall Ed. Absent any information from my parents, I could only guess why Stan asked. One of the girls told Miss Victoria she thought Ed would die. God did not like Philistines, no question about that. But Ed was recovering the last time I saw him.

He introduced Charlotte, his secretary, to Dad and me. He told me to ignore her. She would scribble on a pad and read what I said from it. After conversation and changes Dad signed the letter. The men poured drinks and lit cigarettes; Charlotte and I got Peachtree Colas. Stan said I could have a whole one, Dad interrupted and said I could have a half.

"Hank, that's twenty dollars."

"It wasn't a question."

"You interrupted. Jeb, do you want to tell me what happened at school today?"

"Tall Ed pushed me down. I slugged him in the gut and he messed his pants and rolled around on the ground.

The girls told on me. But it was justified because he hit me first."

"Mr. Wallace is not here about Tall Ed," Dad noted.

"Hank, that's another twenty dollars. I do like you as a client. In five minutes I have made forty dollars and at this rate I'll drink another twenty in twelve year old Scotch… Hank, I have to insist!" Stan looked at Dad, who quickly put his finger to his lip.

"So Tall Ed bullied you and you slugged him in the gut with good effect. Jeb, I think if someone starts bullying me I'm going to call you. "Justified," the word you learned the last time I was here. What did your teacher say?"

"She sent me to the lunchroom to talk to Miss Boyette."

"The principal?"

"Yes, sir."

"What did she say?"

"She didn't come right away. I saw some Negroes in the lunchroom. They were there when the Buick was stolen. I left. Mrs. Boyette saw me and said she would punish me for leaving the lunchroom. It was time to go home so she sent me back to class."

"I bet she did. Hank, this is what I needed to know. Was Tall Ed involved in the slingshot dispute?"

"Yes, sir."

"Your Dad is right. I am not here to talk about Tall Ed but I believe your principal and I should have a little chat."

"Oh, Stan I don't think that's necessary," Dad said.

"I do, read your contract and add another twenty dollars. We talked about this earlier I think it's time to leave us." Exasperated, Dad nodded. He added bourbon and ice to his drink and grabbed an ashtray as he left for the master bedroom down a short hall.

After Dad left Stan asked me to describe how I recognized the Negroes and how I knew they recognized me. He clarified some things but did not put words in my mouth. He expressed surprise I bore no malice to Thelma, LaVonn's Momma. I explained she did not defend LaVonn's pushing me even when I hit him and he cried.

"But LaVonn's Momma is named Thelma and you are certain she was present when your Dad's car was stolen. And the Negro man, whose name you did not hear, had to be there because he said he saw you hit LaVonn." Stan paused long enough for Charlotte to quit writing. "Jeb, I want you to say yes that's right or no it's not."

"Yes that's right." I said.

Stan added scotch to his drink and lit a cigarette in silent thought. When Dad called from the bedroom to see if Stan had finished he called back. "No, Hank," Stan looked back at me. "Jeb, things turned out OK, but your Dad had to buy a new car. You said the Negroes could watch you to see which car you get into. Captain McConnell said not to let the Negroes learn about your new car. You don't want that do you?"

"No, sir."

"Could you pick Thelma out of a line of Negro women?"

"How many? I could pick her from the two at school."

"You didn't see the Negro man who saw you hit LaVonn, but he recognized you."

"Yes, sir, he told Thelma. But he wasn't one of the two Negroes that took the Buick."

"But all of the Negroes together scared you and your Dad."

"Yes there were too many for us, they weren't nice." I wanted to use the profanity I had learned but wisely held off.

"No they weren't Jeb. Did you see your Dad sign my letter and give me a check?"

"Yes, sir."

"I am your lawyer. You and your Dad are my clients. Scaring you, taking your car and money was wrong. All those Negroes, who participated, who took part, should go to jail."

"Well those other men burned the house," I said.

"Yes, and if they are caught they will go to jail too. They called what those men did 'street justice," but it is not real justice. Real justice would be putting the guilty Negroes and whites in jail. Is that what you want Jeb?"

"Is that what Dad wants?"

"Yes," Dad called from his bedroom.

Stan called back, "I won't charge you for that one."

"I know it's dinner time and you're getting hungry. But at this point I would like to ask you what do you think I should do?"

I had already thought of it earlier. "When we have car pool tomorrow have someone watch the Negro cook. If he comes out to identify our car put him in jail and don't let him out."

Stan smiled, "Terrific idea, Jeb. I mean it. If he goes for it, we can sweat the names of the ringleaders out of him. Maybe you should not go to school tomorrow."

"No, I have to go so you can see if he watches me."

"You are right again, but I will have to talk to your Dad."

"Anything else?"

"Thelma was not mean to me."

"Jeb, I am tired of paying you complements, but I have to say one more. Hank, come on back in." Dad returned and Stan continued, "I have tried not to put words in Jeb's mouth but I can't believe he's five. In essence he has given me a plan I believe will get all our rats under one net. He also asked me to go easy on Thelma, which shows equanimity beyond his years. The law does not provide for it but I'll remember it. You don't know that word do you"?

"No, sir."

"It means you are not snarling mad at all those Negroes. The whole mob is equally guilty but you are asking for mercy for one of the Negroes."

"I'm not," Dad said. "The law needs to work."

"I agree with your Dad," Stan said.

The next day as I left school the Negro cook walked out on the porch to take a cigarette break. Two teachers stood together at the steps as always. I walked out to a yellow Ford station wagon borrowed for the occasion. We drove to the Wallace's house to retrieve our new turquoise station wagon. Then we went home and I prayed the 'rats' would fall for the bait. Per plan, Dad called and said to expect Stan Wallace for a cocktail.

From the stairs to the dining room table from the nursery to drinks with the men, I moved up in the world fast and I loved it. I wanted to show I deserved to be there.

Stan let himself in the unlocked front door. "I think I have good news. The Negro cook's name is Elmer Wright, not related to the airplane Wright's," said Stan laughing at his own joke. "When I left Elmer he was a guest of the Atlanta police and state prosecutors. And Mack sent some patrolmen to search for Thelma who did not go to work today."

"Have a drink Stan," Dad offered joyfully. "So the rats took the bait."

"Took the bait is too mild. They jumped all over the bait, took it, and covered themselves up with it. At least Elmer Wright did," Stan said. "Call Jeb in here, he needs to hear this."

"Jeb, come on down, I know you're on the stairs," Dad said and I bounded down. I had already heard.

The men loaded their glasses, Dad his bourbon and Stan his scotch. Absent the urgent note of previous meetings we relaxed. Dad positioned ashtrays and napkins. Once the men lit their cigarettes the cocktail meeting began.

"What a relief!" Dad said as he exhaled his first puff of his cigarette, "Tell me about it?"

"Jeb gets credit too." Stan beamed, "I added to his plan. Mr. Wright did all you could want a guilty man to do and more." Stan pulled his hair back and adjusted his glasses. "Mrs. Boyette helped too. We briefed the two teachers who had the carpool duty to the situation. We asked them to do whatever the cook asked should he come out. They had to stay close enough to each other so they both could hear and confirm any conversation. Hank, it was too good."

"Did he recognize Jeb?"

"Yes, he came out to smoke on the porch when the five year olds left school. He said Jeb looked familiar and he asked one of the teachers about Jeb."

"We got him." Dad said.

"I'm going to fine you another twenty," Stan joked. "Let me finish. Not only did he ask Jeb's name, he handed the teacher a piece of paper and asked her to write it down, which she did. When Kate came in our yellow and white station wagon, he asked them to write down the kind of car it was. Charlotte wrote down the teacher's statements and they signed them at the school office. Our favorite police captain McConnell had two patrolmen stationed down the street. When they picked up Mr. Wright minutes, no seconds, after we called, he had in his possession the piece of paper the teacher had written on. You know the rest, the police and prosecutors have him. It's their case now."

Stan looked at me confounded, "Jeb, your Dad and I are overjoyed. I thought this case had no chance and now I think it's a lay-up, easy. What's troubling you?"

"You said the teachers gave him my name."

"No, no, no, I did say that but we made up a name."

I smiled relieved, "Great, are they going to get Dad's money clip back?"

"We will see."

"Did you know the prosecutor?" Dad asked.

Stan shook his head no. "They turnover pretty fast, they're good young lawyers trying to get a lot of courtroom experience."

Mrs. Hewett replaced all three cooks. Stan told Dad he didn't charge him for the interruptions. He returned two hundred dollars. After the Negro cook implicated himself, rather than go to jail, he ratted out on everyone else in the neighborhood. The police and state prosecutors did the rest. Thelma had taken LaVonn and fled the state. A search of several homes produced thousands of dollars in stolen goods but not Dad's money clip. The two Negroes who had stolen the car had multiple charges. All the Negroes offered to testify against their neighbors until the police refused to hear about another theft. Several went to jail but prosecutors did not pursue any charges related to the car theft. Stan expressed his disappointment I didn't testify. He wanted to get appointed by the court to question me. He wanted to write a book and do a speaking tour on how to question preliterate children in court.

Dad and Stan drank and smiled and joked about events. I was elated. I did not get disciplined at school or spanked at home for hitting Tall Ed, the Philistine. God answered my prayer and life was good.

Chapter 14 Deal

In March after a five month delay Judge Jackson handed down a ruling on Ida Mae Reivers's case. Dad called Stan for the familiar ritual of drinks and cigarettes.

Dad got straight to the business at hand. "Ida Mae Reivers can go free on parole if she can find a job in thirty days. Judge Jackson did not elaborate. He reduced Ida Mae's sentence to make her immediately eligible for parole. She has the option of further legal action to clear her name."

"Did she take the deal?" Stan asked.

"She is considering it. She didn't like it."

"What a mess. Hank, I think I'd rather chase the Klan. At least their leader has some money." Stan shook his head and leaned back in his chair catching a glimpse of me seated on the stair. "Come on down and join us Jeb. Yes, sir I want Jeb in here to protect us from bullies." Stan enjoyed my unsophisticated observations. "Jeb, have you heard your Dad talk about the Ida Mae Reivers case?"

"Is she the Negro woman who stabbed her husband?"

"That's the one. What do you think? This judge will let her out if she signs a paper saying she is guilty of manslaughter. Then she can go to court to prove she wasn't guilty. The next judge will be holding a paper signed by her admitting she is guilty?"

"Stan I appreciate your indulgence of Jeb, but this is a serious question," Dad inserted.

"As far as I am concerned Jeb has won his spurs, his opinion's as good as mine on this one. But I'm not sharing my retainer." Stan said patting the bottle of twelve-year-old Scotch.

"Well Jeb do you remember my question?"

"Yes, sir."

Stan grasped the bottle he had been patting and added scotch to his glass. "I think there are several mistakes here. If she could pay for a serious lawsuit I think we could give her one. Meanwhile the best thing for everyone is for this thing to go away. But she does not want to sign a guilty plea even to get out of jail." He mumbled, "I think I spilled too much water in the first one."

"Any ideas Stan?" Dad asked as he lit his second cigarette.

"None you would like. Send Jeb, I bet he could get it done," Stan said bringing me back in the conversation. "Do you have any ideas?"

"When Freddie, Marvin and Tall Ed apologized for trying to hit little kids, Dad said it shouldn't count because they had to. He said they were under 'duress.'"

"Oh Hell, let's not talk about that," Dad started shaking his head before I could finish.

Stan moved forward in his chair animated, "Hell, yes, let's talk about it." Then he laughed and clapped his hands, "This boy has to be a lawyer. Tall Ed is the boy you thought you killed? Right?"

"Some girls thought he would die but I knew he would be OK."

"And Tall Ed confessed about the slingshots under duress, under pressure, from who?"

"The teacher told them to apologize," I said.

"I like it, Hank, and it won't cost money or time and it is a Hell of a fine point. Ida Mae Reivers can sign and plead it was the only way she could get out of jail. Anyone would have to agree she's under duress. I like it. Can Jeb have some scotch? He's earned it." Stan guffawed and Dad called into the kitchen to ask Mom to please bring a Peachtree Cola.

"Do you think it will work?" Dad asked. "It's too simple."

"Why in the Hell do you care if it's simple or not? No chance to show off your Yale education if it's simple? There are two issues: first, will she sign? And second, can she get a hearing claiming duress? You're done if she signs. You did your job and got your client out of jail." Stan leaned back in his chair and took his glasses off laying them on the table in front of him.

"Could she get a new trial?" Dad asked.

Stan waved his arm dramatically, "If she is out of jail why would she want a new trial? An opportunity to hang! She's free. Damn, she may not be smart but she can understand free."

"I will make your point, but would she have a basis to clear her name?"

"First of all if she is out of jail no one will know unless she tells them. Heck, I never asked any lady if she killed her husband. Maybe I should, it doesn't come up in polite conversation. What I'm trying to say is it won't be an issue unless she makes it one."

"Well she seems to be determined to make it one," Dad said as he added bourbon and ice to his drink. He was quiet but Ida Mae's fate hung in the balance.

Stan looked surprised, "Clear her name now? No, Hank. The straight answer is no, no, not if I'm the judge anyway. If it came to me I would say I have a signed plea deal. You have paid your debt to society if you keep parole. The court is finished with you goodbye," Stan paused looking at Dad deep in his thoughts. "What the Hell, Hank? How much is being a convicted felon going to hurt her? Does she want to be a bank president or a politician? She may not vote anyway. Tell her to get out finish parole stay clean and then come back. Everyone loves a repentant sinner. I'd give her a clean bill then. I don't think this requires a hearing, find a judge to sign off on it. You can forget the 'duress' thing, but she can ask for the pardon."

"Dad, isn't that what Mr. Lockhart said to first get clear of jail then try to clear her name."

"You asked Dirk Lockhart about this and then you asked me?" Stan said clasping his hands over his chest. "Well I am flattered to be called to second guess Dirk Lockhart, but I can assure you it is time wasted."

"No, Stan. I talked to Dirk when I first got the case. His advice was to take any out the judge might give her and worry about the record later," Dad clarified.

"Other than the fact that you have wasted your retainer, I would like to point out I am giving the exact same advice as Dirk. And I want you to tell your friends and acquaintances. When people find out I am giving the same advice as Dirk I will be able to charge higher fees," Stan laughed as he turned up his glass.

"Hank, I have to hit the trail but I can tell you are concerned. It is your client's decision. Your job is to explain the options as best you can. If she chooses a new trial and a new pro bono lawyer and gets hung it won't be your fault. I hope she will sign and be paroled. Good luck."

***

Ida Mae had high hopes of coming out of prison vindicated and free. She made no effort to hide her dismay. After providing the information for the moonshine bust all she got was parole, which she thought was coming anyway. After the sense of her situation sunk in she exploded.

"Mr. McKnight! That ain't right! I gots parole coming. The womens in prison say white people just be trying to put us back in slavery and I aint going!" She slammed her fist down in frustration with the force of a steel driving hammer breaking the flimsy table.

Wardens quickly unlocked the interview room door. Dad was obliged to leave. He had seen a different side of his client. He left an angry and disillusioned Ida Mae in the jail. The required signature was not in hand. He kept the papers for fear she would destroy them.

After Ida Mae had time to cool down Dad sent word to her that he would meet her one more time before resigning as her lawyer. He could not say what the judge would do about a new trial. When he returned to the jail Ida Mae accepted the deal. The parole had been conditioned upon her finding a job in thirty days and reporting back to Judge Jackson.

Ida Mae could not leave prison to look for a job. She had to take turns to use the single phone provided for prisoners. She had to identify herself as a parolee for manslaughter. Job offers did not come rolling in.

Three days remained and she had no job. Ida Mae contacted Dad. He had her released to his custody. He took her to several potential employers. All expressed immediate interest in her. They backed down at the responsibility they had to assume for a parolee. No one would hire her. In the meantime the Lockhart's maid, Hattie had given notice. She had to take care of an aged relative. Dad brought Ida Mae to the house. She had never seen homes like the ones she saw in Buckhead. After her tour of the house, Dad risked the ride to her Auntie's house.

Dad told Ida Mae she could work as a maid three days per week for the McKnights on two conditions. Neither condition was a given. Her Auntie had to let her live in her home and Dad had to persuade Mom to accept Ida Mae as a maid. His pro bono manslaughter defendant was taller and heavier than Mom and she had plunged a butcher knife into her husband's chest. Her resume was brief, a semester of nursing school, six months in a commercial laundry, and four years in prison. I do not know how Dad did it. Ida Mae Reivers was released from jail. On the thirtieth day allotted to Ida Mae to find employment Dad appeared before Judge Jackson. Dad produced a letter from Ida Mae's new employer, him. Ida Mae Reivers had both employment and a suitable place to live. Dad agreed to act responsibly in his oversight and cooperate with parole officers. Parole granted. The judge had not consulted the parole board. After the initial flap Dad jumped through those hoops in time to keep Ida Mae out of jail.

Dad's reputation for criminal jurisprudence and moonshine busting remained a question but he secured his courthouse reputation as a bleeding heart liberal. No judges assigned other pro bono cases to him, ever. Monday morning after Ida Mae went free he found his office reception room full of seekers for pro bono legal work. They refused to leave and the building security guard asked for police help to clear the building. Dad lost a client who arrived for an appointment and found poor Negroes and two policemen in a fracas inside his office front door. His critics at the courthouse did not hide their glee with his discomfort.

Chapter 15 Maid

"Hank, what in the world is going on?" Dr. Pete Flannigan asked his voice full of frustration.

"You said Kate needed a maid. So I got her one. Since I can't afford a full time maid I thought you might help me find someone for some of the other days."

The two men sat in the living room as Mom lay sleeping in her bedroom. Dinner would be at Davis Brothers cafeteria as Mom was tired and the baby was past due.

"I think Kate has been through a heck of a lot and I don't think a maid from jail makes it easier."

The living room was at the bottom of the stairs across from the dining room and Dad had brought the drink fixings in and set them on the coffee table. The men could talk and smoke further away from where Mom slept. Pete registered his concern and disappointment at Dad's choice for a maid. Dad defended Ida Mae as a diligent worker. She suffered mistreatment by life in general and the criminal justice system in particular. She deserved a break.

"Hank, I appreciate your sense of justice and willingness to put your life where your mouth is. I have to ask about the toll this is taking on your family."

"Well Doctor don't forget who prescribed the maid," Dad answered. "And your prescription included driving my new friend, Candy, to and from work. After forgetting her twice and being tied up in court once, I have only lost fifteen dollars in cab fares on the bargain."

"Driving Miss Candy is not working, is it?" Pete questioned.

"The fourth time I forgot to pick her up I told her I would be there in a few minutes. I made the return trip from the house to the medical building down the new freeway in twelve minutes. Sterling Moss couldn't have covered it faster in his Ferrari."

"Hank, how fast were you driving?" Pete asked in an astonished tone.

"Could have been fifteen minutes, I had the MG humming along," Dad added. "A policeman stopped me on the way home and asked me if I was the same red sports car he saw speeding in the other direction. It didn't help that the engine was ticking and the tires were so hot we could smell rubber fumes. I told him I had forgotten to pick up Candy and introduced him to her. After he met Candy and I showed him my veteran's driver's license he let me off with a verbal warning."

Pete could not help laughing, "I'm giving you a warning you need to take care of Kate. She will have four children, starting at five years old and under. They will all be home this summer and she will require some help." Pete and Dad talked longer about their mutual interests until Travis asked me to intervene on the supper issue.

"Dad, Travis is hungry," like I wasn't.

The men graciously accepted the interruption. Pete went home and we went to the cafeteria. Travis and I noted that the Davis brothers, whatever good they may have done in the world, made vegetables way too available for kids at the cafeteria.

***

The new maid arrived. As the oldest I recognized Mom's stress signals. The new maid did not match the neighborhood maid profile. Other maids carried numerous letters of recommendations. If they could not give years of experience, they gave the names of other maids who had tutored them in cooking, cleaning, and the care of children. Ida Mae had experienced several disappointments in rapid succession. She had not been acquitted. She had to sign the guilty plea. She had to accept the conditions of parole, and she had not returned to her former job. Childcare to Ida Mae carried the stigma of being a servant, which in her mind equaled slavery. The doctrine of equality she had heard about in prison was associated with communism. Other inmates had told her the glories of communism and the joy they would share when the workers of the world united. They would split up the wealth and everyone lived as brothers on the same income. The only thing Ida Mae hated worse than her present situation was the thought of prison.

Dad stayed home to meet Ida Mae. Hattie rode the same bus as Ida Mae and tried to direct her to our house. Ida Mae refused instruction. Hattie called from the Lockhart's house to tell us our maid was wondering down Ridgewood Road. Dad retrieved her and reintroduced her to Mom. Ida Mae wanted Dad to stay to tell her what to do. He explained Mom would give instructions about housework. The two dachshunds barked adding to the usual confusion. Mom, nine months pregnant and emotional, could not have picked a worse time to break in an ex-con. Three boys and two dogs aggravated the situation. Mom had to call Dad several times and at least once handed the phone to Ida Mae. Hattie agreed to come two days to help train Ida Mae.

We awoke the next morning to find Mom's friend Jan fixing breakfast and organizing us for school. Dad and Mom had gone in the night to the hospital to deliver Lillie and by prearrangement Jan had come over to take care of us.

Mom had been worn down by events. Her hospital stay lasted two weeks the baby came home before she did.

Lillie had blond ringlets and blue eyes like Mom. She was a girl and three boys had no idea what to expect.

Dr. Pete Flannigan had prescribed another week of vacation then revised it up to two weeks.

In 1950 Dad received an appointment as Attorney General of the newly formed Jekyll Island Authority. He did the legal work for the purchase of the Island from the millionaire's Club and development as a State Park. This position was a reward for his participation in rewriting the state constitution. His administrative position on the Authority of the then uninhabited island, a political and geographical wasteland, was considered politically unimportant to everyone including him. By what Pete described as a "fortuitous concourse of events" Dad had been offered the use of the Cherokee Home on Jekyll Island. The lavish stucco home with Palladium doors was built by Jay Gould for his daughters and had nothing to do with Indians that I could tell. Dad, Mom and Lillie would make the trip.

Mom's friend Jan and her husband Chuck Biden came to baby-sit the three boys. We did not see much of Chuck, a quiet accountant starting his own practice. Hattie came and Ida Mae continued three days a week. Ida Mae had a bad attitude about the whole deal. And the straight speaking Jan and Hattie had to coax Ida Mae to do participate in the chores. Ida Mae exasperated Jan. When the two weeks passed and Mom returned Jan explained in tears her problems with Ida Mae. Jan asked Ida Mae if she did not feel some gratitude to Dad for getting her out of prison and saving her from the gallows. Ida Mae claimed she could not be hung because it was self-defense. She thought the white judge and white lawyer made a deal for her to be a maid. Mom in turn asked Dad to speak to Ida Mae.

Hampton County Negroes appeared grateful to work for Poppa and in his home. Dad understood their plight in the rural segregated south where farm employment accounted for ninety percent of the jobs. Cheap labor was in abundance and labor saving machinery was expensive so backbreaking work for man and beast brought crops to market. Small farmers kept every able-bodied member of the family on the farm and out of school. Few rural job opportunities for whites or Negroes required even a high school education. The value proposition for spending time in even grammar school did not make sense. Few had checkbooks a handshake and cash sealed deals for the illiterate. The opportunities for the unscrupulous abounded.

Ida Mae thought slick whites had victimized her. She had a rough youth and a catastrophic marriage, the killing, and four years in prison had hardened her more. Now she was a servant. Life had been more than unfair.

Dad had been empathetic to a fault. He wanted to change the plight of the poor whites and Negroes and he was willing to work one case at a time. But Ida Mae had embraced some of the teachings of communism. Some in prison saw it as the remedy for the failures of capitalism. She did not understand lending and assumed all the beautiful homes she saw in Northwest Atlanta were owned free and clear by whites. She had also been told all the construction had been done by Negroes. As a white man Dad had no chance of overcoming this perception.

Dad's frustration matched Ida Mae's in magnitude. He had been embarrassed professionally, in the neighborhood and before his friends. He lost his largest client and one potential new one. In addition to Ida Mae's belligerence against Jan and Hattie, Mr. Preston had raised Hell. He wanted her met at the bus by her sponsor to insure she did not slaughter again. Neighbors who had been unaware of Dad's existence now had opinions. Damn, it was enough to make a five year old swear.

The ingratitude born of her suspicions and prejudices made Ida Mae glad enough to be out of prison but not glad to work for the McKnights. This attitude showed up in her resentment of things Mom asked her to do. The most unpleasant home chore was changing diapers. The soiled cotton diapers had to be swirled and wrung out in the toilet before being washed at high water temperature in bleach. Billy and Lillie provided dirty diapers like it was their favorite hobby. Mom grocery shopped two or more days a week, made meals from scratch following directions in her cookbook. She also made clothes for herself and Lillie and cleaned house. A mixer, sewing machine and a Hoover vacuum cleaner constituted her entire collection of electric labor saving devices. Ida Mae exuded a sluggish attitude and communist quips like, "Three or four families could live in this big house." She also thought a second bathroom was extravagant. When the weather warmed Dad put window air conditioners in the upstairs bedrooms. Ida Mae thought this was an excessive waste of money and electricity, but she stood in front of them to cool off anyway.

Ida Mae decided the tub could be used to swirl the diapers. Due to her large frame she preferred sitting on the side of the tub to sitting on the toilet. She thought the refuse would drop straight down as in an outhouse. Mom told her not to do this. After Mom left Ida Mae filled the tub and did a bunch of diapers at once clogging the drain. Mom returned home to find the fecal catastrophe in the upstairs tub and told Ida Mae to clean it. Rather than try to remove the waste from the tub and flush it down the toilet as instructed, Ida Mae tried to pack it down the tub drain. When Mom tried to intervene again, Ida Mae announced she couldn't clean diapers any longer and refused to fix the tub problem.

Mom got on the phone to Dad, "I don't give a damn if she goes back to prison." I had never heard Mom cuss before, "And you can call a plumber to fix the tub drain. She packed it full of crap from the diapers she won't clean properly." We held our breath. "I am not going to say another word you handle it. You handle it!" Mom listened for a while. "I will tell her."

"Jeb" I came running.

"Yes, Ma'am, please run next door and ask Mrs. Colquitt if she could come right over."

"Yes, Ma'am." I ran fast out the door to the new house next door. I asked Mrs. Mary Jane Colquitt if she could come and help my Mom for a few minutes. Mrs. Colquitt went by Mary Jane. She had moved in from a small town north of Atlanta. Mom thought of her because she was tall and had helped manage her father's carpet mill. She sensed some urgency in my voice. She did not change her housedress or comb her hair. She came straight away. Mom had opened the front door for Ida Mae to leave and Ida Mae was arguing. The gist of the argument was Ida Mae did not want Mom to say she would not work. If Dad intended to fire her she did not want to return in the morning. Mom would not involve herself in Dad's case. Ida Mae would have to communicate directly to Mr. McKnight. I stopped on the walkway and Mrs. Colquitt could hear every word through the open door for some distance.

"Hello Kate, is there a problem."

"No problem I have asked Ida Mae to leave my house and go wait for the bus."

"Ida Mae, that seems simple enough to me," Mrs. Colquitt said.

"Well there is more to it," Ida Mae said sensing the two white women would not back down.

"No there's not more to it. If Mrs. McKnight has asked you to leave her house that's all there is. Do you need help getting your things together?" Mrs. Colquitt continued.

"No I don't need no help," Ida Mae said. A minute later she walked out the door toward the bus stop.

Mrs. Colquitt stayed for a short while but Mom did not care to discuss it. "Mary Jane, I must say that Ida Mae is the first Negro I have ever tried to work with and if they are all like her I understand why people hate them. That's all I can say."

Mary Jane spoke in a sympathetic tone, "I grew up around here. I have known lots of Negroes. They are like everyone else, some good, some bad."

Mary Jane had to return to her own house.

After a while I went outside. Travis and Billy remained in front of the babysitter, Miss Philco TV. They watched a soap opera not because it interested them but because the TV fascinated them. Out of boredom I went to the bus stop. The landscaping hid me from their view as I observed the three Negro women sitting on the bench at the bus stop. I could not hear what they said. I soon tired of this activity but I considered the soap opera on TV as an alternative and lingered on.

A lone Negro man approached the three Negro women and engaged them in conversation. After a few minutes he pulled a knife and demanded their money. All three of the women open their purses and pulled out butcher knives. Confronted by a uniform front of knives the Negro man retreated. The women replaced their knives in their purses and continued talking as if nothing had happened. Ida Mae saw me as I moved from behind the landscaping to see where the Negro man went. She called to me to go on home and I did at the run.

The next morning Dad had breakfast and did some work at the dinner table. I sat on the stairs as usual until Dad called me to go see if Ida Mae had arrived at the bus stop. I ran to the mailbox and looked up the hill toward Ridgewood. Nothing. After a few minutes. The 4 Ridgewood, West Wesley Bus came into view over the hill and Ida Mae stepped off. I ran back in the house and told Dad, "She just got of the bus."

"OK, thanks Jebby." He looked dejected and could see by my expression I recognized it. "This is a difficult thing for your Dad to do. I have tried to help this woman but I don't know what else I can do." Dad and I had been through a lot and I felt he wished I could share his burden.

Ida Mae knocked and Dad called for her to come on in. He offered her the chair at the head of the table. Dad felt bad on the way to getting worse. The night before Dad and Chuck Biden, Jan's husband, worked hours to get the crap from the diapers out of the P trap in the upstairs plumbing. It confirmed the problem. Dad had asked Chuck to join him as a witness. Jan returned in the morning to help Mom and was helping in the kitchen when Ida Mae arrived.

Dad asked Ida Mae to sit, "Ida Mae, I have tried my very best to help you. It has not worked out here and you are going to have to find another job."

"Mr. McKnight, I do not know what your wife told you but I done everything she said."

"Jan, Hattie and Kate have all said you seldom do what you're told and then not without arguing."

"That ain't right, Mr. McKnight, I been good."

Jan who had listened from the kitchen stuck her head in the dining room. "Ida Mae, do you remember me?" Jan held one of the breakfast dishes in a towel as she spoke. Ida Mae looked down, busted. Jan continued, "I thought so. This man has done all he could and so has Kate. He and my husband spent half the night trying to fix the tub drain."

"Miss Kate didn't say nothing to me about not putting them diapers in the tub." Dad and Jan stared gap mouthed in disbelief. Jan looked at Dad and went back in the kitchen. "Well I guess that settles it," Ida Mae said holding to her bluff.

"Yes, it does," Dad said. "I have to end your employment here and I cannot recommend you for employment elsewhere. If you can find an employer who will sponsor your parole you will not have to go back to jail. I suggest you try the laundries. They liked your work."

"Mr. McKnight, I can't go back to jail. You going to have to find me another job."

"No, Ida Mae you will have to find your own job."

"No, sir. You my lawyer, you got to do it."

"You have signed a document stating you understand I no longer represent you and that you understand the conditions of your parole. I have prepared copies for you to give to your next employer."

"No. The paper I signed don't say that. I can't read so I didn't know no better."

I could see Dad's complete dismay as Ida Mae told one lie after another.

"Ida Mae, I have a copy of your High School Diploma to show a prospective employer you can read. The Diploma has your maiden name, Norris, and I have arranged for you to go by Norris if you choose. Telling me what I know to be false is not helping."

"False. What you mean? I ain't lying."

"Can you read?" Dad asked.

"Yes, Sir, I can read," admitted Ida Mae; "You supposed to get me a new trial so I can get out of this mess."

"Three lawyers have told you they thought you would lose a jury trial and get life in jail or hang."

"You ain't never told me."

Dad's professionalism had been attacked, his word impugned and he stared in disbelief. "I told you about one hundred times."

"No you ain't."

I could see the struggle on Dad's face. I had remained in the foyer. I do not know if it was my presence but Dad said, "I have listened to more than I can gracefully stand. I will have to excuse myself for a minute. He stood and left the room."

Ida Mae sat stern faced in her faded button up housedress, her hands folded in front of her. She turned her gaze toward me. Emboldened by what had become more frequent input in adult conversations I offered my child's view solution. "Ida Mae maybe you could talk to your preacher and he could help you."

"No, No. I ain't talking to no preacher man," she said, annoyed. I continued to look back at her as her gaze turned into a scowl. "I saw you across from the bus stop yesterday. Did you tell on me too?"

Dad returning asked, "What about the bus stop?"

I answered, "Yesterday at the bus stop a Negro man said he wanted Ida Mae's purse. Ida Mae and two other Negro women pulled out butcher knives and he left."

"Please open your purse," Dad requested.

"Yea, I got a knife," she said pulling out a butcher knife. "And I pulled it out to protect myself," Ida Mae said in a matter of fact tone. "I can defend myself."

"Did you murder your husband?" Dad struggled to control his voice.

"It were self-defense!" Ida Mae exclaimed, "I killed one man and I'll kill another if he tries to do me wrong!"

"How much money do you have in your purse?" Dad asked.

"Almost eleven dollars."

"You would kill a man for eleven dollars?"

"Who going to pay my bus, buy my groceries, and pay my Auntie if he take my eleven dollars? Eleven dollars ain't nothing to you, you is rich. You own this big house and them cars. I am poor I got to defend myself. Nigger thieves be everywhere. You got the biggest rug I ever saw. If I put a rug on my Auntie's floor in the morning it be gone before I come home at night. The only furniture we got is what nobody wants to steal. That's how it is."

"Ida Mae," Dad began in a calm tone, "I appreciate the fact conditions in your neighborhood are very different than here. I wish I could change it but I can't. In time I could have helped you move to a nicer neighborhood. I do not own these things. I own a share in these things, the bank has a loan on the rest."

"Oh, you rent from the bank. I understand rent."

"No, I rent the money from the bank and use the money to buy these things. I must pay the bank every month or they will take these things back."

"Well I don't know. I see what you got," Ida Mae said waving her big arm in the air.

"I know you don't understand and that is a problem. The world is changing. If you could get a good job you might own your own home by renting money from the bank as I have done."

"I don't know about all that," Ida Mae said shrugging her shoulders showing her disinterest in learning.

"Do you understand that you do not work here anymore?"

"Yea, I understands."

"OK, then. Leave the knife on the table and go back to the bus stop. Take these papers and ask your Auntie if she can help you," Dad said handing her a manila folder.

"You ain't going to get me off on the self-defense?"

"No, I'm not your lawyer anymore. I have explained numerous times, I don't do criminal law."

"You done it to me now," Ida Mae said shaking her head. And Dad then shook his.

Jan had been listening from the kitchen and entered the dining room to speak on Dad's behalf. "What he has done for you is get you out of jail and a chance at a new life. What you have done for him is damage his reputation, antagonize his wife and children and it sounds like you could have murdered again yesterday."

"No it were self-defense. You don't understand how it is. Two other women pulled out knives same as me."

"Is this true, Jeb?" Jan asked apparently not having heard my account.

"Yes, Ma'am."

Dad spoke, "Ida Mae, I am sorry for your bad experience. Whatever the reason I will never be able to help someone again as I have tried to help you. It has cost me a great deal. I don't think you understand and I shall not belabor the point. Other women pulled knives to defend themselves but I think you will hang if you stab another man. Where did you get this knife?"

"From the kitchen you got plenty."

"It's time for you to go, you have your papers. I'll keep the knife." Dad pulled the knife away and rose to open the door for her to leave.

"Ida Mae," Jan said, "Whether you believe it or not we wish you well."

"We truly wish you well, Ida Mae," My Mom added coming into view.

After Dad closed the door he looked down and then up at Mom and Jan who still stood at the door to the dining room. He looked so sad I thought he would cry. "I tried so hard to help her."

"We know you did, Hank," Jan said.

"Excuse me," He said and went into his bedroom.

By the time Dad left the house the car dealers in Buckhead had opened for business. That night he came home driving a 1954 black and yellow Ford. It was supposed to be a great deal since it had been a dealer demo car. The black and yellow two-tone turned out to be too much yellow. He returned the car and the salesman asked what it would take to make a deal. Dad said we hated the yellow inside and out and asked him to look for an all-black car. Two days later, an all-black Ford convertible powered by "burn rubber" V8 engine pulled in the drive way. The quintessential used car salesman in a bright plaid sports coat tried to get Mom to sign for it. She called Dad. Then she told the salesman Dad would come by to see it on his way home from work.

The black convertible Ford V8 pulled in the driveway and we piled in for a ride. The Ford had plenty of room for us. The boys stood in the back seat so we could see out. Mom and Lillie fit in the roomy front bench seat. The salesman asked Dad to drop off the car to have the seamstress change out the yellow accent panels in the black front seats to black. Dad did this the following day.

When Dad got out of his car the next night he had a black band across the back of his suit. Mom pointed this out to him and Dad used words not found in the Bible to express his dissatisfaction. The seamstress had been the salesman and black paint. The car dealer found out the next day his salesman had lied about several things about the car. He had done all the paintwork himself.

The next day Dad met with the Ford dealer, who immediately paid for the suit. He did real car paint job on the yellow parts on the body. He replaced the seats with black ones from another car and sent for new ones from Ford. Dad had a one of a kind Ford convertible. We rode in style and comfort, and we usually went fast.

Chapter 16 Vacation

Dad's mind had been occupied with car issues. Ida Mae's future was out of his control. His humiliation as a lawyer, father, and Good Samaritan was complete. He could only pick up the pieces and move on. He thought he would have to sign some papers and Ida Mae would finish her parole time in jail.

Dad was shocked to receive a call from a man who would become a force in the civil rights movement, Reverend Charles Beard, the head pastor at the Auburn Avenue Church. Dad had never met him. Beard pleaded for a meeting with Dad to explain what options Ida Mae might have. To the desperate preacher's amazement Dad said he wanted to meet him and see his church. Beard was delighted. He said he would have Ida Mae and her Auntie and some church staffers on hand. Everyone was determined to try one more time to keep Ida Mae out of prison. Dad agreed.

Dad met Rev. Beard at his large church. There he explained his desire to help Ida Mae but an impossible situation developed at home. Rev. Beard proved a good judge of character. The two men spoke, laughed, cried and prayed together. When they finished Rev. Beard hugged Dad and said he loved him and he would thank Jesus for him every day. He told Dad not to worry; he would do all in his power to fix the situation. He then called in some deacons and introduced them to Dad as the best man he had met in years. Then he told the deacons, "We are going to make things right."

Ida Mae got religion. At no additional charge two Negro women accompanied Ida Mae to our house. The two older women showed Ida Mae how to clean everything and how to prepare some meals. Ida Mae's attitude was transformed. We also received a diaper service for a month. They picked up soiled diapers and delivered clean ones. During the week Ida Mae asked if Dad could be there one day so she could thank him. The preacher had explained the situation to her. She did not understand what Dad had done for her. She said he had been the first person to help her for her sake alone. After the week ended Dad and Mom agreed to hire Ida Mae back for three days a week and help her find employment for the other two.

The new Ida Mae worked like whirling dervish; she had to be held back. She did the laundry and ironed every piece of clothing including Dad's boxer shorts. Mom explained that starched and pressed underwear was not comfortable. She watched us children and in time we grew fond of her, and she grew fond of us too. The Negro minister invited Dad to meet other ministers. He introduced them to other sympathetic whites and all things worked to the good.

***

The Jekyll Island Club consisted of the wealthiest people in America: Astor's, Morgan's, Rockefeller's, Gould's, Crane's, and many more. They reportedly controlled over 90% of the wealth of America. It was a nice place. A few built lavish "cottages" surrounding a hotel for the members and their guests. After the war the island was purchased by the state of Georgia for a park.

In 1950 Dad was appointed the first Attorney General of the Jekyll Island Authority. The position was to be a part time job but it was time consuming. The Authority was created to run the island in a businesslike manner. From the beginning of 1950 until the end of 1954 the island was under construction and closed to the public. The authority operated on a shoestring budget. Dad combined some of his trips to manage affairs with vacations for the family. We stayed in the few homes kept open and maintained by the authority.

Dad envisioned all Georgians, white and colored, enjoying the island as a park and resort. Segregationist fought him all the way. Dad became the sole visible proponent for opening the park to "coloreds." Segregationist used all means to fight against sharing the island with Negroes on any terms. They even opposed providing segregated facilities; Negroes were not to be allowed on the island. Most of the media backed the segregationist. Dad's comments were edited out of a TV debate and he appeared to be mute. Dad's proposal for an integrated beach and public buildings never hit the table.

In 1950 the Island's fate hung in the balance until Dad walked into the Georgia State Senate Chambers. By informal questions to passerby's he decided he had the best chance of support from Senator "Big Heart" Hartman of Benton. Some double entendre was intended signifying his big heartedness. Big Heart owned the largest road building operation in the state. Mike Willis, the head of the state highway department was also an elected official. Senator Hartman had what may best be called a cooperative relationship with "Big Mike" Willis. The two "Big's" did OK. The island needed a six-mile causeway and a bridge.

The base for the causeway would have to be dredged up at low tide by light equipment or mule teams or dug up and trucked in from elsewhere. The last stretch of road to the island would require elevated approaches and a drawbridge. The project would take years at an enormous expense or the State Highway Department could provide a right of way and a permit and the State Senate could approve a toll road. The road builder could borrow the entire amount required for the project from a bank secured by the proceeds from the tolls until paid in full. This was enough road building to make Big Heart a liberal. "Big Heart was all heart" and he loved Jekyll Island. He loved the island more when he found out it did not have a single paved road. Big Heart introduced Dad to another key ally Senator Virginia Darien of Glenn County. The vote was close but roads and improvements for Jekyll Island State Park were funded "and the naysayers be damned."

Big Heart contracted with the state to use convict labor for much of the grading and site prep work. White convict labor built roadbeds and cleared land for hotels using hand tools, mule teams and a few tractors. Dad tried to improve conditions for the prisoners incarcerated on the island. He allowed the guards to hunt deer and wild turkey to supplement the prison food; the island became the top requested work camp in the Georgia prison system both for guards and prisoners. The prisoners put in five years of backbreaking labor.

Dad maintained a close relationship with Big Heart and together they overcame many hurdles. Everything about Big Heart looked flamboyant, his chauffeur driven black limousine, his three-piece suits, and a large Cuban cigar fixed in his mouth. His immaculately landscaped mansion in Benton, looked fit for a king. He was tall, heavy and broad shouldered. He wore a gold watch chain across his vest. He also wore a large gold ring that looked like a tourniquet where the flesh of his right ring finger squeezed out. Folks in the paving business said you could wear Big Heart's ring through your nose or on it. He appeared larger than life, in a crowd people unconsciously made way for him. For someone who appeared to be the center of attention he seldom said a word. When he spoke his voice was low and even toned, other conversation stopped, people listened.

Big Heart appreciated Dad and approved of what Dad tried to do. My brothers and I received gifts from Big Heart of toy road building equipment. Although Benton was forty miles from our house he drove down to personally deliver our presents. His Negro chauffeur dressed in a black suit, black tie and black chauffeur's hat opened the door for Big Heart to get out of the car. He then sat behind the wheel for two or more hours for his boss to leave. Dad wanted Big

Heart to see how much his boys enjoyed the toys. We brought out the yellow colored toy earthmovers and Mr. Hartman explained how each worked in road building. His explanation represented about ten times as much as I ever heard him say at one time. Big Heart told us the toys worked best in sand. The next day one of his dump trucks delivered a full load of sand so the McKnight boys could enjoy their new toys. He was big hearted and Jekyll Island won Senate approval for two of everything, one each for coloreds and whites. Segregation was expensive.

The chain of events in Ida Mae's case that led to Reverend Beard was fortuitous for Jekyll Island. Dad went to his new friend who was the best placed Negro he knew. Would the Negroes support Jekyll? Charles said they would come if he had to drive the church bus himself.

***

After weeks of relative tranquility in early summer of 1955 Dad had business at Jekyll Island and decided to take us for a vacation. The new Ida Mae considered herself family and we did too. Dad left a few days early and Mom, Ida Mae and the four children followed in the station wagon. Mom drove with one year old Lillie in a baby basket between her and Ida Mae in the front seat. Lillie would not cry if she could see Mom. The three boys sat in the middle seat with the luggage in the back.

Mom had packed snacks and a lunch. We left Atlanta at daybreak for the nine-hour drive on two lane roads. Not far outside Atlanta a policeman stopped us. He told Mom Negroes did not ride in the front seat beside white people. He offered to take Ida Mae to the bus. Mom explained she needed Ida Mae to watch her children. He suggested Ida Mae sit in the back to avoid repeated stops. Ida Mae and crying Lillie got in the middle seat for the rest of the trip.

Jekyll was hotter than blue blazes. On the leeward side of the Island the ninety degree plus humid air hung so thick and still I felt like I had to wave it aside to walk through it. To catch some wind and cool off we packed the station wagon full of beach paraphernalia and headed out to the white beach.

The welcoming ocean breeze and salt spray fragrance could not soften Dad's disappointment that no one else was there. The beach cabana had bathrooms for changing had ample parking for seventy cars. The cabana building stood on a long sand dune. Twenty-four year old Ida Mae saw the Atlantic Ocean for the first time as she crested the dune.

"Mr. McKnight where is the other side?"

"It's a long way Ida Mae, thousands of miles over the horizon," Dad answered as he grabbed up our beach gear.

"I can't see nothing on the other side. What holds the water?" she asked. Her sense of amazement and discovery lasted the whole day.

"I'll explain," Mom said, "Hank, you get the baby basket for Lillie," Mom talked about water, gravity and the horizon while Dad made a second trip to unload the car. 1955 fashion demanded cover clothing up to the water's edge. Travis and I wore burgundy boxer swimsuits and our white terrycloth bathrobes with "Champ" written in burgundy on the back. Mom wore a one-piece black bathing suit and lightweight multi-colored cover held by a matching sash. Dad sported Hawaiian boxer swim trunks and matching collared button up beach shirt. The outfit had a white floral design over a navy blue field. The McKnights dressed for success and we would have impressed, but empty beach stretched as far as we could see in both directions.

We walked to the beach where Lillie and Ida Mae sat under our beach umbrella and the boys waded into the ocean. We managed to build credible sand castles surrounded by water filled moats. Mom and Dad had gone for a walk up the deserted beach leaving Ida Mae beside

Lillie's basket. A man and a woman conspicuously out of place in street clothes down to their shoes came down to the beach. The man had dark brown hair combed back and held in place by hair tonic. I heard him yelling at us to get out of there. I turned to see his angry face glaring at us and then at Ida Mae. He wore a blue shirt and kaki pants. The short-sleeves of his shirt were rolled up. He told his female companion who was wearing a large skirt and a blouse to go to the car presumably to avoid the ensuing bloodshed.

"This is the white beach you stupid nigger," he hollered marching across the sand toward Ida Mae. "Tell your kids to get out of the water and you get out of here!"

"Them is white boys. I'm watching them for their parents, I'm the maid." explained Ida Mae.

"Don't sit there talking to me. Stand up when you talk to a white man." Lillie had been sleeping and opened her eyes but did not cry as Ida Mae stood. Lillie was the whitest McKnight; she had fair skin and blue eyes. The boys had crew cuts and dark tans from playing outside all summer. "Those boys don't look white to me." Then looking back at her, "It don't matter. Ain't no niggers allowed here, not even one."

Ida Mae pointed down the beach, "There comes the Daddy and the Momma."

Sensing something was amiss Dad hastened his step. The man raised his voice and asserted Ida Mae was not supposed to be there. He and his companion were so offended they were leaving and he would call the police. Dad told him to do what he thought best. And the man went to join his escort at the car and they drove off. Dad told us all not to be alarmed. Mom was dismayed. "I thought we would have some peace here."

Dad told her not to worry the closest town was twenty miles away and our antagonist would have to find a phone. Dad also doubted the police would be in a hurry to clear the beach at Jekyll of its solitary group of visitors because one was a Negro maid.

Wrong. Five minutes after the man and woman drove off a single policeman in a patrol car arrived to make us leave. "You can stay, but the colored woman has to go," the uniformed cop explained. Dad used the names of the local Sheriff and Senator Darien, but the policeman would not be swayed. He glared at us until we had left. Ida Mae apologized like her color was a fault, some sort of personal failure. Dad said it was his fault and not to worry because he knew where there was another beach close by.

Surprise, at least fifty or more Negro men, women and children frolicked at the beach and in the surf beyond the colored cabana. Dad and Reverend Beard had done such a good job of promoting the Island more Negroes than whites visited. If anything, the colored beach offered more amenities. Twenty picnic tables shaded by oak trees flanked the walk to the beach. We parked and walked down toward the beach. Dad went ahead and asked some people if they minded us coming to the colored beach. The Negroes said they didn't mind and we walked further toward the beach. A few Negroes approached us and ordered us to go to the white beach. They would accept no excuses and reasoned if Negroes couldn't go to the white beach whites couldn't come to the colored beach. And we walked back to our car.

"I done seen it all today," Ida Mae said shaking her head.

"I have too Ida Mae," said Mom. They both laughed at the irony. "So, Ida Mae what did you think of the Atlantic Ocean?"

"Ain't seen nothing like it. Mr. McKnight told me it took a big boat two weeks to cross to land again. I ain't never seen no water you couldn't see the other side," Ida Mae commented. "I ain't never seen or even heared of white people being told to leave somewhere because it was for coloreds." She laughed showing her wide smile, "Yes, Ma'am, I done seen it all now."

A policeman stopped by the beach whenever they saw our station wagon in the lot at the white beach so we had to leave Ida Mae at the servants' quarters behind the Millionaires Club. We also spent some time at the Club, which had been reopened as a hotel for whites. Ida Mae could not go anywhere.

We stayed in the Rockefeller house. Travis and I slept in a bed that was large enough for all four kids. One day it rained and we played tag in Jay Gould's indoor tennis court. And another day we went up to the Atlantic Ocean Club and swam at the pool and beach, all without Ida Mae.

Saturday night we dressed up and went back to the Atlantic Ocean Club for dinner. Ida Mae sat for Billy and Lillie. Travis and I put on white linen pants and blue blazers and made the scene at the exclusive Club. We had fried shrimp, Shirley Temples and chocolate éclairs. Dad wore a white dinner jacket and black tie and Mom wore an evening gown.

A band played while we ate and the grown-ups danced for a while. A lady asked Travis if we were twins. "No, Ma'am, but we're double trouble." Those present smiled and wondered. Travis and I got another round of Shirley Temples and chocolate éclairs from Mom, who thought the sugar rush would be enough to keep us awake, while she and Dad danced.

Apparently Dad did not suspect as the proponent of a colored beach, he might not receive a royal welcome. While our parents danced three men came and stood behind us.

"He's an Atlanta lawyer and a thoroughbred nigger-lover."

"That's three strikes against him," they laughed.

"Yeah, Atlanta, lawyer and nigger-lover. How could he be worse?"

"I don't care. I don't want to see him back here." The man in the middle issued his directive to the other two.

"I can fix that, I'll just ask the boys to move and we can sit down and the whole Nigger-loving family can leave." The man then leaned forward, "Boys your Daddy wants y'all to get up and join him on the dance floor."

"No, sir. He told us to sit right here until he came back." I responded.

"Didn't your Daddy teach you to mind your elders?"

"We are minding him. He said to sit here and don't move." I had enough sand for this situation.

Travis chirped up, "Mister, excuse me but I haven't finished my chocolate éclair." Travis was cuter than a puppy and Mom liked him best. I don't know if that got them but Travis wouldn't quit on dessert for a view of the Lone Ranger riding Silver on the dance floor.

"Never mind the boys."

"I got a better idea." The taller man in the middle spoke again and motioned for a Negro waiter. "These people are finished eating. This table needs to be cleared so other guests can sit down."

Not withstanding Travis's unfinished éclair the nervous waiter replied, "I'll have to ask the maître d'."

The waiter left and men discussed Dad. "He's got some brass coming over here."

"Worse than that."

"How did he get down here, train or car?"

"Car."

"From Atlanta? Well, well, well, I think we can help him have a nice return trip." The man on the left folded his arms across his chest as he spoke.

"What? How?" The other two asked.

"Leave it to me. I'll have a valet identify his car. I've got friends on the county commission here and they have a network of sheriffs and commissioners all the way back to Atlanta. They understand how it is. He may never make it."

I turned around to look straight at them and the tall man warned, "I said I don't want him back. I don't want any part of "never make it," a blink, maybe?

The first man backpedaled, "No, no, I was joking. The good ole boys will just write him a few tickets give him a hard time. You know the business. An Atlanta tag is easy enough to spot. I won't have to give the boys much encouragement if you know what I mean."

The men laughed. They continued small talk about people on the dance floor. I was amazed they made no effort to keep Travis and me from hearing.

Dad and Mom returned to the table. The embarrassed maître d' arrived and assured my parents and the three men that it was our table for the evening and that all guest were seated.

We ran into another problem when we left. We stood at the valet stand for twenty minutes as others patrons received their cars promptly. When our car arrived the Negro valet was so rude Dad sought the manager. The manager said he would fire the valet on the spot. Dad said he did not wish to have the Negro fired but he wanted the valet to come to Jekyll the next day. The valet agreed.

I told Dad that the three men had talked about his car and tag and something about the police. Dad only had one glass of champagne. The Sheriff 'Too Tall' Tom Turner sat in on Jekyll Authority meetings and Dad had known him for years. We were pulled over as we returned to Highway 17. Before Dad could get the car stopped a second set of blue lights flashed. 'Too Tall' got out of his patrol car and pulled a long flashlight from the Billy Stick holder on his belt. He shined it on himself illuminating his neat police uniform and then on the other policeman.

"Where's your badge Bridges?" The sheriff called out, "I'm going to have to write you up for that one."

"Oh sheriff, I must have forgot."

"You have been on duty for hours and you were making a traffic stop? Get out of here." 'Too Tall' motioned the deputy who had pulled us over to drive on.

"Hi Hank, your lucky I'm on duty tonight. I was headed for home when a call came in to look for a '54 black Ford convertible driving to Jekyll from the Ocean Island Club. The call said you were violent drunk and asked to leave the club. I would have let it go but they gave your name and tag number. Are you OK?"

"Sure. Seems some folks weren't glad to see us. Who called it in? Did they give a name? I had one glass of Champagne. We had no trouble but the valet took twenty minutes to find our car."

"I'd guess that gave the boy that pulled you time to come out from Brunswick. I'll check on the call," 'Too Tall' said and walked back to his car.

Another patrol car came up. We could hear the deputy arguing with the Sheriff to let him run us in. Ultimately 'Too Tall' returned to our car with the surly deputy to show him Dad was not drunk. The visibly unhappy deputy left.

After the deputy pulled away 'Too Tall' said, "I have trouble with that one, big family and friends. I can't fire him. Remember I'm elected, at least for now."

"Find out anything on the call?"

"It was anonymous."

"They filed a false report. Do I need to refute it?"

"I think I can take care of it."

Dad was perplexed, "It's hard to believe. We saw so many nice people we know from Atlanta. If anything they approve of what we're doing on Jekyll."

"Hank, it just takes a few folks to cause trouble. I have the hardest sheriff's job in Georgia. The Club has pull, I have bootleggers, probably some moonshiners no one wants me to find, ruffians and smugglers the ships bring to the port and people tell me the Klan is rattling ax handles over the coloreds coming to Jekyll. I still got two prison road gangs in the county with a convict running off about once a month. I told the county if they didn't give me more money for bloodhounds I'm just going to start letting every other convict run free and hope he's headed home to another county."

"Jekyll is bringing in jobs and revenue." Dad reminded.

"Tell my deputies. I think I got some in the Klan on the force. Anyhow it's bringing me more trouble. I'll follow you down to the Sidney Lanier Bridge. If you have any problems with police, tell them to radio me. I have a police radio at the house."

"Thanks 'Too Tall', I truly am sorry for your troubles. I'll give you all the support I can at the state level."

"Thanks Hank, but they don't vote. You let me know anytime you get near this County. I don't care if you're just passing through. It's for your own good."

***

Mom and the rest of the family left early the next morning in the station wagon so they would not have to drive at night. Dad persuaded me to stay and accompany him in the black Ford.

The local State Senator, Virginia Darien had informed Dad many Negroes in the county saw Jekyll as a threat to their jobs on Atlantic Island. The Negro valet showed up to meet us driving in his own late model car. Dad persuaded him to ride with us and he got in the backseat. Dad gave him the tour of the Negro beach, hotel and convention center. The valet asked to be returned to his car.

"I came over here like you asked. You will not ask to have me fired, right?" he was well spoken and neatly dressed in black pants and shoes and a white shirt.

"True, I want to find out what you think and see if you would encourage your friends to come use these facilities," Dad said.

"Mr. McKnight I think what you are doing may be good for Negroes in the state of Georgia, but not Glenn County. We don't want Negroes coming down here and taking our jobs. I don't swim. I do not want to come to the beach. But I do want to work at the Atlantic Ocean Club."

"You sound educated have you been to college?"

"Yes, Fulton Park University.

"Jekyll Island needs educated Negroes to work at the hotel and convention center."

"Do you own it?" the valet asked.

Dad laughed, "No, it's a state park. The Jekyll Island Authority wants all Georgia citizens to enjoy the park and the beach. They are hiring Negroes for good jobs."

It was the Negro's turn to laugh, "Mr. McKnight I got the best job a Negro can have in this county." He reached in his pocket and pulled out a thick roll of bills. "This is what I made last night. White people tip big. Negroes don't tip well, if at all. Negroes don't want to work at the Negro hotel or restaurant."

"Don't you think it would help Negroes across the state to have a place to come to the ocean, and relax and get together?"

"Mr. McKnight, you are a rich Atlanta lawyer, you can afford to have opinions. Opinions are a luxury I can't afford. A white man gave me twenty dollars to give him your tag number and to lose your car for a while."

"Who was he?"

"A white man with twenty dollars is all I know." He pulled a twenty off his roll to show Dad. "Twenty dollars is more than my Momma makes in a week. Maybe it's more than a colored hotel pays in a week."

"You could have lost your job," Dad said.

"Maybe, I didn't think you would raise Hell on me, besides the white man that gave me the twenty said he would cover for me. Coming here today seemed the safest thing for me. I told you how it is, how I see anyway. Mr. McKnight, I need to head home, I did what you asked. Are you going to let me keep my job?"

"Yes, I hope you will change your mind about Jekyll. I think it will help Negroes and it would help to have local support," Dad said hoping for some sign of a changed heart.

"I know your opinion Mr. McKnight. I hope you and your son have a safe trip home. I hear the white people at the Atlantic Ocean Club say if you drive through Pelican Hill have another car follow to witness to the judge you were not speeding. They will write you a ticket if you're walking too fast. Lord knows what they would do to a Negro. I do not know how the Negroes are going to get to the beach. From Atlanta the white folks take the Nancy Hanks train. Even the Savannah people take the train down to Brunswick and the Club will pick them up. I have never heard of someone trying to drive across the state to Atlanta."

"Can you give me an example of the kind of troubles Negroes have experienced in travel?"

"First of all Negroes don't travel out of their own county. My Daddy wouldn't let me go any other way than the train to Atlanta. That was before my cousin on Momma's side had his troubles on the bus."

"What kind of trouble?"

"I'll tell you but I wont give you his name. OK? It's been several years now. Anyway."

Dad said, "As you wish."

"My folks called me to pick him up at the bus station in Atlanta. He never made it to Atlanta."

"What happened?" Dad asked with genuine concern.

"My cousin said the bus driver kept talking about how bad the niggers smelled on the bus and making jokes with the white folks. Then out in the middle of the country in South Georgia somewhere the bus driver said he had motor trouble and for everybody to get their belongings and get off the bus. He unloaded the Negroes suitcases from under the bus and made them stand aside. Then he said he was going to let the white people get back on the bus to be in the shade. When all the white people got back on the bus he just drove off."

"No! You're serious? This is what your cousin said?"

"I am serious. A white policeman came by and said he couldn't do anything for them. He said they would have to take it up with the bus company in Atlanta. And if they stole anything while they were in his county he would put them straight on chain gang."

He continued, "Other Negroes came by and the people off the bus asked for help. They left and came back with more Negroes with knives and stole all their money and all their belongings. My cousin walked down the road crying. He didn't know where he was or what to do. He saw some Negroes at a church and asked them for help. A couple from the church said he could work on their farm for money to get home, but he wouldn't pay him for three months, after harvest. Then he paid only half of what he promised because he said he didn't work as hard as the farmer thought he would. They didn't have a phone. Momma thought he was dead. Three months later he showed back up here, torn clothes hanging on him, looking like a drown rat. My cousin said he's not leaving this county again – ever."

"I have seen rude treatment on buses in Atlanta but nothing as bad as this. I had no idea things like that could happen." Dad shook his head. I knew he was thinking about the Preston's maid.

"It can happen and worse. My cousin said he is one of the lucky ones that got off the bus. He got back home alive."

"I am scared for you and your little boy. Be careful." The young Negro said with heartfelt sincerity.

"Thanks, we will. If you change your mind about working on Jekyll you can say I recommend you. I will remember."

"I have to do what's best for me. Goodbye sir." And he turned to get in his car.

Chapter 17 Gauntlet

Stan Wallace had warned driving the rural highways across the state somewhere between adventurous and hazardous. Any scoundrel who could count could identify an out of county tag and if they couldn't count - out of state tags were different colors. Credit cards were not widely accepted so weekend travelers carried cash. Cash attracted bad cops and bad guys. Dad had highlighted a route on two Georgia road maps and gave one to Mom. Dad wrote the phone numbers for the State Patrol and the home phone number of Judge Matthew Gordon on the back of both maps. Dad had those two numbers and Captain Mack McConnell, Dr. Flannigan, and the GBI access number for the State Patrol. He had advised all on his list that he would drive from Jekyll Island to Atlanta on Sunday.

Dad was serious about the cavalry and fully expected his boys to be in cavalry ROTC in high school. He explained our mission in cavalry terms. We were going to reconnoiter, that meant act as scouts, for people who traveled to and from Jekyll Island. We were not reconnoitering in force; if we found a problem we would not engage the enemy but return to headquarters and report it. Dad told me we would have good father, son time and maybe encounter a speed trap. This view our trip home compared to General Custer guessing the seventh cavalry might see a few Indians at the Little Big Horn River.

Dad had loved the MG but he loved the size and V8 engine of the Ford. The higher top end speed and softer suspension made it a better car for the highway. When I told Dad I hated the Ford because I could not see out, he pulled over and fashioned a pillow of clothes stuffed in one of his tee shirts so I could sit high enough to see. The top was down, the wind cooled and I began to enjoy the trip. Dad had not mentioned my "photographic memory" in a while. He told me he wanted me to pay careful attention and remember our trip, especially any stops we made.

I saw Georgia. We headed up highway twenty-five first through the marshes that smelled of brackish water then past fields of planted pines all in rows. They all looked the same.

"Dad, they're too many trees to remember."

"Don't worry, I'll tell you what I want you to remember."

We passed through quiet towns and some small factories and saw mills. The highway in flat South Georgia could be straight for miles at a time. Unbroken lines of pine trees lined the highway for miles. Occasionally, a farm would break the monotony of the plantation pines. We saw more farms as we drove inland. We saw more than one man working barefoot, wearing bib overalls and a straw hat.

"Dad, why doesn't that farmer wear shoes?"

"Good shoes are expensive, he's saving his shoe leather. Besides his feet get hard and calloused and you hope the dirt is soft. He probably has a job at a sawmill or cutting timber during the week so he works his farm on evenings and weekends."

We passed some clapboard houses and Dad guessed at the age of the house based on the architecture. Dogtrot homes and those with detached kitchens, he thought were the oldest. Dad shared his thoughts about what he did and why. He asked what I thought of the Negro man from the Atlantic Ocean Club. I thought he looked smart and he spoke well. He made it plain he did not appreciate the provision of colored beach at all.

Dad asked if I understood Judo and how it differed from boxing as a style of fighting. He explained in Judo a fighter tries to take the blows aimed at him by his opponent to flip the opponent using the opponent's momentum. Dad hoped to use the incident at the Atlantic Ocean Club to flip the valet from being a hater of Jekyll Island to being a supporter. He had not been successful, but he had gathered valuable information. Negroes did not desire to work at the colored facilities. Though the salaries were comparable, the tipping was not. He wanted to make the most money he could and keep others from taking his job. This simple reality of life would come up time and time again.

We also had a discussion about the price of opinions. Dad said he took the long view on opinions. This meant at the end of his life he wanted the personal satisfaction of having made the right decisions. He desired to help others and make his life a positive influence. He gave examples of short-term decisions that seemed like a net loss but later paid great dividends. Our discussion did not solve the valet's problem. If he kept his nose clean he could work at the Atlantic Ocean Club the rest of his life. He could become the richest Negro in Glenn County.

Dad talked about the value proposition of education. Though the valet may never use his education for profit it would always be a personal treasure. Education would add enjoyment to his life in awareness of arts and letters. He would be able to pass on to his children an appreciation for books and knowledge. Negroes and whites would benefit from public education that provided for more than their agrarian jobs required. Prekindergarten was not enough education to appreciate his observation, but he was working on me.

When he moved to Atlanta, Dad taught College at night. He now had a captive student. Despite my youth, Dad did not hesitate to bring up complex subjects. He explained radio waves, aerodynamics, synthetic materials, and hydraulic plane controls, all related to Granddad McKnight's patents and inventions. His favorite topics included theology, education and character. He taught a course on the economic causes of the Civil War and argued that all wars could be viewed this way.

We seldom turned on the car radio. But we were curious to hear the local programing. A minute sample was enough. Since it was Sunday, we caught some fire breathing preachers and gospel singing. Neither one suited our Anglican tastes in preaching or music. Dad was uncritical and glad that people sought the solace provided by the Good Lord in whatever manner spoke to them.

When Dad mentioned great-great-grandfather Jeb Lee he had my interest. He required succeeding generations to learn two axioms. "Don't fight an Indian unless another Indian will fight on your side," and "A single neighbor ready with a rifle and dry powder is better than the whole British Navy," Dad's own corollary of this axiom expressed his bias for action in crisis, "Do something, and do it Now!"

***

We headed right through the speed trap of Pelican Hill. Dad had me slide across the bench seat next to him so I could watch the speedometer to see that he wasn't speeding. We saw the police car sitting in a vacant driveway watching us as we passed. The police car pulled us over. One officer approached the car and told Dad to get out leave the keys in the ignition and go sit in the back of the patrol car to speak to the police captain. Dad told me not to worry but to remember what happened. He advised the policeman that we both had watched the speedometer and he was certain we were not speeding. The officer said he did not know why we were pulled and to discuss it with the captain.

After Dad went to sit in the patrol car the officer looked admiringly at our new Ford convertible. He was an older man with a clean-shaven, lined face and worn uniform and hat.

"Your father is right. Don't go a crying on me. Everything will be fine. I may have to drive your car down the station so your father can pay his fine," The officer made his comments then folded his arms and leaned against the car.

Sheriff 'Too Tall' had raised questions about his deputies but I did not grasp that there were "bad" cops. As per my precocious nature I chirped up. "Oh, no, sir, I am not worried. My father knows the Governor and he is the Attorney General of Jekyll Island. The State Patrol is going to follow us all the way to Atlanta to make sure the road is safe for tourist to come to Jekyll Island."

I could have told the man there was a giant spider crawling up his shirt and received a calmer response. At the mention of the State Patrol the officer lurched from his leaning stance to take a hard look at me, he asked, "Are you telling the truth, boy?"

"Yes, sir." And I added somewhat offended, "I always tell the truth." Before I could remind him of the ninth commandment or about George Washington and keeping my options open for the presidency, he was moving quickly toward his partner.

The officer interrupted the captain and pulled him from the car out of earshot of my father. We were immediately freed and the captain offered to do a speedometer check for us. He followed us for a few blocks then advised us that our speedometer did not register properly at low speeds. According to the captain when we thought we were going fifteen miles per hour we were actually going twenty. The State Patrol came up as we received the bogus information about the speedometer. The

Patrolman stopped but after a brief conversation we continued toward Atlanta. When I told Dad what I had told the officer he warned me to let him be the one to share the information about who he was. He did not use the term "bad cop" but said some believed that policemen in some counties did not perform their job properly. He said we would not likely be stopped again but I was to be quiet if we did.

As we passed though the town we saw whites and blacks dressed in their Sunday best talking and joking together outside a church. Dad was so impressed he asked a black man accompanied by wife and children waiting to cross the street. "Is that your church?"

"No sir. That's the white church ours is behind it. But we're all friends in Jesus."

"Yes, I can see that. Y'all have a nice Sunday."

"Yes, sir, we will. You too."

We resumed our trip and saw a group of white and black boys playing baseball as we pulled out of town and back up to highway speed. The country seemed friendly enough at least in Pelican Hill.

The father to son talk started afresh. Dad talked about growing up in Hampton County during the depression. Most Georgians were so poor the depression made little difference in their lives. Schools in the county did not require children to wear shoes until after Columbus Day, in the spring they took them off again. Dad reminded me of his seventh grade class picture showing him barefoot in the front row.

Dad developed asthma as a child. In high school he caught pneumonia and the doctor ordered him south to warm weather. Dad went to live the rest of the year in Havana, Cuba. A family there nursed him back to health.

His Cuban experience further convinced him that under the skin all people were the same.

"A man's got to do what a man's got to do," Dad's Poppa used to tell him. When Dad entered Hampton Military School he turned this axiom around, used judo, on Poppa. He asked to join the cavalry. Dad met all requirements but parents or guardian had to pay for boots, saber, and a horse allowance. Parents had to sign a liability waver, a fatal riding accident occurred two years prior. Dad told his father and Poppa, he was a McKnight and knights fought on horseback. He did not want to go back on his name by not accepting the challenge. The boots, saber, horse fees, and wavier found their way to Hampton.

I wanted to hear more about the cavalry, but a bullet whined through the air across the front of our car. We both flinched and ducked. We heard the rifle bang from behind an unpainted clapboard house about forty yards off the road to the left. Dad and I knew the sounds of hunting, the whiz of bullets and the different reports from rifles and shotguns. Dad looked over his shoulder but continued driving north on highway twenty-five. The next little town had a police stand at the single stoplight. Two policemen sat on a park bench outside the one room police hut smoking cigarettes.

Dad stopped to report the incident. The uninterested policemen listed excuses including hunters and the locals did not use the road much. Dad pointed out it was not hunting season. He also said if they did not respond he would call the State Patrol. One of the policeman decided he would accompany us the three miles back because it was on his way home.

Dad said, "Remember this." I did not recognize the man who spoke as a policeman at first glance. He was dressed in brown street shoes, khaki pants and tan shirt but no hat. He pulled a small tin badge out of a pocket and pinned it on his shirt. He noted for our benefit he was on duty. By agreement the policeman followed five minutes behind us.

I registered my concerns about going back. I had been in more than one tight spot with Dad leading the charge. On the short ride back Dad explained a lawyer was an officer of the court. Among other things this meant he had to report suspected crime or illegal activity. As Attorney General of the Jekyll Island Authority he wanted to make certain the road from Atlanta was safe for coloreds and whites. In short, he was doing his job.

We arrived at the farmhouse and Dad got out. No need to knock. A defensive older woman and a young man dressed in farm clothes came out the door. The young man asked who Dad was and what he was doing there. Dad explained about the rifle shot and they acknowledged the man of the house was out with his gun. From where he stood on the porch, Dad could not see the man advancing carrying a rifle around the house. The man wore bib overalls, straw hat, shirt and lace up work boots. When he saw me he put a finger to his lips to shush me. I was going to "Do something, and do it Now!"

"Dad there's a man with a rifle walking up." The man glared at me like I was supposed to sit there and do nothing.

"Where is he?" Dad asked.

"Coming around this side of the house," I said.

"What do you want me to do, Paw?" The farmer's son called from the porch.

"Does he have a gun?"

"NO, I don't have a gun," Dad called out.

"Well? Does he?" The farmer called out.

"No, Paw, I don't see one."

The man rounded the corner of the house and began scolding Dad about using the road in front of his house. He did not notice the police car until it was speeding up his driveway. The policeman pulled up past Dad's car and blocked the farmer from returning around the side of the house.

"Put the gun down, Clell," the policeman called out. The policeman was unarmed but Clell put the gun down.

"This man been driving up and down my road," Clell answered. He laid the gun down. It was an Army surplus 1903 Springfield .30–06, a powerful rifle with a effective range of several hundred yards. It was a deadly weapon.

"It ain't your road, Clell," the policeman argued with Clell while Dad was silent.

"It is too my road. My property is on both sides."

"Clell, you can't be shooting across the road."

"I ain't hit him. I could have if I wanted to."

"Clell, I'm going to have to take you in, this man is an officer of the court from Atlanta."

"You can't take me in, Louis. We is kin, I was born in your Momma's family."

"Momma ain't got nothing to do with this," the policeman said and began to advance toward the old farmer. The farmer ran toward the woods on the other side of the house. No one made any effort to follow.

Dad looked around for guidance. The policeman stood gazing at the fleeing farmer like a buzzard on the phone line waiting for something to die. He put his hands on his hips and looked back up on the porch at the woman and young man. "Tell Clell to come into the station and see me on Monday or I'll have to send someone out here to get him." As an afterthought he picked up the rifle, "Tell him I got his rifle."

"Ow, Cousin Louis, he' going to be madder than Hell. Remember we is kin," Clell's grown son said.

"Larry's right," the woman added. "Don't be going back on your raising."

"I know my own. You ain't got to remind me. I got his rifle, means I'll see him Monday."

Dad walked back to the car. The policeman's clean-shaven face showed his discomfort. His dark hair thinned out on top and he put a hand to the side of his head. "Mr. McKnight I ain't going to chase him, he'll be in on Monday and I'll have the judge talk to him. He's been a problem to us before."

"Do you have a piece of paper?" Dad asked.

"My ticket book."

Dad opened the trunk and got out a yellow legal pad. He asked for the policeman's name and contact information and Clell's name and address. The policeman hesitated but provided a business card.

The policeman said, "Mr. McKnight, people around here like Clell, he was in the first war. They will not like it if he gets in jail, besides people here use other roads."

"I was in the second war and I don't like being shot at. I pay taxes and this is road belongs to all Georgians. As an officer of the court it is my responsibility to see that all citizens can travel safely on Georgia's highways. I will check on this Monday. If you are unable to apprehend Clell I will ask the State Patrol or GBI to come down and help you out." Dad looked down at the card to read the name then looking up, "Officer Louis White, correct? Do you understand?"

"Yes, sir, we'll take care of it." He rubbed his lined face and did not let his anger show.

Instead of "going on home" as he had said, Officer White followed us back through the town. We noticed that he stopped at the little police stand. If Dad suspected something he did not say.

As we drove Dad gave me a brief quiz on our stop and what the people looked like. I understood that he thought it was important and I was his only witness. I was not just along for the ride.

Chapter 18 Magnolia

We needed gas but could not find an open gas station. Dad had been driving easy to save gas. A man in a green Ford sedan signaled us over by flashing his lights and waving his arm out the window.

"All right everyone out of the car," the man ordered.

"Who are you?" Dad asked.

The man looked down at his clothes as if he had forgotten what he was wearing. There was no mark of rank on his khaki pants, white oxford shirt, or gray sports coat. He was fit and tall with blue eyes and close trimmed blond hair. He glared at Dad. "I'm the Sheriff around here. Everybody knows that get out of your car and I'll show you."

As we walked behind our car I smelled the scent of fresh cut pine and noticed a small lumber operation off the highway. I was not concerned until I looked up at Dad. An anxious expression crossed his face.

The Sheriff pointed to his car, a light green Ford sedan with the word "Sheriff" in gold letters on the door. "Mister, my car says 'Sheriff' on the side and the people of this county don't give anybody this car unless he's the Sheriff. That's going to have to be good enough for you. Let me see your identification."

"I am a lawyer. You are supposed to identify yourself as an officer. What is your name and what county is your jurisdiction?"

"A lawyer huh?" He glanced down at the number one on our license plate and added, "Atlanta, big city lawyer." "All you need to know is I'm Sheriff here."

He cocked his head and looked askance at us like a big yellow coyote considering his prey. Dad had already pulled out his driver's license and held it in front of him. The Sheriff reached forward and snatched the license from Dad's hands. "All you need to know, Mr. Lawyer, is I am the Sheriff like it says on the car. I help watch this stretch of road and I caught you speeding. I'm going to keep your license and you will follow me to the jail to pay your fine."

"I was driving under the speed limit, I am low on gas."

"It ain't far. If you such a smart lawyer you ought to know to keep gas in your car."

"Many gas stations are closed on Sunday."

The sheriff got in his car and drove toward town.

"Jeb, this could be another important stop. Remember all you can."

We followed the Sheriff. The little town had a wrought iron sign announcing "Magnolia, friendliest town in the South." On the far side of the central park a large green dinosaur sign announced a Sinclair gas station. It was open. Dad said, "Thank God," the station was no more than twenty yards past the end of the jail property. Dad flashed his lights to signal he would stop for gas. The Sheriff stood by his car and waved off the gas attendant.

Dad started the pump. The attendant came back out, "Hold your horses, Mister, I'll pump your gas."

"Thank you. I am in a hurry to follow the Sheriff and I am below empty," Dad said as he continued.

The attendant, a small man with a toothy grin, light brown hair and friendly blue eyes said, "OK, Yes, sir. You are the one in a hurry around here. If you turned on the pump I guess you can turn it off."

We went in the small office. It was connected to the mechanic's bay and smelled like gas, oil and grime. Dad and I both needed to go to the bathroom. What had to be the fattest white man in southeast Georgia and a Negro boy about twelve years old went in the men's room in front of us. The attendant explained that he let the Negro boy in the white men's bathroom because the white man was so fat he couldn't reach around his stomach to hold his pecker. This was more than we wanted to know. Dad said we would not pay for the gas until we had gone to the bathroom.

"I just done cleaned the White Ladies Room. I'll let you in there but don't pee on the seat," the attendant said with his happy smile. I noticed his oil etched hands with a black line of grime under each fingernail and wondered. I thought if he had cleaned any bathroom with his hands he could have only made it worse.

We returned to the office to find the fat man and the Negro boy standing by the cash register. The attendant wore a soiled striped shirt with his name above the pocket. He wiped his hand on his shirt before changing a dollar for the fat man to pay the Negro boy. Both men joked. The fat man gave the boy a quarter the attendant said, "That's a lot of money for not much work."

"Don't be talking down to my nigger," the fat man said in mock anger.

"No, sir, I ain't," the attendant responded in the same vein, perhaps for the Negro boy's benefit.

"We got in there and my nigger told me he couldn't find it," the fat man said and paused as he and the attendant laughed.

The fat man continued, "I said boy you better find it. You was the last one had it."

They laughed hysterically, "I told him, I ain't the one lost it."

The fat man paused again as they whooped with laughter. "I says, boy, it's wherever you left it." The attendant bent over laughing and holding his stomach.

The fat man was on a roll. "I says if you want to stay dry you better find it quick. He found it all right." Dad and I smiled awkwardly.

"My pants is dry, ain't they? I can't see, I got to check a mirror. I don't pay if he wet's my britches. I can do that myself." The attendant and fat man roared with laughter again. After some time the fat man and the Negro boy walked outside.

"If it was lost, the boy lost it," the attendant recalled laughing. He opened the cash drawer and added, "Fat people is jolly, ain't they?... Let me cipher on this...looks like you owe $3.50 for the fill up. You must have been empty."

"Running on the fumes," Dad said.

"Well I got to check the bathroom. If it's messy I got to charge you to clean it again."

When the attendant left I asked quietly, "Do you think that fat man was pretending - just to be funny?"

Dad answered quietly, "I don't know. He's awful fat. Don't talk about him."

The attendant returned. "It wasn't too bad I guess I wont charge you much." He took Dad's ten-dollar bill and said he didn't have change.

"I'll take the dollar you took in." The attendant "found" three dollars. Dad paid double and thought it was a bargain.

"You can tell the Sheriff I owe you," he chuckled. "Got you over there on highway twenty-five, didn't he? Ain't a hundred yards of highway through this county but he sure do cover it. He tore out of here a little while ago and come back with you lickity split."

He rubbed his hands on his dirtier and darker green pants as he looked out the door at the Ford. "Yea, he wants your car. If you ain't got the money for your ticket, he'll impound it. If he does you better pick it up the next day or it will be gone. Won't make you spend the night in the jail, y'all being quality white folks."

"I would like to use your phone," Dad said. Dad's face showed his concern from the moment we stopped. I thought he was worried about gas and now I knew it was something more. I paid close attention to Dad and he had me worried.

The attendant chuckled and looked around. "Where do you see a phone? I'd like to use our phone too. Only we ain't got one. The Sheriff got him one, maybe he'll let you use it. If he locks you up send your boy back over here. I'll take him to stay at a widow woman's house a few blocks from here. You can settle up when you get out."

"Dad I don't want to stay here." I did not like the suggestion.

Dad spoke to the attendant again, "Let me give you a phone number and a message. Its long distance and I will pay for the call and ten more dollars.

"Ain't no use. Mister, I don't read."

"You know someone with a phone who reads?" Dad asked.

"No, sir, I am a nobody."

"What about the widow?"

"Awe, Sir, I was going to take the boy myself for a sawbuck. I figured you wouldn't give him to me so I said I knowed a widow woman. The Sheriff won't keep him in jail no how." I marveled at how nonchalantly he admitted his lie about the widow.

"The sign said Magnolia for the town. What is the county?"

"Cross Keys County. Don't worry, y'all will come out fine."

Dad wrote a message, name and number. "If you can get this call through I'll give you twenty dollars when I come back."

"For twenty bucks I'll try."

We walked to the car, "Dad, I don't like this place."

Dad managed a smile, "Me neither. We'll leave here soon."

"I'm glad. Why did the attendant say he was a nobody? Like it didn't matter if he lied? He had to be somebody?"

Dad explained a "nobody" was a man without a "name." He had no reputation to protect and people expected him to lie so he was not ashamed when he did.

Dad had to follow the one-way streets around the park moving away from the jail before circling back toward it. The Sheriff appeared on the raised porch of the jail and called out to us as Dad parked.

"You can pull it on around back," the Sheriff said.

"Am I under arrest? I thought you said I was here to pay a ticket?"

"Yea, right. Come on in. But, you ain't carrying a pistol? No guns allowed in the jail."

"No."

"You got a pistol or gun in your car?"

"No, I do not own a pistol."

"How about that boy? Sounds stupid but I have to ask. We've had grown men let their kids carry for them and tell me a pistol belonged to the boy. I have seen it all."

"No, my son is not carrying a pistol."

"That right boy?" the Sheriff smirked.

"Yes, sir, and my name is Jeb."

"Smart boy, maybe an Atlanta lawyer too."

We followed the Sheriff in the jail and he explained, "I got someone coming to get a prisoner."

The jail looked like a typical public building with large windows in front. A wide set of steps led to a concrete porch running the length of the red brick building. The entrance of the one story building was located far to the left of center. Inside there was well-lighted open area with a high ceiling that looked like a small gymnasium about the size of one basketball court. A small sign listed the public services available at the counter at the far back right corner of the room. Two ladies helped the few people at the counter. There were a dozen chairs in the area in front of the counter. The same sign said Sheriff and pointed to two desks perpendicular to the entryway with two chairs facing each. Behind the desks were several rows of head tall filing cabinets. On the back left wall in line with the Sheriff's desk was a steel door to the cells. It had a small glass window crossed with steel bars.

A deputy handed the Sheriff the phone and we were directed to sit in the two chairs across from the first desk inside the door.

The Sheriff hung up, sat behind the desk and stared at us.

"May I ask your name?" Dad asked in a relaxed tone.

I pointed to the nameplate on the desk, "What does that say?"

"It says Sheriff William Verdon, Son. That must be this man." Dad said calmly.

"Verdon?" I asked not having heard the name before.

"That's right, Verdon. My people are from Holland. Verdon was shortened from a longer Dutch name. I come from Harlem outside Augusta. I went to two years of college there. I've been here ever since this is my county now." Sheriff Verdon lifted the nameplate from his desk and threw it in the drawer as he spoke.

"I got to get a prisoner ready. The Sheriff in Kennedy County called. He's sent a deputy to pick him up."

"Is that the jail?" I asked curiously.

"Yes, would you like to see it?" Verdon asked smiling. I was used to helpful Atlanta policeman and the good cops on TV.

"It isn't as big as the Atlanta jail," he said as he looked at Dad, "Mr. McKnight do you want your son to see the jail?"

"Yes, if he wants to."

"Come on back," Verdon said as he walked to the door, jingling a large ring of keys. He motioned for the two mismatched uniformed deputies, young stout men, to accompany us. "Bring leg chains and those handcuffs, you will need them both for Hayes. You know which one he is. If the Kennedy County deputy doesn't have leg chains to swap you take those off when you get him in the truck. I'm going to let this lawyer and his son see our fine jail," he said by way of explanation. He added, "Don't try to bring Hayes out until the Kennedy County deputy gets here. Sheriff Davies will probably send that mean, ugly S.O.B., Jim. He can help." By way of feigned politeness the Sheriff lowered his voice when he said "S.O.B."

Behind the airtight steel door the smell of puke, excrement and body odor hit the senses like a fist to the face. The stench was punctuated along the tiled hallway by small pools of disinfectant. The interior of the jail consisted of barred cells approximately twenty feet square lined by two stacked bunk beds around the walls. Fifteen white men crowded each of two cells. In the first cell there was a ruckus between three youths. The Sheriff laughed and commanded the other prisoners to break it up. In the second cell the Sheriff pointed to confirm Hayes to the deputies. Hayes was tall with a medium build and like the other prisoners he wore street clothes, a shirt and jacket. Fear shone across his face; he stood back to the wall as far as he could get from the cell door.

Hayes called out, "You can't send me to Kennedy County, a judge got to say so. I am from Cross Keys County all my life. They'll kill me down there."

Verdon laughed, "They got judges and lawyers in Kennedy County."

"They are all the same thing," he pleaded. "I'm from Cross Keys County, my people are from here, I want to talk to a Cross Keys County Judge."

"Talk to me," the Sheriff taunted and laughed through the bars.

Then walked further back and turned and saw the last cell was for Negroes. "It smells real bad back here. We give prisoners a turn in the shower every three days if they want one. Niggers won't take them."

"Not the way you give them," I heard a Negro mumble.

"One of you niggers say something?" the Sheriff said. Not one of the dozen Negroes spoke. The Sheriff addressed the two deputies, "When we leave, teach that nigger," he said to the guards then back to Dad. "One of them is a murderer. You tell me which one I'll forget the ticket. We got twice as many niggers as whites in this county but I got twice as many whites in jail,.. more than twice. When something happens in a nigger neighborhood they don't talk, so I can't do anything."

After a pause the sheriff stood in front of the cell and continued, "Niggers did tell on a white farmer carrying labor to his farm. Said he ran over another nigger before daylight. He had six niggers riding in the back of a pickup. Three didn't see nothing, two said they heard the thump and one said he saw the boy hit by the truck. So, I put the poor man in jail. Took me a week to get the coroner from Savannah up here." He raised his voice at the Negroes in their cell, "He told me that nigger wasn't killed by a truck. He said he must have been dead for hours. The boy died from twenty stab wounds and dropped dead after running for a ways. Coroner said the way the truck ran over his legs wouldn't of killed him anyway. But nobody round there knows the dead boy or what happened. That nigger fell dead right in front of that one's house." Verdon pointed, "Probably yelled his fool head off. But, the niggers that stay there said they didn't hear or see nothing."

Magnolia was a rough place.

As we walked back by the first cell a young white man asked us to help him, claiming he hadn't done anything. He said the Sheriff picked him up for the other prisoners to abuse. The sheriff ignored the conversation.

"Got any questions about my jail?" The sheriff directed his question to Dad and could have been alluding to the young man's comment.

But I answered, "Why are the prisoners so young?"

He laughed, "Not enough jobs or enough workers. Depends on who you ask. The men don't go forty miles from here, either south to join up at Fort Stewart or north to Reidsville state prison. Folks joke the world is flat and drops off at the county line because wherever people go they don't come back."

Why would they? I thought – I was barely smart enough to keep that thought to myself.

We returned to the Sheriff's desk. Dad and I sat in two chairs facing across the wooden desk.

"Mr. Lawyer, if you have any ideas on how to get through to those niggers and solve my murder case… Well, I'll forget your ticket."

"Are you serious?"

"Of course I'm serious. I'm not going to have an unsolved murder in my county. Somebody will swing high for it. Well you want to give it a try? I've tried and got nowhere. I've been Sheriff five years with only one unsolved crime. Someone stole the appliances out of a new house. Only new house in the county in two years I had my deputies spending the night in it when it was under construction. Folks move in, next week thieves hit. I looked everywhere; those appliances are not in my County. Do you have any experience with nigger murder cases?"

"Just one."

"That's one more than I have. I'm like you. You're a lawyer and you tell people. I'm the one that say's how it is here. We have two things in this county, what the farmers grow out of the ground and what I bring off the highway. That's it. You would do the same if you were me."

Dad appeared perplexed, "You have a witness that said the farmer hit the Negro with his truck and killed him."

Sheriff Verdon chuckled and rocked back in his chair, "So that's what a smart Atlanta lawyer thinks. And what about the five that didn't see it and the coroner's report? Well, I tell you what I think; I figure you were going eighty miles an hour in a sixty mile an hour zone that is reckless driving. You being a lawyer you ought to know. It's more than fifteen miles per hour over the speed limit."

Dad said, "I was driving 60 miles an hour or less. I wanted to conserve gas because I was near empty. Driving faster would have made the gas go quicker."

"Are you disputing my word?" the Sheriff asked in a threatening tone.

"Yes, I am," Dad's voice was calm.

"Well then you will have to post bail for me to hold 'til your trial. Bail would be $400," the Sheriff said smiling and chuckling.

"I do not see the humor in this. Can you explain it to me?" Dad asked.

"No! Give me the $400 dollars and I will schedule you for a hearing at the judge's convenience."

"I will have to write you a check."

"We don't take checks. Too many people run off on bad checks and we don't have the time to track them down."

"How much is the ticket?" Dad asked.

"$200, And I'm adding another $200 for trying to escape. You tried to drive off when I hollered at you, $400 total."

"It is a one way street, I had to go that way. If you will not accept a check for the bail, I assume you will not accept one for the ticket either."

"No, but I will impound your car and help you get a room with a widow woman tonight. You will have to get someone to come get you. The bus to Atlanta does not come through here. We don't want one, too easy for everyone else to leave and go to the big city. You can come back for your hearing or to pay your ticket. Rich Atlanta lawyer like you probably has two cars." The Sheriff leaned back in his chair, folding his arms across his chest and looking at Dad.

"I would like to make a call," Dad said.

"The phone we have is for police business."

"This is police business," Dad said. "I am allowed one call by law."

"Who do you want to call?" Verdon asked.

"Judge Gordon," Dad replied.

"He won't be at work on Sunday," Verdon tried to end the conversation.

"I will call his home."

"You can't call long distance."

"I will pay for the call," Dad offered.

"I don't think you got the cash. Beside, I don't know the charges until the end of the month. A long distance call is too much trouble."

"An operator will assist you and Judge Gordon will accept the charges," Dad said.

"You are pretty sure of this judge," Verdon paused.

"I am."

Dad overcame the Sheriff's objections and Verdon made the call. Thank God, the judge answered the phone and accepted the charges. The Sheriff would not let Dad speak to the judge and reported to the judge that Dad had tried to escape.

"That's not true," Dad said loud enough to be heard on the other end of the phone. "I am in Magnolia in Cross Keys County," He added before the Sheriff could cover the mouthpiece of the black rotary phone.

Then Verdon said he didn't have to talk to the judge because he could be anyone on the phone. Judge Matt Gordon on the other end of the phone took in the situation and told the Sheriff he was ordering the State Patrol to take Dad into his custody and he would handle the speeding issue.

"He's my prisoner at my jail. If the State Patrol does come we will work it out." The Sheriff slammed down the phone. He leaned forward, "Judge Gordon, if he is a judge, said he was sending the State Patrol here to take you into their custody. We'll see." He thought some more, "I'll keep your car in case the State Patrol forgets where they got you." And he put out his hands for the keys.

Dad, looked concerned, "Are you going to give the keys back when the State Patrol gets here?"

"Yea, sure, I don't want you to escape. My car can't catch that V8."

"Jeb, remember he said he would give the keys back." Dad looked at me as the Sheriff took the keys and dropped them in his desk drawer.

"Yes, sir," I said. The Sheriff had the keys and I was scared.

"I might have to put you in a cell anyway in case you try to get out of here on foot. Can you run fast?" Verdon smiled as he taunted Dad.

"OK," Dad said, "But I will ask the State Patrol and GBI to investigate what you do here today."

This comment angered the Sheriff. He muttered to himself that the State Patrol did not have enough information to find us. He had trouble but he wanted to save face in front of the deputies. "Let's keep our big Atlanta lawyer locked up in the hallway."

"Are you sure, Sheriff?" asked the deputy. The sheriff glared back. "What'd I say?"

Dad followed the deputy back and signaled "OK" to me through the small barred window.

After the deputy took Dad, the Sheriff opened the drawer and took out Dad's keys and put them in his left shirt pocket. When he noticed I was watching he said, "I'm taking my keys, I don't want them mixed up with your Dad's keys. He walked over to the deputy and said, "I may have to move the lawyer's car so it won't be in the way."

As they talked the deputy from Kennedy County walked through the door. He had a face to scare the white off rice with short cut black hair with no sideburns. His black eyes peered out of a rough shaved pockmarked face. If he wasn't "the mean, ugly S.O.B." referred to earlier I didn't want to meet him.

"Where is he?" the deputy growled.

"In the back. We got some paper work," the Sheriff said.

"We ain't got no paperwork until I see it's him," the Kennedy County deputy said. Like Sheriff Verdon he did not have much of a uniform. He was dressed in black from head to toe including a black snap-brim hat and a six-inch barrel .38 revolver in a black holster on his belt. The single identifying mark was a five-pointed tin star on his shirt pocket that looked like it came from a box of Cracker Jacks. His evil demeanor emanated not from any physical deformity but straight out from his dark soul refracted in darting glances from his coal-black eyes."

"Sheriff Davies wants him now," the deputy in black demanded.

"He ain't no boss to me," Verdon bowed up.

"You want me to tell him?" the deputy sneered back.

"No, we got a lot going on. The State Patrol is supposed to be coming and I don't want no trouble!" The Sheriff yelled back.

"Your problem, Bill," the deputy sneered. "Sheriff Davies said don't let him talk to nobody and get him right now." He pulled off his belt and pistol holster and placed them on Verdon's desk, "And this is right now."

"Don't smart off to me," Verdon said. "My desk isn't the place for your pistol. Lock it back in your truck."

The deputy in black moved quickly out the door and came right back. "OK, Bill, you know what I need. Take care of it or I'll have to tell Davies you can't carry your end of the stick."

"I got it, so shut up," the Sheriff was rattled. He opened the locked door to the cells and motioned Dad out. He instructed one of the Magnolia Deputies to help the Kennedy County deputy and the other to stand with Dad out of the way.

"Mr. McKnight, I need you to sign for your court date and then you can wait outside for the State Patrol. But they need to report to me, you are still my prisoner," the Sherriff told Dad, who stood out of the way with the second deputy.

Dad read the ticket. He placed the ticket book and pen back on the Verdon's desk. "There is no court date specified."

"I must have forgot. I'll get it later." Verdon was annoyed.

The Sheriff and I walked ahead toward the front door. A prisoner had asked Dad a question. Dad sought clarification from the jail deputy and paused for his replies. I noticed through the front windows a young man looking at our Ford. He wore a collared shirt, short-sleeves rolled up and dark pants. He looked at the rear quarter panel where Dad had the yellow accent painted black to change the car from two-tone to solid black. The Sheriff opened the exterior jail door and looked back to see Dad talking to the Magnolia jail deputy. Then he asked the man around the car. "What do you think? Can you take it?"

"No, it's got custom paint and seats. They would find it the first day."

"That V8 will out run nine out of ten police cars," Verdon said.

"It's the tenth one I'm worried about."

"I got the key in my pocket," he pulled his coat wide open and patted his left shirt pocket. I noticed his shoulder holster and a pistol butt I had not seen earlier.

"You can take it now," the Sheriff encouraged.

"It's a nice car but I don't want it."

"If you change your mind it may be here a few days."

The Sheriff noticed me listening, "The man is admiring your Dad's car."

"We need to go home," I said as Dad finished his conversation and came toward us. The Sheriff returned to his desk. Dad and I sat in the two chairs in front of the Sheriff's desk.

The Kennedy County deputy came to the jail door that led to the cells and angrily demanded some help getting the irons on the prisoner. The Sheriff told us there would be trouble getting the prisoner out and for us to go outside and sit in our car.

We went out and sat in the car. Dad leaned over and checked the glove box for his extra set of keys and spare cash under the maps. They were there. Outside nothing moved in Magnolia, not even a breeze. It was like the town itself was holding its breath. After a few minutes the door to the jail flung open. The Sheriff came out to hold it as his two young deputies and the deputy in black wrestled Hayes toward the Black Maria.

The prisoner in street clothes, handcuffs and leg irons struggled with all his might screaming, "Don't let him take me! He'll kill me! I'm from Cross Keys County same as you. Help me!"

The three deputies got the prisoner to the open door at the back of the truck. Each time the deputies tried to lift the prisoner in the back door he struggled, putting his chained feet up on the truck and pushing back. "He'll kill me, damn it! I'm serious. He will!"

"I'll handle this," the mean looking deputy said, walking around to the driver side door and returned swinging a long Billy stick. Dad and I watched from ten feet away sitting in the Ford. The deputy looked like death himself. He came around the back of the prisoner who screamed, "No, don't let him hit me!" The deputy swung the stick with all his might hitting the prisoner in the back of the head and knocking him to the ground. The prisoner groaned in pain and blood seeped through his matted brown hair.

"Shit, Jim, shoot me and get it over with," the prisoner said, clearly acquainted with the deputy.

"You would like that, wouldn't you? You sorry piece of white-trash, you been nothing but trouble for us." The deputy hit him again and knocked him unconscious.

"That's enough!" Verdon commanded, "Don't kill him in my county! I'm serious about that."

The prisoner's limp body was lifted into the back of the Black Maria. They unlocked his leg irons and handcuffs and then locked the truck. The deputies walked back in the jail, carrying the leg irons and handcuffs belonging to Cross Keys County. They remained in the jail where the Kennedy County deputy did the paperwork. Enough time passed for the prisoner to regain consciousness.

"Oh God. I'm in Hell. Oh God help me!" He wasn't in Hell, but he could smell the brimstones burning. Dad and I saw two hands grip the bars in the window in the back of the Black Maria and the prisoner pulled himself up to look out the window.

"Oh please, Jesus, get me out of this and I'll be good," His eyes focused on Dad, "Please help me, Mister. They sure gonna kill me."

I held my breath as Dad opened his door and moved to the back of the Maria to hear what the prisoner had to say.

"Mister, I ain't bad. I made some moonshine for these people. They said they wouldn't make me run it. Now they gonna kill me." Dad tried to get his name and some more information. In a few sentences the prisoner gave some personal messages for next of kin and where he thought his body could be found. Dad promised to tell the state patrol.

The Kennedy County deputy came out. He saw Dad talking to the prisoner. I did not think it possible but he made an even uglier face than before as he flew into a rage.

"You want to talk to my prisoner? Well, god-damn-it you can just ride along!"

He started for Dad, who tried to explain he was a lawyer to no avail. The deputy opened the back of the Maria to reveal his prisoner chained to the wall. He wrestled Dad toward the open door. Dad pushed back but he was loosing the battle.

I gasped aloud. All I could think is Dad is dead too if he gets in that prison truck. I leaned on the horn. The earsplitting blast pierced the absolute quiet of Magnolia. I did not let off even when the Sheriff came out of the jail. For all I knew he would help the deputy put Dad in the truck.

Verdon pulled the deputy off Dad and yelled at me, "Shut that horn off!"

I let off the horn and the Sheriff started in on the deputy, "This here is an Atlanta Lawyer. The State Patrol is going to be here any minute to get him. Get out of here fast."

"Sheriff Davies ain't going to like this. He was talking to the prisoner. Ain't no telling what he said."

"That prisoner is white-trash. Ain't no problem. Nobody cares about him. Now get." Verdon responded.

The deputy insisted, "Nobody gonna miss that lawyer neither. Get out of my way."

"That's his son sitting right there," the Sheriff said pointing to me, and asked, "you going to take them both? The State Patrol is supposed to be coming for them."

"You need to bust a cap on both of them. Say he pulled his gun." The deputy pointed at Dad as he railed against us.

"He ain't got one, neither do that little boy."

"The State Patrol boys will. Nobody like them either, get the drop on them. It's your county, your judge. Davies is gonna find out. Make him happy or he'll send me right back up here," the deputy said in a menacing tone.

"What do you mean, bust a cap?" Dad demanded.

Verdon pushed Dad back to the Ford, opened the door and shoved him behind the wheel knocking me over to the passenger side. "You sit there and don't move," the Sheriff commanded. The deputy paused and decided to leave. He climbed in the Black Maria and drove off. Dad said nothing. We had seen and heard too much.

The Sheriff then opened the car door and took Dad back inside the jail, "You need to tell me everything the prisoner said to you. It's police business."

The State Patrol came in like the cavalry to the rescue. They passed the Black Maria going in the other direction. The Patrol car had two Troopers in it. Seeing the one prefix on our tag they called out to me, "Jeb McKnight?"

"Yes, sir."

"Was your father in the Black Maria?"

"No, sir. He's inside."

"Come on, son, we're here for you both," the lead Trooper said. "Jeb, can you tell me how many people in there? And do the policemen have guns?"

"Sheriff Verdon and two deputies, there are two ladies behind a counter to the right. Dad is the only regular person. There are no walls inside. The two deputies stay on the left by the jail door, they don't have guns. The Sheriff has a desk to the left and my Dad is probably sitting in front of him. The Sheriff has a pistol under his coat in a left shoulder holster."

"Got it, Barrett?" The first Trooper said.

"Heard him clear. Hope he's right."

"Thanks, good report Jeb."

The Sheriff was questioning Dad about what he had seen and heard outside. I walked in behind the two State Patrol officers. They wore Smokey Bear hats, dark gray pants and lighter gray tunics. Their pressed uniforms of lightweight wool gave them a professional look far above the Sheriff and his mismatched deputies. The Troopers wore polished black shoes and black belts. They opened their holster flaps for their 1911 Colt .45's and gripped the handles. They meant business. They opened the door and entered scanning the room.

"I am Lieutenant McClain and this is Sergeant Barrett of the Georgia State Patrol." The Troopers kept their hands on their pistol grips. "Would you two deputies stand together by the barred door? Ladies, would you please keep your hands where I can see them and come out from behind the counter?" Everyone obeyed. The two ladies moved to the seating area away from their counter and McClain signaled for them to sit.

The Sheriff blustered out, "This here is my jail. What do you think you're doing giving orders here?"

"Are you Sheriff Verdon?" McClain did the talking.

"That's right."

"Are you armed?"

"Nobody carries in the jail," Verdon acted offended.

"Would you slowly open the left side of your jacket using your left hand?"

The Sheriff obeyed exposing his shoulder holster and pistol. McClain and Barrett pulled their 1911's clear of their holsters at the sight of the Sheriff's gun but kept their pistols pointed down at their sides.

The Sheriff mumbled, "OK, I guess I forgot about this little thing. It's not a regulation pistol."

"It shoots. Remove the gun using two fingers and place it on your desk." McClain ordered. Sergeant Barrett will hold it for you. Barrett took the snub nosed .38 off the Sheriff's desk and put it in his belt. McClain holstered his 1911 but continued to grip it at the ready. Barrett's pistol remained out pointed down at his side. It was confusing to me to see the one law enforcement agency pull guns on another.

"Sergeant Barrett and I are here on official business by order of Judge Matthew Gordon of the Georgia State Court. You are to remand to our custody Mr. Henry L. McKnight and his son Jeb L. McKnight."

"He is my prisoner, I caught him reckless speeding and he tried to escape and he's been talking to another prisoner who has been transferred over to Kennedy County. I need to investigate. And I don't know nothing about no Judge Gordon."

The Troopers did not blink. The Sheriff and deputies shrunk back from their stare. McClain looked around. His partner was positioned to cover him. Then he began in a firm voice looking the Sheriff in the eye.

"Let me be clear, Mr. McKnight is no longer your prisoner. By order of Judge Matthew Gordon he has been remanded to our custody and his car too." McClain glanced at Dad but kept the Sheriff in view. "Mr. McKnight, were you speeding?"

"No I was not. I was going a few miles an hour under the speed limit," Dad answered.

"Mr. McKnight, did you try to escape custody."

"No, I did not."

"I had to holler at him to come back, my deputies saw," the Sheriff interjected.

McClain looked at the deputies and one said, "I heard him holler but I did not see anything. The Sheriff was standing on the porch."

"You were on foot and he was in a V8 Ford. I believe he could have escaped if he wanted to. What about the other prisoner in the Black Maria?" I noticed McClain was writing things down on a pad.

"The Sheriff of the next county had a warrant on him. I don't know anything about him."

"Mr. McKnight, what did you see?"

"It took three men, handcuffs, and leg irons to take him from the jail. He repeated a number of times he was from this county and he would be murdered in Kennedy County. They had to beat him unconscious with a Billy stick to get him in the Black Maria."

"Dang, how big was he?" Barrett asked.

"He was a big monster. Toughest S.O.B. we ever had in this jail," Verdon blurted out. "We had to keep him in solitary. He scared the other prisoners to death."

"Mr. McKnight, is that correct?" McClain turned to Dad.

"I don't know about the other prisoners. He was of average build and a bit taller than me. He kept saying they would kill him. After he regained consciousness he said through the truck bars they planned to kill him. He said he made moonshine but didn't deliver it."

"He's a fool, he ain't no moonshiner," Verdon raised his voice.

"How would you know?" McClain asked.

"This is my county, I know what goes on here. There's no moonshine."

"We will need his name," said McClain, putting his pen to the pad.

"I forgot, we don't keep paper work on transfers," Verdon shrugged.

"Toughest man you ever brought in and you don't know his name? Mr. McKnight, did you get his name?"

Dad volunteered, "I wrote his name down. Lonnie Hayes. I think the GBI should follow up."

"Oh, shit," the Sheriff, muttered. "Lonnie wasn't his name, I believe it was Willie. Yea, Willie something, lot of Willie's in this county."

McClain looked around and then his eyes landed on Barrett. "I think we are done." He turned to the Sheriff, "We believe Mr. McKnight. His story makes sense, yours doesn't. Judge Gordon will hold court to hear your charges unless you want to drop them."

"I can't be leaving here over a traffic ticket."

"Sheriff Verdon, are you dropping the charges?" The Trooper's question rang like a challenge.

"Yes, I'm dropping the charges. You can consider it a warning."

"I believe I can contest a warning. I would like to do so before Judge Gordon," Dad said.

"Sheriff Verdon, are you going to write up a warning?" McClain asked.

"No. Y'all can leave."

"We need Mr. McKnight's car keys and any paperwork on Mr. McKnight."

"I didn't do any paperwork. I was too busy."

"May I see your ticket book?"

"I don't know where I put it."

"Hand me the one on your desk." McClain extended his hand.

"Oh, here it is," Verdon complied.

McClain opened the ticket book and tore out the top page and carbon copy. "I'll keep these. I am going to guess you forgot you wrote him up."

"Must have," the Sheriff smiled and scratched the back of his head, unconcerned to be caught in another lie.

"I'll take the keys now," McClain held out his hand.

The Sheriff opened the drawer and said in a surprised voice, "Those keys are gone." He looked at his deputies, "Y'all saw me put them in the drawer. He must have taken them out in the confusion."

I pointed to the Sheriff's left shirt pocket. "He put them in his pocket."

"Let's see those keys in your pocket, I can see the imprint in your shirt," Barrett had the angle to see them.

"These are my keys, I got a Ford too."

Barrett took the keys and held them in his left hand and with his right hand still griping his pistol he watched as McClain put his pad in his belt and griped his own pistol. "Clear?" and McClain responded, "Clear."

Barrett walked outside and seconds later we heard the Ford start up then turn off. The Trooper walked back in.

"I must have got those keys mixed up with mine," the Sheriff shrugged.

McClain asked, "Jeb, did you see anything else?"

"The Sheriff knew he had Dad's keys. He told a man looking at our car he had the keys in his pocket and the man could take it. The man said he didn't want it because it had custom paint."

"You going to let that little boy call me a liar," Verdon acted insulted.

"Almost everything you have said has been a lie," I said, surprising everyone including myself. The Troopers stifled their laughter. Verdon was a joke, a bad joke.

"What?" Verdon gasped.

"How often do you auction off the cars you impound?" McClain said, gazing steadily at the Sheriff.

"I don't know what you mean. It cost the county to keep cars and I don't have much room."

McClain turned and asked Dad then Barrett if they had anything to add before we left. Barrett fixed his steel gaze on the Sheriff. "I guess I have one thing to add. He stepped toward the Sheriff and said, "Sheriff Verdon, you are one of the worst liars I have ever met, both as to content and as to manner of lying."

The flummoxed Sheriff ranted, "You can't talk to me that way!"

"Do you want to take your hogwash story in front of Judge Gordon?" McClain demanded.

"No, I have to stay here in my county and do my job."

"Barrett will leave your pistol on the hood of your car." The Troopers signaled for Dad and me to go outside. They backed out of the door.

"I can't thank you enough," Dad said.

"Jim was the name of the deputy from Kennedy County, who drove the black truck." I said.

"Thank you, Jeb. Mr. McKnight I must say your son helped us with a description of the jail and warned us that Verdon had a concealed pistol. We will lead you out and then follow you once you're back on highway twenty-five."

Judge Gordon had ordered them to follow us all the way to Atlanta. When we hit highway twenty-five again the State Patrol car motioned us around and said they would follow about a mile back until we left their district.

We rode in exhausted silence for a while. Dad broke the silence, "Judge Gordon was better than the whole British Navy."

Chapter 19 Roadkill

In the afternoon sunshine we headed north to Atlanta. Everywhere we went there was trouble. Chances of making Atlanta by evening were gone. It disturbed Dad to discover I saw peace as the exception and capricious violence as the rule. Dad tried to assure me about the Fatherhood of God and the Brotherhood of man. He had a tough sell on the second part. In Dad's series of lessons for me, we had got up to playing football at Georgia Tech. He only played one year and did not start at quarterback. Dad sprained both ankles in a touch game and had to be carried by his roommate to classes.

We rounded a bend to find the road was covered by red clay mud, which is slicker than ice. Dad down shifted the V8 and our tires spun, but we passed through. Dad stopped where a skinny old farmer had his mule team standing alongside his house. This was an old country scam to get cash. A farmer made a stretch of dirt road, or in this case paved road, impassable by putting down a layer of mud. When travelers got stuck he would offer to pull them out for a fee. The amount was based on how much cash he thought they might have. As expected, the State Patrol pulled up behind us. When the farmer saw the State Patrol he exclaimed, "You ain't supposed to be up here today!"

The Troopers got out, "Mr. McKnight, we will handle this one. Good luck. We will radio ahead to the next State Patrol Station, but we can't say where they might pick you up."

Highway twenty-five somehow got subtracted by two and became Georgia State Highway 23. There was a perfectly good reason for this. The State Highway Commissioner, Big Mike Willis, said so. If Big Mike wanted to change the name of your road to Mike's Highway 55 that's what it was if you wanted a highway.

At sunset we stopped to put up the top and I looked down the dirt road on my side of the car to see a group of boys, whites and blacks, fighting each other. Dad did not notice and I did not want to point out more random violence. The sky darkened with rain clouds and we had to drive in the pitch-black country night and light rain. The centerline was the only line painted on the road. There were no white lines on the edges. In daylight we could see where the black top turn to red clay but not at night. Dad tried to hug the centerline and hope. A film of oil and mud sprayed up from the road covered our windshield, impairing our vision even more. I noticed a dark form as it rose out of the roadside drainage ditch.

"Dad, cow!"

Dad slammed on breaks. It was not a cow; my farm animal recognition skills were diminished in the dark. We slid into a three hundred pound sow knocking her end over end in front of our car. She lay dead almost on the centerline of the road. Dad tried to roll the huge pig to the side, but couldn't budge it. He turned on his left hand blinker hoping another car would not hit the dead animal.

A pickup truck came up skidding on the rain slick road, the driver was unable to stop behind us so he went around. He turned sharply back in front of us barely missing the pig. In Dad's headlights we could see the longhaired woman hand him something from the glove box. The man in his thirties wore khakis and a short-sleeve shirt. Dad showed his empty hands to the young farmer as he exited his truck and walked toward us. The farmer held a long barreled revolver at his left side.

"Lordy, Mister, you trying to get killed!"

"No, there is a pig in the road and I thought I might save you from getting killed."

Because he swerved around us, his headlights never hit the pig. The startled farmer jumped like he had stepped on a snake as he recognized the pig close to his feet. "Mister, I'm sorry if I hit that pig I'd flipped for sure."

He put the pistol back in the truck for the woman to put away. "Sorry, I got to be careful, my wife's in the car."

"I don't blame you at all. Can you help me get it out of the road?"

"She's too big for us. I got a chain, we can sling her into the ditch with the truck."

"We should try to find who owns it," Dad said, ever the Good Samaritan.

"Where you from, Mister? I can tell you who owns it, nobody. If unfenced livestock causes an accident, it is the responsibility of the owner, no one claims to own road kill. Did it hurt your car? It looks like a new one."

He and Dad examined the front bumper. The Ford's chrome covered steel bumper appeared undamaged in the dim light. The farmer attached his chain to his trailer hitch. Together the two men pulled the pig's back legs together and wrapped the chain around them. No other cars came by. As the two men worked to secure the pig I caught a whiff of the blood and offal, roadkill smells bad fast.

"Mister, this pig is still warm. Do you know how long it's been here?"

"Two minutes," Dad said.

"It's fresh. I'm going to dress it out. Do you want any of the meat?"

"No thanks. I need to get home."

"I ain't got a phone but I can tell you where I live. My brother-in-law can dress it out better than any grocery store. You deserve a share."

"No thanks. If you clear it off the road you should have it all."

"Could you give me your name and address so I have a witness as to how I got this pig."

"Certainly." The men exchanged business cards.

"Thanks, Mr. McKnight."

The farmer got back in his truck. He speed away then swerved the truck left then right and hit the brakes hard, the pig rolled into the right hand ditch. He jumped out and disconnected the chain from his truck. He threw it in the ditch alongside the pig and drove off. Dad and I got back in the car and drove on.

"Jeb, how do you like the Ford now? If we had hit the big pig in the MG it would have mangled the car, and us too."

"I think the MG had better windshield wipers."

"Maybe. We need to do something."

If it had rained harder it might have cleaned our windshield. After a few miles we came to a cinderblock roadside bar. Four cars were parked in the gravel lot. Dad was weary by this time. He checked for his spare keys and cash in the glove box. He took two extra twenties out of his money clip and put them under the floor mat.

He went inside to see if they had any soap to clean the windshield. The bartender suggested a Peachtree Cola, which Dad bought and threw on the windshield. The wipers knocked much of the Peachtree Cola off before the carbonation could cut through the oil. So he returned for a second P.C. Some ruffians followed him out. Dad noticed the VFW hand painted on the concrete block wall and said he was a veteran too. They watched him clean the windshield.

"We ain't no veterans, they don't use this place no more."

"We veterans of Reidsville prison."

"Yea, they wouldn't let us out to fight in the war," another said.

"But we can fight."

They beat, robbed, and shoved Dad around. I was scared half to death. I remembered the horn and gave it a blast. The bartender came out and rather than help, he demanded a share of Dad's cash. The ex-cons continued to beat and shove Dad around. They let him get back up only to knock him down again. The men began fighting each other over the split of Dad's money. He managed to get back in the car and lock the door.

"He ain't going no-where. I got his keys."

Dad fumbled in the glove box for the extra set of keys and started the car. They chased the car on foot. Dad almost lost control of the car where the driveway crossed the drainage ditch. It was ugly.

We drove on in the dark and drizzling rain. Dad no longer cared to talk and strained to see the road ahead. He did not complain but I knew he was in pain.

"I needed an Indian on my side at the last stop," he vainly joked.

"I'm on your side Dad, I honked the horn."

No one followed us. We turned on forty-two and drove until we saw Fresh Air Barbeque on the left. Dad went straight to the bathroom to work damage control on his face and mud splattered clothes. We ordered our food from the counter and sat down at a wooden table. We ate a feast of pulled pork, white bread, potato chips, cole slaw, Peachtree Colas, and vanilla ice cream in a cup with a little wooden spoon. The ice cream softened while we ate our Barbeque. Dad got up and ordered two hot fried peach pies to put our ice cream on and two more six-ounce bottled PCs.

Dad looked the worse for wear. He had cleaned up the best he could using paper towels in the bathroom. Small bits of mud and debris splotched his clothes and his pants were torn at the knee. Bruises rose on his face, and the knuckles on one hand trickled blood. I hoped he caught one of the bastards in the teeth. He tried to keep a good front on things. He kept his torn pant leg under the table, and his bloodied hand in a napkin in his lap.

We had not eaten a meal since breakfast. We had passed the day on one adrenaline rush after another. We savored our barbeque in the security of familiar surroundings. I had achieved a new level of tired; my bones ached.

I took stock of out situation. I seriously doubted we could finish the three-hour drive to Atlanta and I saw the same doubt in Dad's face. We had a memorable father-son talk.

"Dad, do you think we are wearing the wrong clothes?"

"What do you mean?"

"It seems everybody wears short-sleeve shirts rolled up. You wear long sleeves with a jacket. Maybe if you wore a short-sleeve shirt and khakis we'd get by better."

"Jeb, I don't think it matters."

"Dad, you have told us one hundred times to dress appropriately for church or for school or to box. I think we are wearing the wrong clothes. Something's wrong."

"Jeb, we are dressed fine for our trip," Dad said, too tired to express his impatience with my inane line of reasoning.

From one crisis to the next, it had been a close run day. We were several hours away from Atlanta on two lane roads in the rain on a moonless night. Five-year-olds believe their Dad can do anything, but my Dad's humanity glared through the circumstances. I was not destined to be a teenager before I though my Dad was fallible. Something hit me in the sugar rush of ice cream, Peachtree Cola, and peach pie. I guess I was goofy. I wanted Dad to pay attention to this problem we still weren't home and despite a meal our chances did not seem much improved. Out it came, adult words.

"Dad! I mean Damn, Hell! We have been shot at, put in jail, drove through a mud trap, hit a pig, and robbed! We are doing something wrong!"

People turned to look at this foul-mouthed kid. Dad started to yell at me and he laughed so he wouldn't cry. I used up most of the profanity I knew. My remarks caused a disturbance.

The owner came out from behind the counter, "We don't allow cussing in this restaurant. Church people are here and it's Sunday. Mr. you're going to have to control that boy."

"Don't worry, I will. He's had a rough day."

"Did all what he said happen to y'all?"

"I'm afraid so."

"That explains it. The state patrol came by here before y'all asking if a man and boy had been through. When y'all came I didn't say anything. I don't want trouble. Maybe they're trying to help y'all."

"Yes, they are."

"I got a number. I'll call them."

"Thank you, thank you so much," Dad said.

"If you get them tell them we are headed north."

When we started driving I asked Dad, "Do you think Mom and Ida Mae made it?"

"I hope so." Seeing my concern he added, "Don't worry, Jebby. We would have passed them if they had a problem." Not if they were in jail I thought.

Dad told me to get in the back seat and go to sleep on my improvised pillow. I awoke to find we had been pulled over by a car with a flashing light. I thought, "Damn, not again." But on Judge Gordon's orders the state patrol had continued looking for us to escort us home. They were better than the whole British Navy. Dad asked one of the patrolmen to drive our car. After midnight my Mom awoke to see two sets of car headlights pull in the driveway, a State Patrol car and Dad's Ford. I slept through it all and I woke the next morning in my own bed.

The next morning I didn't wake up until Ida Mae had arrived for work. She fixed me two poached eggs, bacon and toast that I gobbled down like I hadn't eaten in days. Dad tried to put the best face on our trip home and I ate.

We found out Mom had escaped all but the mud trap. She hit the brakes and slid into the ditch. The skinny old farmer said he would pull her out for ten bucks. After he pulled her out she opened her wallet, and handed him a ten. When he saw her cash, he told her it was ten dollars to pull her out, but twenty more dollars to disconnect the mules. As

Mom argued Ida Mae got out of the car and disconnected the mules from the car. As the red-faced farmer harassed Mom, Ida Mae leaned over and honked the horn. The unencumbered mules took off. The farmer cussed and chased after his mules and Mom sped off.

The relief of being with the whole family in the security of my own home spilled out as I cheered, "Hooray for Mom and hooray for Ida Mae!"

***

Our reconnoitering mission had been a close run thing but we survived to report. The artillery was called in. Stan Wallace came after dinner Tuesday to meet with Dad and me. The meeting was never anything but serious. Stan shook his head often and spoke in frustrated tones about our run through the gauntlet of rural road hazards. Dad wanted to make sure he had enough evidence for the State Patrol or GBI to investigate. He did. Dad selected events that he wanted me to verify. Stan "knew" me and my account was all he needed. Stan was openly critical of Dad for including me as witness and pointed out that both our lives were in jeopardy. Stan said Dad could thank two people for saving his life - me for honking the horn and the engineer that designed the Ford's horn to work with the ignition off. I was sent to bed. Their conversation continued with occasional raised voices and I heard Dad sob out loud.

Wednesday Dad spent the day at home preparing notes for his meeting with law enforcement people. Two Troopers in uniform and a GBI agent in a black suit arrived in the late afternoon. I was called in from outside and Dad offered everyone cold drinks. Judge Gordon arrived later wearing a dark suit. Like Dad, he had played football at Georgia Tech and had traveled north to law school, the University of Chicago. Stan Wallace was there to represent me as a child witness. The meeting was somber as a funeral home. Dad focused on violations of the law that could be proved, and he had suspects in mind.

I did not field many questions because I could not read. I did have to swear I heard a rifle shot and some stuff about the Sheriff of Magnolia. The patrolman blanched when I told them the Kennedy county deputy had advised the Magnolia sheriff to "get the drop on the State Troopers." and then rely on his county judge. I did not understand but they did.

The GBI swung into action. They made arrests. Clell was the first one in jail. His shooting scared people away from his moonshine operation. The criminal enterprise included his wife, son, and cousin, Officer Louis White.

The prisoner Dad and I saw transported from Magnolia in the Black Maria never made it to the Kennedy County jail. Someone took the prisoner to a bridge over a creek on the county line and beat him to death on the Kennedy County side of the creek. The culprit also shot the prisoner twice to make sure and then buried him in a shallow grave not twenty yards from the bridge, no witnesses. Before the GBI could question Jim, the heinous looking Kennedy County deputy, he fled to L.A.- Lower Alabama.

We heard that Sheriff Verdon did not lie any better at his trial than to the Troopers and he was sent to prison. The loyal citizens of Cross Keys County did not elect a new sheriff and Verdon tried to run the county from behind bars. Evidence mounted against the Kennedy County Sheriff and he killed himself before going to trial.

The State Patrol apprehended the men who robbed and brutalized Dad. The men used the unlicensed bar as a hangout. They were all parolees except the bartender. A state judge revoked their paroles and returned them to chain gang to serve time on previous convictions. The illegal bar was closed and the bartender sentenced on a liquor charge.

The State Troopers explained they circulated an open public service letter to local sheriff offices with their monthly schedule for the highway sections they would patrol. Their schedule was virtually public knowledge. With Stan's support the adults indulged me for one suggestion. From TV's Dragnet I recommended they allow the Troopers to 'follow their hunches.' They listened and decided to continue sending the schedules but go elsewhere. Arrests of moonshine runners and mud trap operators spiked. Moonshine cars, tractors and harnessed mules were impounded.

Animals on the road and speed traps were statewide problems. Some towns had posted limits of fifteen miles and hour. Dad got Big Heart's support for a bill to require fencing along all state highways – road construction crews would add them. Another bill was introduced to set forty miles an hour as the lowest speed limit a municipality could post on a state highway.

Weeks later, a handsome couple traveling back from Atlantic Ocean Club failed to return to Atlanta, ever. The State Patrol recovered their new Cadillac but no bodies. This crime drew attention and added support to the efforts Dad had started to make the roads safe.

Heretofore Dad's reputation involved helping Negroes, which gained him few friends. Securing state highways to Jekyll Island made Dad more popular with everyone, including Atlantic Islanders. Dad had a special concern for the Negroes who he hoped would use the colored hotel and beach facilities. Dad asked his Negro preacher friend Reverend Beard to get the word out. The State Patrol would provide an emergency number for them.

Chapter 20 Rogues

All Apostles Church supported all things charitable. The educated, and affluent, congregation possessed the southern patrician attitude that they should care for those less fortunate. They took the lead in doing "the right thing." In 1955 it meant asking a Negro to preach.

The priest searched for and found a "suitable Negro" to invite - Reverend Doctor Shadrach P. Martyne. He had preached to other white congregations. Our congregation prized the Negro family and two single Negro women who attended, making us integrated. He preached that we could bring in God's millennial kingdom by sharing our wealth. It sounded a lot like communism. Some in the congregation cared little for what he said, but they were pleased to report a Negro preached at our church.

After the service Dr. Martyne graciously acknowledged our praise and thanksgiving for his sermon and visit. Blue sky and sunshine attended the celebration of this historic event. Sweet tea, punch and sugar cookies were served on the lawn. I boldly greeted Dr. Martyne. I proudly told him Dad had given Ida Mae a job so she did not have to go back to jail. Dr. Martyne asked if he and his associate Mr. Beetlebrow, not in attendance, could meet Ida Mae at our home. Dad said an introduction could be made. He hoped they would not resurrect the prospect of a trial to clear Ida Mae.

On the appointed day for the meeting a short man in a suit and tie showed up at our front door. Beetlebrow engaged Mom in a conversation about the large homes and spacious landscaped lots. They talked about the dogwoods, tall pines, camellias and other blossoming plants and trees. Mom dodged pointed questions about our family and net worth. Beetlebrow asked to speak to Ida Mae in confidence, so Mom called Ida Mae from the kitchen and went to another room.

Ida Mae came into the hallway and Beetlebrow walked toward her from the front foyer. She stood a head taller than the short man, looked down at him, folding her large arms in front of her.

"What you want with me?" Ida Mae asked in a suspicious tone.

Noticing me by the phone stand, Beetlebrow said, "I would like to speak in private."

"Right here is fine, I got chores to do. What you want?"

Mr. Beetlebrow claimed to have come south to save poor Negroes from exploitation. "I know Mr. McKnight is abusing you, and we can help you?"

"What? What you mean, "abusing"? Ida Mae asked.

"Show me where he touches you."

"He ain't ever laid a hand on me nowhere."

"Do you like this house?" Beetlebrow asked cocking his head to the side like a weasel.

"Yes, I like working here," Ida Mae said.

"This house could be yours. All you have to say is Mr. McKnight is forcing you to have sex. I am handling another case like this one. We would win."

Ida Mae then called out, "Mrs. McKnight, you need to come out here."

"OK, you had your chance," said Beetlebrow as he headed for the door.

At Dad's request, the GBI instantly opened an investigation of the preacher and the lawyer. They had initiated a lawsuit against another family. The maid initially cooperated for the promise of money and then recanted her injurious testimony. Beetlebrow had hired a Georgia lawyer and the rules of Georgia law had been observed. The two lawyers denied they promised money to the maid, who's credibility could be an issue. Mr. Beetlebrow fled the state and returned "up north." The GBI sent out inquiries but "up north" no one would claim him.

Dr. Shadrach Martyne paid a visit to our home to apologize and blamed Beetlebrow. He admitted Beetlebrow offered to pay him to locate abused Negroes, but claimed he was not a party to the fraud. Dr. Martyne said he had done it to help and not for the money which he never received. Ida Mae and Mom heard his apology and promised to pass it along to Dad. They declined the offer of his return visit.

I sensed Ida Mae had stood up for us. The children of the family had become more accepting of her and she of us.

"Ida Mae, you helped Dad and I am glad for it." I said.

"Me too. Your Daddy been good to me. That little man was no good."

***

People joked our neighborhood had more horses than people; but city folks encroached. The week after the Beetlebrow affair Dad was thrown from his horse as he road with Travis. A teen driver honked spooking the horses. He had to spend a few days in bed before returning to work. The McKnight cavalry squad of the Militia want-to-bes was out of commission. Mom delayed a trip to take Lillie to Chicago.

On Ida Mae's day off my two younger brothers' were at a neighbor's house and Lillie was sleeping in the nursery. I heard the noise of barking and looked out my second story window to see a man in a suit and tie feeding treats to our Dachshunds. The dogs wobbled and fell down. I thought they were dead. I came downstairs as he knocked on the door. Mom opened the door.

"Do you remember me?" We recognized him. He was the menacing man who had come to the door and threatened Mom the day Dad and I were taken by the Klan. He was average size and the grey was taking over the brown in his hair. His sour face matched the man who directed Lukey.

"I have business with you. Your house is too nice for you. I know people who should live here."

"The house is not for sale." Mom held on to the door.

"You talked to the police. What did you say?"

"My husband talked to the police. Talk to him."

"Yeah, I got your husband back alive. Remember?" He said as he pushed the front door open.

"I don't want you in my house."

The man reached for Mom. She twisted free. He chased her but I stepped in his way it slowed him enough for Mom to get in the downstairs bathroom and lock the door. When I heard the door lock I locked the front door, shut it behind me and ran for the neighbors. I scooted on my hands and knees through the hedge. The Klansman caught me by the ankles and I yelled at the top of my lungs for Mrs. Colquitt. He pulled me up and held his hand over my mouth.

We would have been locked out of the house but he had not closed the door behind him. He noticed the door locked when he shut it and asked me to open it. I couldn't turn the ancient brass knob. He pushed me down the hall to the back door, which had the same style ancient brass lock. He tried it and assumed I could not open it. He asked about the phone and I said I wasn't allowed to use it. The Klansman smiled an evil smile and took the receiver off the hook. He left me in the back foyer and returned to the bathroom to talk to Mom through the door.

The man was no damn good. I had to do something and do it now! What? Ida Mae was a woman she backed a thief down at the bus stop with her knife.

I ran into the kitchen and selected a knife with an eight-inch stainless steel blade that came to a point. It would do the job. The man stood at the bathroom door trying to persuade Mom that he would not hurt her.

Holding the knife in my left hand down out of his view I stood by the man and asked Mom to open the door so I could give her something.

"Jeb, run to the Colquitt's house I'll be fine."

The man half laughed as he grabbed my right shoulder, "Now I can't allow that. Calling the police is the whole reason I'm here."

I thought if I could cut the man he would have to leave. I spun clockwise shifting the knife into my right hand and then turned hard left back toward the alarmed man. I aimed the knifepoint straight at his left hand pants pocket but he chopped down with his left hand. Instead of stabbing the knife went four inches down the side of his leg tearing his pants and cutting his leg.

"Ow! Shit! Your boy stabbed me!" He wrestled the knife away and looked at his torn pants and lightly bloodied leg. "You need to see this! You're going to have to pay for theses pants!

Mom called out, "I don't believe it. Jeb are you OK?"

"Yes mam."

He held the long blade straight down my chest. I thought this is the second time this year a full-grown Philistine has had a knife on me. I prayed silently, Jesus, it's me and I need saving again so does Mom. Amen.

Mom's choices were limited and she came out of the bathroom and sent me upstairs. Again, we needed an Indian or a neighbor on our side and fast. I rejected a run to the neighbor's house – too far, the man could easily catch me, and they might not be home. I had to do something and do it now! Call the police – Captain Mack.

The only phone was in the back hallway. No one in the history of the world had ever sneaked up or down our stairs. I had tried I was aware that each stair had its own signature creak. I was a heck of a good tree climber and jumper – out of trees, over bushes and the stream. I considered several jump locations but I was afraid to jump out of a second story window. There was another option, a plan I had considered to get by Ida Mae when I had been sent to my room. I had rejected it as too risky. I could break up a jump to the first floor with a stop half way down.

The upstairs hallway was shaped like an 'L' with a bannister rail along the stairwell. I climbed over the hall rail and hung from two second-floor banisters letting myself down on the top of the banister railing coming up the stairs. I could hear Mom and the man talking past the dining room and bathroom. Rather that risk a single step on a stair I slid off the railing holding on two bannisters sliding down them until I dropped onto the hallway slate floor with a small boy thud. I froze and held my breath. Nothing.

I sneaked to the rotary phone, got a dial tone and lifted the receiver. I turned the dial from the 'O' and slowly let back.

A lady answered, "Hello, this is the operator."

"There's a man in the house and my Mom doesn't want him here. I want the police to come."

"What's your name?

"Jeb"

"How old are you?"

"Five, almost six."

"Is there an adult I can speak too?"

"No. I want Captain Mack to come. Do you know him?

"No. I don't."

"Do you know Roy Rogers?"

"The TV cowboy?"

"Yes, he helps people."

"No. What's your address – the road you live on?

"Nancy Creek."

"A creek is not a road."

"That's what people call the road." Exasperated I tried something I had heard Dad say, "Let me speak to your supervisor."

A man's voice answered. "I'm the supervisor and I'm on the line. The police will come to Nancy Creek Road. What should they look for?"

"Our house is red and the man's car doesn't have a number one on it?"

"What?" the woman's voice asked.

"His license tag, he's not from Buckhead the first number is not a one." I was going on memory of the cars at the house fire. I did not notice Mom coming through the kitchen. She took the phone.

"Hello... Yes, I'm Jeb's mother... There is someone here but there is no problem... No, I don't want the police."

Mom hung up the phone. She seemed relieved. "Jeb the man won't hurt me if you run back upstairs to your room.

I ran up to my room and I can only assume the use of the phone unnerved the Klansman. I heard raised voices but he left. I ran downstairs; successfully turned the front door knob and went outside. Our dogs awakened when I poured cold water on them like they did to the unconscious cowboys on TV. The phone supervisor had called the police and a police car pulled in the driveway. Mom told them the man had left and they should go look for him. She said Dad would file any report we made. Mom called Dad and he arrived home as she put an early supper on the table. Mom lasted OK through most of dinner. She began to sob and left the table. Dad followed. Lillie was in her room; Dad returned to tend to Billy. He told Travis and me to finish our supper and put our plates in the kitchen. Stan Wallace was called.

After bedtime I was awakened and called to the dining room in my pajamas. Mom was not in the smoke filled room. The long knife I used and ashtrays were on the table but there were no drinks. Dad and Stan were both furious and steeled for action. But what?

Dad found fault and Stan didn't know what to say. He asked some clarifying questions about my use of the knife and he examined my route down the bannisters to the hallway and shook his head often. Back at the table the men were dismayed when I said the man looked like one of the men in the road at the house fire, maybe brothers. Stan surmised this would be an identification problem.

I pointed out. "If he's caught, he would have a cut on his left leg running straight down... Maybe as long as my hand." I held up my right hand.

Stan looked at me as if he would say something then shook his head again and put his hand over his forehead shading his eyes. "I can't speak..."

"About what?" Dad asked.

"About any of it!"

We sat quietly looking at Stan before he spoke again, "Jeb, I appreciate why you acted the way you did. I am upset and I can't say anymore than that now. You should be in bed." Then he turned to Dad, "I can't help you on this one. It's way out of my wheelhouse. You'll have to see what the police come up with and decide. I can give you referrals."

Dad sat in silence.

"Hank, I am going to try not to repeat anything I have said before. You are a lawyer and thought you could fight with these people in a courtroom. They don't fight that way. They chose the fight. I am surprised I have not heard anything about the Klan doing this kind of thing but then they don't publish their manual of arms."

"The law applies to all and goddammit they're part of all!" Dad punched the table with his finger.

Stan replied. "We had laws in the Pacific – the Geneva Convention, the rules of war. The Japs didn't want to fight that way. They chose their fight. Many men at arms and civilians suffered hideous things and those choices came back on the Japs. It was heinous and you know it so I'm not going to mention it. Jeb does not need to hear anymore. It's eleven o'clock and you need to look after Kate. Under the circumstances I am loathe to mention my own situation but I have trial to start in the morning."

Dad signaled and I went up to bed. I was not sleepy and stayed in the upstairs hall a while. The men lowered their voices; I could not hear.

At one point I heard Stan raise his voice, "Damn it! The boy's five years old!"

I wanted to holler down, 'I'm almost six.' My TV influenced worldview suffered from a dose of reality - the good guys didn't always win in thirty minutes. Other than scared and upset I didn't know what happened to Mom. But I did know that despite my best efforts in a matter of weeks Dad had been beat up and Mom had been terrorized in her own home and I worried that a new episode in this series could occur 'same time and same TV station next week.' Exhausted. I went to bed. Nothing was to be said about that day to anyone.

Lunchtime the next day Mom and I were stunned when the police called to ask her to bring me to Mr. Hickok's house across the street. No, I was not in trouble but it was police business. Ida Mae was off so Mom watched me cross the street and remained home with the other kids.

Mrs. Hickok had heard my disturbing yell the day before but could not place it. She called Mr. Hickok to come home. The police sent to Nancy Creek Road stopped him for a license check and his information was sent to police detectives. Mr. Thomas Hickok had the obvious nickname of 'Wild Bill'. He developed Real Estate and his office was in Cobb County. With nothing else to go on the police asked Mr. Hickok to meet them at his house for an interview. A police car was parked in the driveway. Mr. Hickok's dark green Buick Roadmaster was parked behind. He had a Cobb County tag, no number one.

Mr. Hickok and two uniformed policemen stood by the open door of the garage smoking cigarettes. The policemen's pressed uniforms had all the accouterments; they were tall, fit and alert. Mr. Hickok wore a blue blazer, kakis and brown leather boots. He was over six feet tall and strong as new rope. Unfortunately for this meeting he had the same hair color and fair complexion as the unwelcome Klansman of the day before. I was in my broad striped tee shirt, shorts and high top sneakers.

"Hi Mr. Hickok." I said as I walked up."

"Howdy, Jeb. How you been doing?"

"Fine. How about you?"

"Fine. Seems like these policemen want to talk to us."

We all politely shook hands. "I'm officer Stetson and this is officer Inman. If you two know each other this shouldn't take long." Inman pulled up a clipboard and arranged forms and carbon paper for copies. He set his ballpoint pen to write and Stetson did the talking.

"Jeb Lee McKnight do you agree to answer truthfully to the questions I am about to ask? Your answers will be read back and you will be asked to sign that they are correct. Did you understand what I said? It means tell the truth, OK?"

"Yes, sir. I always tell the truth but I can't write yet."

"OK. You can make your mark." Stetson continued, "Can you identify this man, Mr. Thomas Hickok, as the man that came to your house yesterday?"

I looked puzzled. "I thought his name was Wild Bill?"

Stetson asked, "People call you that? Do they Sir?"

Mr. Hickok flushed, "Yes, its more of a joke."

Stetson asked me again about identifying him. I had to ask, "What does identify mean?"

"Let me put it this way it means does he look like the man that came to your house?

I studied the uncomfortable Mr. Hickok, "Yes he looks a lot like him…"

Before I could finish the two policemen had come on guard. Stetson had his hand on his pistol and said in a firm voice to Mr. Hickok, "Don't run; keep your hands where we can see them."

"Wait a minute! I can prove where I was all day yesterday!" Mr. Hickok exclaimed.

"It wasn't Mr. Hickok!" I called out. "He looked like Mr. Hickok only smaller and not as strong.

Stetson looked at his partner, "We have a boy saying he looked like him; that's enough to take him in." Mr. Hickok groaned in disbelief.

I sprung to his defense, "It wasn't him and I can prove it. I cut the man's left leg. He's got a cut long as my hand down his left leg." All three men's eyes popped as they focused on me. Stetson was the first to speak, "What did you cut him with?"

"A long kitchen knife." I held my hands apart to show how long. "Ask Mr. Hickok to show his leg if it wasn't cut it proves it wasn't him."

Mr. Hickok dropped his Kakis inside the garage and Inman walked around him. "Not a cut or scab or nothing. But I have already written Jeb said he looked like the man."

"Write what he said about cutting him and Mr. Hickok has no leg wounds." Stetson said.

"Lukey knows him. He could tell you who the man is."

The relieved Hickok pulled his pants back up as Stetson asked. "Who's Lukey?"

"When the Klan took Dad and me to burn the house down Lukey was the man in charge. The man that came yesterday was with them. Lukey knows him."

Three men's mouths dropped wide open; their chins would have hit the pavement if they could have reached.

Inman turned his back to us and muttered to Stetson, "Sweet Jesus, did you have any idea? I am not writing that down. You think he's telling the truth? We need an adult."

Stetson muttered back, "Yes. He's telling the truth and no, we don't want an adult even if there is one."

I tried to clarify, "Y'all might know Lukey. I think he's a policeman. He's as tall as you and he has solid black hair."

Inman muttered, "Luke Blanchard?"

Stetson flashed a flinty look at Inman. "Don't write another word. I know how to handle this."

I could hear everything they said but Mr. Hickok did not. He wanted to know more, "What's this about the Klan and a house fire?" In disbelief he added, "In Buckhead!"

The police cut me off after a few remarks about the Klan and the fire. "Mr. Hickok as far as this meeting I think you understand the need to keep it absolutely confidential. You will not hear anymore about this. Thank you so much for your cooperation. We have new information that we will have to evaluate with detectives downtown. Would be so kind as to move your car? That looks like a new one I'd hate to scratch it backing out of your driveway."

"Sure officer." Mr. Hickok walked to his car.

Stetson studied me for a minute, "Jeb, I know you told the truth. Don't speak to anyone about this. We will talk to your father. We will get that man. Thanks for your help."

"Yes, sir. You're welcome."

As Mr. Hickok backed out I heard Inman addressed Stetson. "The Klan, are you serious? We stepped in it now."

"It will be OK. I told you; I know what to do."

I would have shaken hands or waved or something but the men flushed out of there like a three bird covey of quail. I told Mom the policemen's instructions. She did not want to hear about it anyway and she didn't from me.

The following day Jan Biden came over and took Mom shopping for her trip to Chicago. Ida Mae was left with the children. The boys played outside in the afternoon sun. Ida Mae came to the front door and called me in.

"Jeb a man on the phone wants to talk to you."

"Me?"

"You're the only Jeb here, ain't you?" She handed the phone to me and stood by.

A man's voice at the other end began, "Are you Jeb?"

"Yes, sir."

"Are you the oldest boy? The one with your Daddy when the Klan burned the nigger house?"

"I don't think I should talk to you." I handed the phone back to Ida Mae.

She listened and shrugged, "Yes, Jeb's the oldest. I can do that." She handed the phone back to me. "The man say he's with the police and he need to tell you something. I'm going down into the dinning room."

I took the phone, "Hello."

"Is you maid gone from the room?"

"Yes, sir"

I need to ask you just a couple of things all you have to say is 'yes' or 'no.' OK?"

"OK"

"When the Klan took you and your Daddy some men came to your house. Have you ever seen one of them again?"

"Yes, sir."

"Three days ago?"

"Yes, sir."

"Did he scare or hurt you or your Momma?"

"Yes, sir."

"Does anyone else know about it? We need to talk to an adult." I felt like cussing. Damn it! Why do adults keep asking me when what they want is to talk to an adult?

Instead I answered, "My Dad and Stan Wallace know. Mr. Wallace is a lawyer. Mr. Wallace is not going to take our case. You could hire him and he can't tell about his clients."

"Hum,… well something might work. I read a report that says a boy cut the man's leg. I knew that was you. Wasn't it? You're not in trouble - we're glad you did it."

"Yes, sir, it was me. How did you know?"

"I saw you when we burned the house. You do have sand. I was proud to be with you. I really was. The men still talk about it."

"Are you Lukey?"

"I can't say… I know Lukey."

"Jeb, you're going to remember that fire the rest of your life. I mean you're never going to forget it. Right?"

"Yes, sir. I wont forget."

"I don't know what you have been told about the Klan but we don't hurt women and children ever. That man is a bad man and no part of the Klan. He will be severely punished; he will go to jail. You wont read about it; but that will protect your family. All of us at that fire were proud to have you ride with us. That's what we call it. I know it wasn't your choice. But punishing this man is something we are doing for you. Will you do something for me?"

"What?"

"When you remember that fire remember too that the Klan doesn't hurt women or children. We try to do the right as God gives us to see the right. We'll be watching over you; we're on your side. One day when you're older if you think like we do we'll be waiting for you to join us."

"Should I tell my father? He thinks different than you."

"It's up to you. He might get mad. We will get word to him when the time is right."

No one told me if anything else happened.

Mom took Lillie and left for Chicago. Dad had an asthma attack and missed work again for a few days. Ida Mae rose to the challenge of caring for everyone. Hardened by her own life circumstances, she had never shown much affection for us. In Mom's absence in word and deed Ida Mae began to demonstrate tenderness toward me and the other children. Her support of Dad and the family made our support for her more love than duty. Ida Mae was becoming family.

I told Ida Mae I didn't understand the rapid string of calamities that had struck us 'good people.' "We try to be good but people are mean to us? The Klan man called us "nigger-lovers" but the short lawyer acted like we didn't love you enough. And some Negroes don't like us even though we try to be nice."

"Jeb, its too much for a little boy to understand. Shoot, I'm big and I don't understand it. We have to do the best we can and leave it to the Lord. My preacher says the Lord be watching over us all the time. When they put me in the jail I felt like you do now. Sometime you got to wonder but that's when you got to believe. That's called faith."

I hoped Ida Mae's preacher was right because we sure needed watching over.

Chapter 21 Convicts

Blue Shoes, Boot Head, and Willie Rat had been arrested in the moonshine bust precipitated by Ida Mae's conversation with Captain McConnell. The judge in the case sentenced the trio to year on the chain gang for their first moonshine offence. He ordered they serve their sentences in different facilities. With time off for good behavior they would be out by late summer. Through bureaucratic neglect and trickery, the moonshine trio reunited at West County Colored Correction Center. Willie Rat and Blue Shoes started their time at West County together and arranged to get in the same dormitory.

Boot Head needed a little help. The minimum security colored correction center occupied a site adjacent to a poor Negro neighborhood. Inmates received credit at the prison store for roadwork. Cigarettes and candy bars could be traded for a night in the company of the prostitutes in the neighborhood next door. Willie Rat and Blue Shoes pooled their resources and persuaded Aurora, a prostitute to write a letter to the state warden of prisons claiming that Nathan Smith a.k.a. Boot Head, whom she had never, met, was her stepbrother and ask that he be transferred to West County so she could visit him. The staff approved the minimum-security transfer for family reasons without investigation.

Through the grapevine the gang heard Ida Mae had made parole. Fellow inmates constantly insulted them about the gang's inability to kill Ida Mae. They let a teenage girl kill their partner, and done nothing. The criminal code required vengeance. Humiliated daily and mad for revenge the gang determined to escape with only two months left on their sentences so they could murder Ida Mae.

Blue Shoes led the group and developed a simple plan of escape. They bribed the usual guards for a weekend out. Fellow inmates agreed to stand in for them until the Monday morning road gang call when their absence would be discovered. They hoped to be drinking moonshine in Atlanta by Sunday night. They knew there would be no great manhunt for three moonshine runners. Their names would be sent out on warrants and the law assumed they would be in trouble again.

Friday night they went to the popular whorehouse close by the prison and traded cartons of cigarettes for street clothes. Blue Shoes wanted to buy at least one butcher knife but the whores would not come down on the price so the gang kept their prison shivs, sharpened metal blades wrapped with black electrical tape. By agreement Aurora saved their prison clothes in case the law chased them back. They struck out in the waning summer light across country northeast along Moccasin Creek. Blue Shoes had a crude map made by another inmate showing dirt roads following the creek until highway fifty-four crossed it. From there they could find their way back to Atlanta. The plan called for the light of the three quarters full moon to illuminate the back roads. The inmate estimated the distance to the bridge to be about sixteen to twenty miles. Blue Shoes thought they could cover the distance in five hours. After they walked for several hours they decided to sleep for a few hours. Blue Shoes reasoned they could better see road signs and find their way in the morning light.

They left prison bent on revenge. After a sleepless night of swatting mosquitos and wandering dirt roads, Boot Head and Willie Rat wondered about Blue Shoes leadership. They wanted to murder Ida Mae, but revenge faded in importance to the exhausted, bug-bit gang members.

At dawn they awoke to the sound of the clomping of a mule team. Blue looked down the road from behind a tree.

A large shirtless Negro in boots and overalls wearing a straw hat loomed in the low morning mist, leading an unhitched team of mules. The mules snorted when they got wind of the convicts.

"Good morning to you," Blue Shoes called out as his companions came from the trees to the road. "I hope we didn't startle you. We are a little ways from home. Could you tell us how far it is to the highway bridge over Moccasin Creek from here?"

The Negro farmer spoke with relief. "Mules been snorting, I knowed they was something up ahead. I'm glad you ain't a rabid dog or no wild boar hog, hard to see in this low mist."

"We supposed to meet our cousins where the highway fifty-four bridge crosses over the creek."

"Highway fifty-four ain't two miles. Go up this dirt road another quarter of a mile, turn left on the paved road. They's a bridge on that road, but it ain't the one you want. Cross that bridge and less than another mile the road comes into fifty-four and you'll see the new bridge back down the highway a piece to your right."

"Think we can catch a ride on the paved road?"

"No, don't nobody use it. It's the old highway. On Saturday could be people fishing."

"How 'bout it, boys?" Blue Shoes said with relief. "Do you mind if we ride on your mules?"

The farmer laughed, showing his broad smile. "No, heck no, I don't mind. But them mules would mind and you'd be plenty mad at me when they throw you. Besides, I got to turn off on the next dirt road. Fifty-four ain't far."

Willie Rat could resist, "Say, you got some change you could spare? Help getting down the road... You know how it is?"

The farmer laughed nervously, "No. Sorry, I ain't got nothing between me and the Lord Jesus but except my boots and overalls...and my hat."

Seconds of uneasy silence ended when Blue said, "We got plenty. Willie you so embarrass me sometimes. We keeping this man from a hard day's work. Thank you, have a nice day. And hey, if anybody asks, you ain't seen us."

"I don't see nothing, never. Nobody ask a poor darky no how. You'll make the paved road in no time. Giddy-up mules."

After a breakfast of candy bars and colas carried from prison the gang walked in the early morning quiet. They dripped sweat in the hot humid air. Despite all the moisture each step kicked up a small cloud of red clay dust.

Boot complained, "I got mosquito bites on top of mosquito bites."

"I believe they done sucked all my blood out." Rat retorted.

Blue was lost in thought, "That was one big nigger back there."

"Sure enough," Rat agreed. "Skillet black."

"He reminded me of the first man I killed."

"Blue?...Go on with your bad self. You ain't killed nobody... Has you?" Boot asked.

"Why you ain't told us before?" Willie Rat rubbed his head as if trying to remember.

"I told Brick Man. He said keep that on the down low. He say he's the NIC 'cause he the badest. I think I'm the NIC now cause I be the badest. That be what y'all be thinking? Ain't it?"

"That's right Blue. Looky right here! We be with you." Rat exclaimed.

"Yea, that's right." Boot Head added.

"I figured it's time I told y'all so you know I got the nerve." Blue Shoes picked up his story, "Yea, I was staying with my Momma out in the country. Be a new nigger on top of her every night."

"Awe man, we know how that is. Come on, you ain't killed a man for taking his pleasure?" Boot whined.

"Hell, we all be dead for that, wouldn't we," Willie Rat punched Boot playfully as they chortled.

Blue insisted, "Shit no, this one gambler he come around a lot, and stay in the house. Another man come around wanting to cut him 'cause he won all his money. They took to fighting and the other man cut him, but the gambler cut him better, so, the other man, he ran off.

"Knife fight?"

"Yeah, the gambler told me to fetch him some well water. I did. I'd seen his big roll of cash. He sat on the porch, you know, to doctor his self. Then I doctored him with my wood chopping ax, split his head wide open, blood everywhere."

"What he do then?" Boot head asked.

"He got dead, fool, what you think he did?" Blue frowned, "Didn't make a sound just fell over. I took the money, the knife and his dice. I left straight from the porch ran and walked all night. Next day I hitched a ride with a man with a load of watermelons to Atlanta – took me down to the Farmer's market. He gave me four bits for unloading the melons. Brick Man was there rolling dice with every darky that had some cash. Yes-sir-ee! Brick Man be rolling them bones." Blue smiled at the memory, "I was fifteen, he took my two bits and my money roll with my own dice."

"Shit yeah, Brick Man would get a man's roll," Rat agreed.

"Them dice was bad luck on account of that gambler being dead." Boot Head added thoughtfully.

"Yeah probably so, had some hex or something." Blue Shoes continued his story, "Brick Man told me I had promise, only man ever told me I might be worth a damn. Took me to work in the brickyard. Ida Mae killed him. I'm gonna make that bitch dead."

"Police didn't come looking for you?" Willie Rat asked.

"No, I run off. They had that other man to look for. One less darky in the county, the police don't care."

"Sheriff usually like to hang somebody for a killing."

"Yeah, probably hung that cut up fool that lost his roll."

"How big were you? Why you ain't told us before?" Willie Rat gazed at Blue Shoes.

"I was already six foot, big enough to kill a man! See for your self, I'm a badass six-three nigger-man walking here today. I'm NIC now and I'm gonna get our turf back, or one better."

"You gonna use an ax on Ida Mae?" Rat thought out loud.

"You don't believe me?" Blue stopped and stared at Willie Rat.

"No, Hell no. I mean yes, Hell yes, I believe you. You the NIC. We with you."

Any doubts about Blue's story remained unspoken. At the paved road they tired to hitch a ride north to Atlanta. There was no shade along the road and temperature and humidity rose quickly. They joylessly listened to the birds singing and smelled fresh cut grass. They were a long way from Atlanta and no cars passed.

"Now what? Ain't nobody use this road to pick us up," Boot-head complained.

"Oh yes they has. Look yonder." On the far side of the old highway bridge a faded green Ford pickup stood on three wheels and a jack. A gray-haired white man in a short-sleeved shirt and blue jeans leaned against the truck. He was tired and sweating from the exertion of pulling off the flat tire. He continued to lean on the truck as the three Negroes walked up to him.

Willie Rat muttered, "Blue we can steal that truck."

"Yea, but I think maybe we too far from Atlanta for that. We'll get further with that Cracker driving us." Blue then called out to the old man, "Hi, Mister, could we give you some help?"

The old man cut his eyes suspiciously at the three escapees. He answered with an offer, "I'll give you a quarter to put my spare on."

"You headed north?"

"Up to Parson's Corner, about five miles from here. I came down to fish and blew my tire. I hope my spare can make it."

"We'll put the spare on for a ride in the back. How about it?" Blue Shoes was out of himself with friendliness.

"Deal, getting those old lugs off wore me out."

The trio made short work of putting on the spare and climbed in the truck bed. The truck engine wouldn't turn over.

"Don't worry, boys. She'll roll start real easy."

"We'll push."

Boot Head and Willie Rat pushed from the back. Blue Shoes opened the passenger side door and pushed from the side. The truck started and then stalled again. The road bank sloped away from the highway to a dirt track along the bottom of the slope.

"We can turn her down the hill. She'll start and then we hit the dirt road down yonder," the old man called out to his three helpers.

He opened his own door and pushed, holding the wheel and jumped back in as the truck bumped down the incline. When the truck gathered speed Blue Shoes jumped in the passenger seat. A police style .38 special had been hidden under some maps in the uncovered glove box but bounced into view as the truck pitched on the rough ground. Blue decided to steal the truck when he saw the pistol. The truck started again. Blue grabbed the pistol.

"Don't shoot," The startled man tried to steer and raise his hands at the same time. He took his foot off the gas and hit the brakes. The truck lurched and stalled again. Willie Rat and Boot Head slid across the bed into the back of the cab. Blue Shoes pitched forward hitting his head on the windshield. As he rocked back into the seat Blue fired the gun twice into the man's middle.

"Shit! Rat, Boot, get him away from the road." Blue ordered.

"You done killed him, Blue!" Boot Head snorted. As they pulled the dead man from the driver's seat.

"What you done, fool? Peoples could hear that all the way back to the prison!" Willie Rat flung his arms out as he groaned in exasperation. "Why didn't you use your shiv?"

"He dead, we in it now," Boot Head lamented.

"What you think we gonna do when we find Ida Mae? We gonna kill her."

Boot Head scowled at Blue Shoes. "The law don't care 'bout no colored gambler or nigger woman been to prison. That's a thoroughbred white man," Boot Head pointed his finger at the corpse.

"Catch hold to yourself. Beside, I don't think it be so loud. Now we got us a ride all the way to Atlanta. That's what you wanted, ain't it Rat? Check his pockets for money."

There was no turning back and the gang fell into line. Willie Rat went through the dead man's pockets and showed the other two his findings. "Looky here, you shot the poorest cracker in this county. He had two whole dollars, a quarter and a penny. Is that enough to make Atlanta? He be packing a blade, a little pocketknife wouldn't scare a roach," Willie Rat continued to check the dead man pockets. He stood back up examining the pocket knife, "Matter of fact, I believe I saw a roach back in Atlanta where Boot stays carrying a bigger knife. You know the roach I's talking about, Boot? Here, you can have this knife in case you see him again." Rat threw the small penknife at Boot Head who let it drop to the ground.

"Fool, pick it up if you want it," Boot Head responded not hiding his disgust at the whole situation.

Rat pulled the dead man's driver's license from the wallet. "Oh shit! Oh shit! Oh shit on us, he ain't no farmer. He got a card says, William B. Cutler, Atlanta Police Department."

Boot Head shook his head and waved his arms. "This be bad luck killing a lawman."

"No it ain't. It be good luck, one less lawman we got to worry about. And when we get back to Atlanta people gonna know not to buck us. And we got a brand new to us pick'em-up truck."

"All the law peoples gonna be after us when they find him!" Boot exasperated.

"So throw his cracker ass in the creek." Blue ordered. "It's so muddy you couldn't see it if you stood on it, no body no murder."

"Come on Boot. We'll be way away from here before anybody can find him anyhow." Rat tried to smooth things over.

Boot and Rat grabbed his hands and feet and carried him to the waters edge. "OK we gonna swing him and let go on the count of three," Rat instructed.

"Don't fall in, I can't swim." Boot cautioned. They tossed the body and it quickly sank out of view.

Willie Rat used the old man's fishing hat to rub the blood on the ground into the red clay. Then he scooped some dirt into the hat and threw it into the creek. He stooped and washed his own hands and declared, "This mess is cleaned up."

As they walked back to the truck Blue called out from the driver's seat, "Get pushing."

They roll started the truck again and Blue Shoes kept his foot on the gas to keep it running. They went up the road past a gas station grocery store. Blue Shoes noticed some white men in a new Jeepster stopped for gas. He went a few hundred yards up the road and stopped. He ordered his two companions out and said he would pick them up in a few minutes. "I'm gonna have to loose this pistol. Maybe we can get some cash. We'll see."

"Yeah, and pick me up some pomade for my hair," Willie Rat called out. "I don't want peoples in Atlanta seeing me look like some ditch digger."

Blue Shoes drove back to the grocery store and parked the truck on an incline sloping back to the road and shut of the engine. He stepped a few paces from the truck.

"Can coloreds buy gas here?"

"Have to ask inside," a man by the Jeepster answered.

"I'm out of money anyhow," Blue whined.

"Then I don't believe you can buy gas," said the well-dressed hunter in a tan shooting jacket walking toward his burgundy Jeepster. Two other white men stood by the Jeepster with the doors opened. Blue Shoes saw encased shotguns in the back of the truck. An attendant called from behind the screen door that he would be out to pump gas in a minute.

Blue Shoes addressed the man in the tan coat. "Mister, I is down on my luck but I got a pistol from my old Daddy and I shot it to see if it works and it do. I'll sell it to you for fifteen dollars."

Curious, the man walked toward Blue Shoes then stopped. "Go get it out of your truck and hold the pistol with two fingers so I can see it."

Blue Shoes did as instructed, "I need some money." Blue Shoes walked back to the man and handed him the pistol. He noticed the man wore expensive leather boots and wished he had asked for more money.

"This gun does smell like it has been shot and like oil. Did you try to clean it?"

"Yes, sir, before I shot it."

"I'll give you five dollars for it."

"Oh come on, Mister, it's worth twenty and I got a sick baby at home. I need the money real bad for medicine for the baby"

"I'll make it eight dollars. It's what I got to give, take it or leave it."

"I got to take it."

The well-dressed man handed Blue Shoes the cash and put the pistol in his station wagon and drove off.

Blue Shoes took the money and walked back to the old Ford. As he opened the door to roll start the truck the attendant walked out and called to Blue Shoes, "You the one wanted gas?"

"No, I can get by."

"That looks like old Billy Cutler's truck."

"Yea it do, lot's a people done told me," said Blue Shoes, not wanting to talk as he rolled the truck and popped the clutch to start it. He picked up Boot Head and Willie Rat.

"Boys, we got some problems. The cracker at the store knows this truck so it ain't no good for us. That dead man being a policeman means all the cops in the world gonna be looking for us."

"You mean the policeman you shot, fool," Boot Head lamented.

"Shut up, we gonna sit right here a few minutes. Then we going back down by the old bridge and drive the road we come on back toward the jailhouse. We gonna loose this truck and go back to West County Road gang where we be safe from the police."

"What, nigger? We come from there," Willie Rat exclaimed, wrinkling his nose.

Blue smiled a smug Cheshire cat smile, "And we going back before anyone miss us. The law ain't going to look for the people what killed their buddy in no road gang. I is one smart nigger. I done killed a lawman and next I'll kill Ida Mae. When we get's back to Atlanta peoples gonna know we is for real. We gonna get some good turf and men gonna want to join up with us. I should have been the NIC from the get go."

Blue Shoes managed to keep the truck running. They drove the truck back to the old bridge and took the south side fishing track. They drove along the creek several miles closer to the prison. They managed to drive the truck through the brush to the water's edge. They pushed it into the creek. The creek was deep enough for the muddy water to cover the truck but the wheel tracks through the brush were obvious. At Aurora's they reclaimed their prison clothes. The gang enjoyed Aurora's favors at two dollars a whack and blew the rest rolling dice and drinking moonshine. They returned to prison with the other Saturday night partiers. The guards never officially missed them.

Chapter 22 Clue

Cutler's wife reported him missing that afternoon. An effort to find him in the waning Saturday evening light turned up Willie Rat's efforts to cover the blood trail under the bridge. As Boot Head predicted, 'All the law peoples' turned out Sunday and using dogs, divers and grappling hooks they found both the truck and the body. The community was enraged at the senseless murder. No witnesses came forward. The attendant at Parson's Corner reported seeing a truck he thought belonged to Cutler but he had not seen the pistol purchase.

Arthur Mansfield, the well-dressed hunter who purchased the pistol, returned to Atlanta. He did not hear of the murder. He owned a grocery company in Atlanta and decided to keep the pistol in his truck for protection.

Mansfield often received parking tickets when he double-parked to make a quick delivery. He considered the convenience of double-parking worth the risk of a mail in two-dollar ticket. He owned a commercial truck license plate. He could park in loading zones downtown and sometimes he ran other errands.

Within a month after he purchased his pistol he returned to a downtown loading zone to find his truck had been towed. Mansfield stormed down the short walk to the police station. He saw his truck parked in front of the new jail building; a police cruiser blocked it in its spot. When the jail greeter invited him to wait by his truck with a policeman, he assumed he could be gone in short order.

Captain McConnell strolled toward the truck joking with two more uniformed policemen who carried their guns out but down by their sides. Mansfield did not notice the guns as the men zigzagged though parked cars. When he saw them he pulled his head back and his eyes bulged like a bullfrog caught in a flashlight's beam. They didn't gig him but they could have.

"Sir, are you Arthur Mansfield." McConnell did the talking.

"Yes I am."

"Mr. Mansfield, are you carrying a weapon?"

"No, sir!"

"Patrolman Connors will frisk you. It's jail policy."

"He's clean." Connors said and they holstered their pistols.

"Mr. Mansfield are you certain this is your Jeepster?" McConnell asked cheerfully.

"Of course I am certain. And I must say this seems like quite a fuss over a parking ticket. I know I have had many, but I have paid them all." Mansfield had recovered enough to complain but he was still flummoxed by the policemen's seriousness.

"This Jeepster was towed from a loading zone on Luckie Street. Did you leave it there?" McConnell continued.

"Yes, I dropped off some produce for Loeb's Delicatessen, then left it in the loading zone while I got a haircut. I have a commercial license and should not have been towed."

Mack noticed the tan line below the freshly trimmed side burns, "Nice haircut."

"Thanks. But my truck should not have been towed."

"Please bear with me," McConnell gave his best public servant smile. "Your truck was towed because you could not be found and another truck needed to unload. Does anyone else drive this vehicle besides you?"

"No, it's a standard shift, my wife won't drive it. She doesn't even like to be seen in a truck."

"I wanted to make sure before we arrested you," McConnell spoke in a serious tone, looking the startled Mansfield in the eye.

"What! For a parking ticket? I usually mail in the fine on time."

"These officers will escort you to my office. Do we need to hand cuff you, sir?"

"No, but you need to explain what this is about."

"Follow me please, sir." McConnell's gut told him that Mansfield was not Cutler's killer but he wanted to know about Cutler's pistol.

Mansfield sat angrily in the Captain's narrow office. McConnell held up a police style Smith & Wesson .38 Special revolver with a six-inch barrel. "Mr. Mansfield, when the tow truck operator lifted your car he noticed that a pistol slid from under the driver's seat. Do you recognize it? And keep in mind you have told me you are the only one to use your car of late."

"Yes, I recognize the gun. It looks like the one I bought several weeks ago. Is something wrong?"

"Possibly, Could you tell me where, when, and from whom?"

"Yes, I can tell you where and when but I bought it from a Negro I never saw before or since. He said it had belonged to his father."

Mansfield pulled out a pocket journal and determined the date. He showed McConnell the location of the store on the policeman's map and gave the names of the two men accompanying him.

"And I presume those men were with you all day Saturday."

"Right, we went down to the farm to shoot skeet and fish in the pond, we spent the night, and came back Sunday."

"Could you describe the condition of the pistol when you bought it?"

"It had not been cleaned, so I cleaned it and kept it under my truck seat. I carry money. Produce is a cash business. I was robbed once at knifepoint and I have had things stolen out of my trucks before including another pistol. I reported all that to the police. I figured if I have another pistol stolen I'd just be out eight bucks."

"Sorry for your bad experiences. What would you say if I told you the serial numbers on this pistol shows that it was issued to Officer William B. Cutler of the Atlanta Police Department?"

"I doubt that was the colored boy I bought it from."

"Cutler was a seventy-one year old white man. He was retired. On the date you say you purchased the gun he was found shot to death by a .38 and I predict our ballistics test will show it was this gun."

"Oh God,.. I swear,.. I'd never,.. I had no reason to hurt anyone. It must have been the Negro." Mansfield felt sick to his stomach and gasped for air.

"Calm down. I believe you..." After a few moments McConnell continued, "Were you aware of officer Cutler's murder?"

"No, I don't follow the news there, my property is the next county. I usually bring everything I need from Atlanta. I was detoured by Parson's Corner because of some kind of road repair. I hadn't been there before or since. I didn't need gas I only stopped to let one of my guests use the bathroom. And we bought some cold drinks."

"OK. Mr. Mansfield I happen to have a lot of pictures of men convicted of at least one crime. Would you be so kind as to look through them? One might be the man we are looking for."

"Sure, I'll be glad to. Officer, I'll do anything to help."

Parker walked up to the open door to the office and McConnell motioned him in. "Mr. Mansfield this is Detective Parker. He will call your friends to verify your story. I believe your story, but we have to follow procedure."

"No problem. When you call please tell them I'm not under arrest."

"He won't. I'll buy you a cold drink, Peachtree Cola OK?"

"Thanks, I'd love one."

"You collect yourself, your truck will be fine parked where it is. So you can look as long as it takes. It may have been random but the killer may have a record."

Mansfield looked at one Negro mug shot book after another. He stayed at it. At five o'clock no one was moving and he received three more books.

"Do you want to leave? I can come back tomorrow," Mansfield asked.

"No thanks, these are the last ones. It's important. Atlanta P. D. can't allow people to go around shooting policemen even retired ones."

"Did you know him?"

"Yes I did. He worked under my late father-in-law. I don't think Cutler spoke to me until I married his Captain's daughter. From then on I was family."

"I understand. I want to help but they are all starting to look the same to me."

McConnell smiled, "Yeah, happens to me too."

On the third page of the next book Mansfield found the picture of Alphonse Howard a.k.a. Blue Shoes. "Here he is! Yes, sir, I am sure that's him. I recognize the narrow face and it looks kind of crooked. Can't be another one like him."

"No, I don't believe there is," McConnell read the description under the picture. "Yes, Alphonse Howard, a.k.a. Blue Shoes. Unless I am mistaken he is doing time on a road gang."

"Well I don't know what to tell you. If that's not him I won't recognize him when I see him."

"Mr. Mansfield, thank you for your time. You are welcome to go now. After you make a positive ID we stop there. I appreciate your efforts, if this one is not where he is supposed to be I will call you. I will have to keep the pistol, it's evidence."

"I hope you get the guy."

"We will."

***

The following day the staff of the West County Corrections Center assured Cheryl over the phone that Blue Shoes worked on the road gang paying his debt to society.

They also noted for her benefit that he would finish his sentence in August, less than six weeks away. She reported the information to Captain McConnell.

McConnell asked, "Six weeks? I remember this case. Seems like yesterday the judge sent them up."

"If the A.P.D. wants to pay for another long distance call I'll recheck?"

"No those road gang operations take convicts in when they need them and let them go when they don't. Parole is used liberally or not at all. I'm sure your right." McConnell thought for a minute, "Cheryl, how about doing a little police work for me? The X's on my map show where Cutler's body and truck were found. I believe West County is two counties over from there but I'm curious as to where the colored corrections center is. Make an X for the corrections center and figure the shortest route to the murder site, I'm guessing Cutler was murdered where they found the body."

"Yes, sir, when do you want it?"

"Next thing."

Cheryl estimated thirty-five miles to be the shortest distance by paved roads from West County Colored Correction Center to the murder site. When McConnell saw the X's he guessed the distance as ten miles as the crow flies.

"Well those West County boys put the coloreds out on the edge of the county. Call down to the warden and ask if I might have a tour of the facility. Tell him I'm coming by myself on police business. I don't care what the outhouses look like or what they're feeding the coloreds. I do not want to see any prisoners."

"He'll have questions." Cheryl raised her eyebrow.

"Yeah, tell him part of my police business is to scout out a hunting lease for friends of the A.P.D. Tell him I might like to talk to some guards who are hunters. I'll get the lay of the land that way. He'll believe that's why I'm coming at all. I'll wear some tromp around in the woods boots and clothes."

"Anything else?"

"Yes, please find out where the other Negroes we arrested with Blue Shoes are serving their time. Get someone else to make the call and make it sound like routine. You know, we just want to know when to expect them back on the street or something like that or relatives asking. Cheryl, I know you'll do perfect."

"Yes, sir."

Parker followed up by phone with Mansfield's companions and the attendant at Parson's Corner. He gathered no new information. The attendant who had seen Cutler's truck said he did not get a good look at the Negro driving.

***

The day following the trip to West County, McConnell and Detective Scott Parker walked to the downtown Dobb's House Coffee Shop. The familiar aroma of bacon on the griddle and hot coffee eased their angst over Cutler's unsolved murder. The men went to a back booth away from the window and the few other mid-morning patrons. Out of habit McConnell had taken a seat with his back to the wall watching the front door.

McConnell began their meeting by handing Parker copies of mug shots and ID information on Blue Shoes, Willie Rat and Boot Head. "That's the whole gang. Blue Shoes is the one Mansfield identified."

"You knew Cutler?" Parker asked.

"Yes, he was the best. He joined the A.P.D. in the 1920's. He had some time as a deputy before that he chased bootleggers up in North Georgia. He made clean arrests and was there when needed for backup. They say he was a heck of a wheelman, knew the roads. He had the right reputation with the bad guys if you know what I mean."

"I guess you knew him through your father-in-law."

"Yeah, he was good to me. The ballistics report was on my desk this morning along with your report. You met Arthur Mansfield he had the murder weapon and he puts himself and two other righteous citizens barely five miles from the body on the day of the shooting. It would be real convenient if he did it. Unfortunately, I'm certain he didn't. Doesn't have the killer look in his eye."

"I agree." Parker nodded, "Repeat parking violator – yes, murder – no."

McConnell looked pained, "Word I get from the street is that a old Negro moonshiner named Cotton Top did a revenge murder on Cutler. No details. They'll do it but nobody on the street can place him near Parsons Corner."

Parker said, "I don't believe that either. Two more bad guys have claimed the murder but my street people don't believe them they think it was personal, someone out around Parson's Corner."

McConnell offered, "Our other lead is Alphonse Howard a.k.a. Blue Shoes. You got to have faith to go with this theory. Cutler's truck was found ten miles as the crow flies from the colored chain gang, the body maybe fifteen by dirt roads. I discovered the inmates get out to visit prostitutes a quarter of a mile through the woods. They give the guards cigarettes and the like, it's a minimum security prison for short timers – they don't chain them on the road or nothing."

"You think he got out, killed Cutler, and went back in?" Parker puzzled, "I don't understand. With the gun and truck he could rob his way back to Atlanta... Maybe they struggled for the gun?"

"Good questions. He is stupid enough to drink and sell moonshine, stupid enough to get caught, stupid enough to escape with about two months left on his sentence, stupid enough to kill a retired Policeman with his pistol. Then stupid enough to sell the gun on the day he used it to a potential witness? Then all of a sudden smart enough to go back to the one place no one would look? Or maybe they panicked when the Parson's Corner attendant made the truck. The man who bought the gun sure as heck didn't do it, airtight alibi and no motive. It's a lot of stupid crap but it is all tied to Cutler's gun."

"This story's got everything but a flying saucer," Parker grimaced.

"Your skepticism is noted," McConnell frowned in agreement.

Parker guessed, "Maybe somebody in the prison wanted to kill this Blue Shoes and he needed out?... Could you tell me a little more about the man who bought the pistol?"

"You met him, rich Atlanta man with a farm past Parsons Corner. He was out there to shoot and fish in his brand new Jeepster with two respectable friends. You made the calls; they vouched for him. He personally makes some cash deliveries for his grocery business. You noted that it's no fluke he got a parking ticket, he's had a bunch. Said he wanted the cheap pistol in the Jeepster in case it got stolen. He did not drive by the murder scene; he turned off toward his farm. No way he shot Cutler and kept the gun under his car seat. It's not him."

"Any idea why he didn't come forward earlier? He bought a pistol from a Negro for below half price five miles from a murder scene. He couldn't put that together?"

"Apparently not. Said he didn't know about it. We have the murder weapon, maybe a witness and a possible, if I grant you implausible, story. I didn't ask you here to waste my time and yours. The sheriff knew Cutler too. He asked me what I was doing with this one. I told him I had my best man on it."

"So why are you telling me about it?" Parker kidded.

"Ha, ha, nice joke, it's your case. You have the mug shots of the prisoner and his two moonshine accomplices. Against all prison policies and the judge's instructions otherwise, they all ended up as guests of the state in the same facility. I don't know how that happened, smarter than we think? Maybe the others are connected to the murder. Anyway, they are due to be released in about a month. Cheryl has the date. At this point we have one connection to the murder weapon, Mansfield, and he identified the one called Blue Shoes."

"If it wasn't for the obvious facts I could solve this case," Parker pondered as he stared blankly at the paperwork he had been handed.

"Stay in touch with the County sheriff out there. Tell him don't quit looking but we have a suspect, who does not reside in his county – but that's all for now."

"So I got nothing and the Sheriff wants results tomorrow."

"But Sheriff says he is always looking for a good detective to promote to Captain." McConnell smiled and put a quarter down for a tip on two nickel-coffees.

Parker slid out of the booth, "Yes, sir, I'm on the hunt. I'll be listening; if the jailbirds did it they will be bragging when they get out. I want to use the colored detail."

"Sure I'll have Cheryl type it up. It will read anything you want from my colored detail on my orders. You will have the same authority as me."

"Thanks."

"I know you've worked with the coloreds a lot. They know what they're doing. I catch some grief for them every now and then but they're fine policemen. I'll tell you two things I have said before. Show confidence in them and they will rise to your expectations and don't let some jackass from another department give them any crap."

Mack rose and stood by the table thinking then added, "I told you the sheriff will be watching, but I will be the one reporting to him."

"You're the Captain, I'm clear on that," Parker said and the men shook hands before walking out the door.

Chapter 23 Revenge

Blue Shoes, Boot Head, and Willie Rat served out their time rather than try another escape. They returned to Atlanta in August and found their old street contacts eager to help them get back in the sporting life. Three former moonshine runners straight from the chain gang needed no other recommendation. They had not snitched to lessen their time nor did they have the complications of parole. They quickly re-entered the racket of moonshine sales and sugar and money collection. The game had not changed at all. Blue Shoes wanted to live up to his elevated status of ex-chain gang.

Their new moonshine source was a fat, lecherous Negro called Smokey. His moonshine operation was an exact copy of the one they used before. Smokey had a gas fired still in a dugout basement. He used his runners to supply sugar and corn for his mash. The bootleggers normally paid cash up front for their moonshine. Smokey wanted new turf so he loaned the Blue Shoes gang some money to acquire a well-worn sedan. The black paint had been touched up by hand and an old blanket upholstered the front seat. When they punched the accelerator, a blue cloud of burnt oil came streaming out of the tail pipe. The cavernous trunk could hold more moonshine and sugar than the car could pull. If they couldn't sell off the whiskey they could sleep in the spacious interior to guard their load. Decks of cards and dice jammed the glove box. Dishtowels inserted in the rolled up back windows provided privacy. They were back in business and living large.

Their new boss did not want trouble for any police killing and they had been on chain gang at the time of the murder. A moonshiner named Cotton Top had done ten years in the penitentiary after a Cutler arrest and he and a couple of others claimed credit for the murder. Their reputation suffered because they had not avenged Brick Man. Their ambition was to be known as "multiple bad." Who wants to partner up with men who couldn't avenge their partner, knifed by a nineteen year old girl?

Ida Mae did not want to be found. She had changed her name back to her maiden name, Norris, when she moved into her adopted Auntie's house in another neighborhood.

Blue, Boot and Willie all had sharpened butcher knives. Blue Shoes bought another stolen .38 Special and six bullets from a moonshiner. He considered this plenty of ammunition. He did not need to practice, any shots he took would be from point blank range and if he used the gun he would throw it away or sell it quick. They caught a break when a lookout spotted Ida Mae getting off a bus and watched her go to her Auntie's house. The next day Blue Shoes and his partners found Ida Mae. Her fists were not enough. The three men beat and abused Ida Mae all night. But they did not kill her. First they wanted to rob her employer, the rich Buckhead lawyer that sprung Ida Mae and landed them in jail.

***

Back to school shopping topped Mom's frenetic agenda. She waited for Ida Mae to arrive to make one more trip to the store. She would leave Billy and Lillie and take Travis and me clothes shopping. She put off shopping to the last minute vainly believing that Travis and I could not ruin the new clothes in the few days remaining before school started. Nine o'clock came and went and no Ida Mae.

"Jeb, run down to the end of the driveway and see if the bus has come."

I covered the distance from the front door to the street in record time. A couple of Negroes had passed our driveway headed to other homes. I ran back to the house. Out of breath, I announced the bus had come and Ida Mae was not in sight.

Phone service had proliferated in Atlanta and the gravity of phone use lessened. We changed to a single party phone line. This had been a necessary. The six-party line was never clear when needed, a nuisance. When Dad discussed a case with his client and an eavesdropper offered legal advice, the change became a necessity. We had a phone but Ida Mae did not. She knew our number and Mom hoped she would call to let us know her situation. She did not.

About ten thirty, an antiquated black sedan pulled in our driveway but stopped back from the house. A Negro got out of the driver's side front door. Blue Shoes stood and looked at the house for a minute. When no white man appeared he opened the back door from the outside to let Ida Mae out. Mom assumed Ida Mae had a ride. When Ida Mae came in the front door Mom could see bumps and bruises on her face and arms.

"Why, Ida Mae, what happened to you?"

"Mrs. McKnight, some bad men got me. They want to come in the house but they say they ain't going to hurt you or the children. And, Mrs. McKnight, I got to have something to eat I ain't had nothing since lunch yesterday."

"Ida Mae! what happened?

"They got me yesterday and done whatever they wanted to me ever since. One of them has a pistol."

"Oh, Ida Mae, how terrible!"

"I got to have something to eat." Ida Mae passed by Mom headed for the kitchen. She grabbed two pieces of bread and spread peanut butter and jelly to make a sandwich. She poured a glass of milk while she held the sandwich in her other hand.

"I'm going to call Mr. McKnight."

"They said they won't hurt nobody long as you don't call the police. One of them got a gun."

Mom had already dialed Dad's office. "I don't care if he is in court! You go get him! Tell him three Negro men are trying to break in our house and one of them has a gun. I'm here with the children and Ida Mae. You go! This is an emergency!"

"Ida Mae, you go out there and tell them I am not letting them in this house."

"No, Ma'am, I'll holler to them. They want to kill me. They is friends of my dead husband. Mrs. McKnight, if they come in I gonna run out the back door 'cause they will kill me sure."

I had seen the car and the Negroes. My other two brothers were in the kitchen and Lillie was in the nursery. I ran to the hall closet and pulled out Poppa Lee's double-barrel shotgun. We had no ammunition for it. The gun was heavy for me but I dragged it the short distance to Mom and Ida Mae in the foyer.

"Put the gun away. I don't think it works," Mom warned.

"Don't tell them," I said.

"Give it to me," Ida Mae said.

Blue Shoes approached the house with the pistol in his hand. Ida Mae swung the top of the Dutch door open and leveled the empty shotgun.

Blue stopped in his tracks twenty yards away and called back to the other two, "She's got a big gun!"

"Shoot her from there!" Willie Rat called out.

"I don't think I can hit her and there's white people, kids." Blue Shoes was looking at the working end of a double-barreled twelve-gauge shotgun and it was frightening.

"This is a shotgun it will blow a big hole in you!" Ida Mae called out.

"Mom, let the dogs out, they will bark. They might even bite them," I said.

"Yes, Ma'am, let the dogs out," Ida Mae encouraged.

Mom was panicked and let the dogs out the back door. They did not move. I waved my arms and told the dogs to go around front. The dogs stared uncomprehending at me. The Dachshunds were German. I didn't speak a word of German and apparently "come to supper" and "eat what's on the floor" were the only English words the dogs understood. We looked blankly at each other until from the front they heard Blue Shoes calling to Ida Mae.

The two dachshunds took off around the house. The barking dogs ran the startled man back to the car.

"I'll shoot them dogs!" Blue called out from his open window.

"Go ahead!" Ida Mae yelled.

"Ida Mae?" Mom implored.

"It's all right, Mrs. McKnight, he won't shoot. That will bring the police for sure."

We could hear Boot and Rat hollering through the open windows of the car, "Shoot the dogs!"

"Shoot Ida Mae!"

"She got a big gun. Shooting will bring the police. We know where she's at," Blue Shoes lost his nerve. He shifted the car in reverse and backed out of the driveway.

"Ida Mae, what happened? Do you know those men?"

"They's moonshiners, just got out of jail, friends of my dead husband. They is no damn good."

"You are right about that."

"They after me 'cause of killing Nate. They found me and they had knives and a pistol. Mr. McKnight won't let me carry no knife; I couldn't defend myself. They took me and done what they wanted until they made me bring them here.

"Ida Mae, how did you stand it?"

"Ma'am, you don't understand how it is."

Dad's secretary took a cab to the courthouse where she breathlessly explained the situation. The judge seized the initiative and sent patrolmen and at Dad's request Captain McConnell to the house.

The phone rang and the judge talked to Mom and Ida Mae. He told them not to go outside and Dad and policeman were on the way.

Mom told Ida Mae to shower and gave her some of her maternity clothes to wear. She gave her an ice pack for her bruised face and several Band-Aid's.

Mom called the dogs in and gave them each a dog treat. The dogs enjoyed their reward. They scared something larger than a squirrel, a memorable achievement. Blue Shoes drove back by the house at least one more time leaving a cloud of blue exhaust.

Three police cars contained two detectives, four uniformed patrolman. Captain McConnell and Detective

Parker came later in an unmarked car. Dad and eight law enforcement officers filled the foyer and crowded around the dining room table. All the men smoked and Dad opened a window to allow the smoke out. Mom sent me upstairs. I went to the top stair. I slid down a stair at the time to hear the conversation around the dining room table. Mom and Ida Mae recounted the morning's activities. Ida Mae identified Boot Head, Blue Shoes, and Willie Rat as her assailants and added Blue Shoes had a gun and claimed he would kill her.

They asked Ida Mae about the abduction. "I'll tell you; but ain't no way I'll testify! They'll kill me or some other NIC will."

McConnell said, "I understand. We will protect you."

"Boot Head came down the street one way. I saw him and turned around. Then Willie came at me. I reached in my purse like I had a knife but it weren't no good. They held a knife on me and Blue Shoes pulled the car up and they got me."

"Why didn't you pull your knife?" a policeman asked.

"Mr. McKnight won't let me carry no knife." She answered.

"Mr. McKnight, why won't you let your nigger carry a knife?"

Dad responded, "I did not want Ida Mae charged for carrying a weapon or injuring someone or even killing them."

"Mr. McKnight they sure would have killed her on the spot. The only reason they didn't was they thought they could steal something from you. These niggers are no damn good."

"Yes, what do we do now." Dad patiently replied.

"All niggers carry something to protect themselves, the police can't be everywhere. If these men are out to get her she needs a knife, good sharp butcher knife."

"I agree," said Ida Mae.

"We don't need to get between Miss Norris and her employer," Mack interjected using Ida Mae's preferred last name.

But the patrolman continued, "Mr. McKnight, they told me in the car that you fought in the war. I am sure you had a gun. The streets in colored town can't be much safer than fighting the Japanese."

Dad did not appreciate this characterization of the streets of Atlanta and started to respond but Captain McConnell preceded him, "Patrolman Kelly, please no more commentary. And please bring your report to me. Everyone but Parker may leave now."

The police shook hands and offered condolences and left McConnell and Parker to council Dad, Mom, and Ida Mae.

"Mr. McKnight, I have to be honest. We don't have a lot here," McConnell said.

"Kidnaping carries the death penalty," Dad said in a defiant tone.

"You're absolutely right. Your wife and maybe one of the children might be asked to testify? You have to decide about that. I don't know what a prosecutor will do.

"What do you recommend?" Dad asked.

"You're in unincorporated Fulton County so I can order a patrolman to come by once an hour and that should keep Blue Shoes away. We can get them in custody in twenty-four hours. If you press charges on what we have now, I am afraid they will walk outright or draw a minimal sentence."

"I have to press charges, they came to my home." Dad rose to accompany McConnell and Parker to their car.

Outside, the policemen consoled Dad. The only thing between his family and a catastrophic criminal attack had been two horrified women with an unloaded antique shotgun, two small dogs and an almost six year old boy trying to be a TV cowboy. Inside, Mom gave the dachshunds extra dog treats in spite of their poor English comprehension.

***

The next day the three gang members sat down for lunch in the Atlanta jail. After being warned by Dad not to talk about the case to anyone Mom received a call from a Negro. It was Mr. Franklin, the gang's lawyer, who called the house to try to get the charges dropped prior to the preliminary hearing. Mistaking the Negro voice for one of the gang members, she told him that her husband knew the judge and he would throw the book at them. Ida Mae had spent the night for safety. Judging a gang member was on the phone she picked it up and railed against the caller saying among other things she and Dad had put them in jail before and now they were going to hang and the judge had agreed to let Ida Mae watch. When Ida Mae paused long enough for the Negro lawyer to identify himself she assured him that if he was Blue Shoe's friend he too was no damn good and Mr. McKnight and the judge would hang him too. Dad was not advised of this conversation.

Captain McConnell thought the gang might walk free, but no one was prepared for how it happened. At the preliminary hearing Mr. Franklin asserted he had talked to Ida Mae Reivers and Mrs. McKnight, a witness to the alleged attempted break in and she agreed with her maid that her husband had communicated with the judge in the case. Furthermore, according to Mrs. McKnight, her lawyer husband and the judge agreed beforehand to hang his clients.

Dad was shocked. The report of Mom's comments caught him totally off guard. The judge required Dad to call home. After talking to Mom, he had to confirm that his wife had indeed made the comments to a caller she believed to be a gang member. The judge knew he had not discussed the case or anything else with Dad. But the judge had been accused of *ex parte* communication, that he had talked privately with one party to the hearing without the other party present. He would have to *recuse* himself, take himself off the case.

Dad came straight home accompanied by a single policeman. The policeman took Mom's statement about the phone call. After ripping the phone cord out of the wall Dad explained to Mom in a surprisingly composed voice that, due in large part to her remarks about him and the judge the Blue Shoes' gang walked free without entering the courtroom. Dad added in a controlled tone, "Based on your comments, the lawyer for the gang said he would file a suit against me and the judge, for what I don't know."

"That's crazy. I don't believe it." Mom was flabbergasted.

"Sweetheart, what don't you believe?"

"I don't believe any of it. You're joking, right? They're in jail."

Dad shook his head no.

"They would have robbed us blind and killed Ida Mae and God knows what else."

"The prosecutors dropped the case. And I agreed to it. The judge would have recused himself. McConnell has a better plan for dealing with these people.""

Mom stared in disbelief, "I want to move back to Chicago."

"I can't discuss it now."

"We can't live here! Those men are still on the street." Mom was about to meltdown.

"We are going to have to. I don't think they will be on the street long."

"What makes you think so?"

"I can't say now."

"I need to know it now."

"It is a confidentiality issue," Dad did not need to explain his statement. "I have to return to the office. I'll be home for supper."

"I don't want you to leave."

"You will be safe. Captain McConnell ordered three patrol cars out for us. One is parked up the street two more are cruising the neighborhood. Your name and mine are on his emergency contact list. I left the number on the phone stand. You will have to use a neighbor's phone until I get someone to repair ours. We can call McConnell twenty-four hours a day.

Dad did not have to go to Stan's house. He had heard the news and came by the house on his own initiative. Dad explained the situation to Stan in the front yard. I opened my upstairs window above the front door to listen. Stan was apoplectic with disbelief at the whole situation and critical of Dad's response, which included not advising Ida Mae of the gang's release from prison after being notified by the Atlanta Police Department in a letter.

"You didn't tell her they were back on the street?" I did not have to lean out the window to hear Stan. "What were you thinking? They told you because you were her parole officer! There could be some sort of negligence here."

Dad was sinking, "I did not want to upset her. She had moved, I thought they couldn't find her. I didn't want her carrying a knife."

"Damn! Damn! Damn! and I mean Damn! Have you looked at Ida Mae? She killed one man. She might have taken all three with a knife or backed them off. They wouldn't have made it out here. You home missed being a murder scene by a whisker. Not just Ida Mae's!"

Dad covered his face for a few seconds but I could not see that he cried. "She said they had a gun."

"Well then there was nothing she could have done." Charitably Stan continued, "Hank, I know you were assigned this case. It was the judge's mistake to give it to you. You have proclaimed that you were doing the right thing but you have miscalculated your suitability for criminal work. You have to do right by your family too."

"Don't lecture me Stan I know the lay of the land."

"For friendship sake we'll not discuss it. Two legal points: First, based on what you told me I would not have dropped the case. Let the judge recuse himself and get another judge. Second, for a retainer of two hundred and fifty dollars I will defend you if the gang's lawyer files a suit. Did you get his name?"

"No."

"I can get the other lawyer's name easy enough. If that suits you get a check and I'll grab an engagement letter."

"Thank you Stan, I would appreciate it very much."

Dad hastened inside and returned from the house with a check. The two men exchanged papers and a handshake and went their separate ways to attend to business.

Ida Mae slept at our house that night and was picked up by two policemen and a plainclothes Negro policewoman the next day. Ida Mae would not get in the patrol car until they promised her they were not taking her back to Buttermilk Bottom. Mom wanted assurances; but the police would not give her any information.

The whole situation was scary and awkward. As a kid I watched the tall and muscular Ida Mae leave and looked hopelessly at my short and petit Mom. Everyone's nerves were frayed, the whole family and the dogs. It was like we had been asked to all sit half way down the slick twenty-foot sliding board at Piedmont Park and not slide down further. Mom would have thrown in the towel had she known where to throw it.

***

Captain McConnell called in Arthur Mansfield for a blind line up before releasing Blue Shoes from the jail. He and Parker stood in the soundproof viewing room with the reverse mirror so those in the line up could not see the witness.

Mansfield pointed out Blue Shoes, "Officers, I am pretty sure that's him. I got a good look in broad daylight."

"Pretty sure?" McConnell asked.

"Yes, He looks different now, but I think that's him." Mansfield said.

"You forget about it. Don't say anything about this to anyone, including your wife. We'll take care of it. I'll call you when we get him."

After Mansfield left Parker turned to McConnell, "Pretty sure? That's what we have?"

McConnell sighed, "I wish I was sure that 'pretty sure' would get him hung - a cop killer who supposed to be in prison, we can prove that he could have got out for the weekend, but all we have for selling the murder weapon five miles from the crime scene is 'pretty sure.' And no clear motive: steal the truck? Money? They wanted the fish he caught? I'll talk to a prosecutor. Let Blue Shoes find our decoy, attempted murder and what we have already will take him down hard, maybe the rope.

Parker looked troubled, "Law enforcement including our Sheriff wants him now."

"I have been through these things before. I'd rather take the heat for going slow than see Blue Shoes get off light or worse walk free again." McConnell smiled at Parker, "Besides I'm not worried about 'our' Sheriff, I have already told him my best man is on it."

"So I've heard. Your best man doesn't want to end up directing traffic."

McConnell assured, "I got your back. Did you get the decoy?"

"The decoy starts tomorrow."

McConnell said confidently, "The bad guys will go for her. Get your ears out."

McConnell assured Dad that around the clock protection for Ida Mae was part of his plan and she would not be returning to work until Blue Shoes was back in jail. Dad knew not ask for details. A police car was posted on Nancy Creek Road. The McKnights were under siege.

Chapter 24 Crossfire

Captain McConnell made arrangements for Ida Mae. She would stay in a safe apartment with a Negro policewoman.

Blue Shoes had beaten the rap in court. The gang's multiple-bad street reputation soared. Informants told McConnell the moonshiner threw the gang a get out of jail party with several prostitutes, a live band and plenty of moonshine. They partied like it was new years eve, but Ida Mae had done it again, a little boy, and two wiener dogs had humiliated the gang and no party was going to make that better. The embarrassment intensified the gang's fury and determination to kill Ida Mae.

Dad began doing as much work as he could from home. He managed to get same day service to replace the phone with a phone that plugged into a wall outlet. It remained unplugged when he wasn't home. A Negro woman began calling our home, Mom answered; Dad listened. The woman on the other end would say she was Ida Mae's Aunt and ask questions about Ida Mae's whereabouts. Mom's story was that Ida Mae had found new work at a commercial laundry. The calls became threatening. Blue Shoes and his criminal pals had everyone looking. They would find her. Dad told Captain McConnell about the calls. McConnell had the calls traced, a time intensive, but doable thing. The caller turned out to be the moonshiner's sister. Police watched her house.

In addition to the colored detail Parker relied on informers, "Street People." He had some of them leak Ida Mae's "new" bus route to the right bad people. He soon had results.

Cue Ball, a loathsome but reliable informant, phoned Parker, "Blue Shoes says Ida Mae will be shot dead when she comes off that bus tomorrow afternoon. He had to get permission from Smokey One because her bus stop is on his turf."

"They have guns?" Parker inquired.

"I know they got one six-inch barrel .38 from Smokey. I don't know about anymore guns – butcher knives for sure."

"Are you absolutely sure about your information?"

"Yeah. You kill Blue Shoes tomorrow that Nigger needs to be dead. And you don't know me."

"You need to be right on this one – You know that?"

"Yeah, I ain't stupid."

"Smokey One? Is he Smokey the moonshiner?" Parker inquired.

"No, you know how it is, a street name is better if a hundred people got it. Police don't know who's who. You owe me fifty for that bus stop address. For twenty more dollars I got a moonshine tip."

"OK."

"They got people on the street trying to sell liquid shoe polish mixed with wood alcohol and some other stuff. Don't use no still, they say convicts learn to make it in prison. They call it 'double kill' because it kills the man that drinks it and the man that sells it. Moonshiners are out to kill them. It's bad for their business when someone goes blind or dies from bad shine."

"That's the tip? I'll give you and extra ten."

"Twenty. Some coloreds gonna get dead soon and you'll know why."

"Ten. That's not news. Be drunk at your corner on Auburn Avenue at ten tonight. Patrolman Walker will stop you. He'll slip sixty dollars in your pocket when he frisks you. Then you pass him the address written on a piece of paper when he asks for ID – nothing verbal I want it in writing."

"OK, OK. I know the routine. Tell Walker I ain't resisting arrest. I'm serious about that. I don't want my drunk bald head beat down."

Parker assured him, "I'll tell him. You be there. I don't have to worry about you being drunk."

"Oh, I'll be drinking double rectified B&T, Block any road Tackle anybody. I don't do anything half-assed. You get the street address for the bus stop when is see the sixty bucks. If Walker confiscates the shine that's another two bucks."

Both men laughed and Cue Ball added, "Have the money right or I won't remember that bus stop."

"Don't get uppity on me. You make more money than I do. You better be right; I got your name and picture." Parker spoke in a jocular tone but his message was serious.

"Don't go off on me. I know you're a kickass cop." Cue Ball kidded back; but both men spoke the truth in jest.

After Parker hung up he called Sargent Leroy Peabody of the colored detail. "I'll call you tonight after ten.

You'll be in charge of a stake out to bring in a gang of three Negros armed with at least one pistol."

"I'll be listening for your call." Peabody answered.

Parker then walked down to McConnell's office.

"Got a minute for the Cutler case, Captain?"

"I only have all day for that."

"It's Blue Shoes. Looks like shooting tomorrow. I'd like you to be there," Parker requested.

"Shooting? You do plan to make arrests tomorrow? We are the law."

"Yes, sir," Parker accepted the mild reprimand. "I suspect Blue and his gang would rather shoot it out than hang. We know they have at least one gun possibly more. I am requesting that you join us for gun out of the holster back up."

"You certain about your information?" McConnell looked hard at Parker.

"It's from a reliable informant. I had agreed to pay fifty and he beat me out of another ten. He knows better than to be wrong. Blue shoes will make his move in the afternoon."

"That sounds right. Still better watch that stop in the morning in case someone's on the look out to see if the Negro woman goes to work.

"Peabody asked about that. We already have a Negro woman decoy lined up. She looks as close to Ida Mae Reivers as we can make her. She will get on the bus in the morning and off in the afternoon. She's been doing it with a plainclothes back up since we put Reivers in protective custody. We'll be the back up tomorrow.

"Good. I'll ride with you in the afternoon." McConnell thought for a second and added, "Peabody, good choice. Average, nondescript, perfect plainclothesman blends right in with the street Negros. Nothing average about him, though, he's one tough cop, smart too. Shook his hand a few times, like gripping a piece of steel. He told Captain Milner, my father-in-law, he was tired of watching the NIC's and moonshiners destroying people's lives. The Captain brought him on the force. He told me Peabody was the best hire he ever made white or colored. As a rookie Leroy went after one of the biggest Negro moonshiners in town."

"Did he get him?" Parker asked assuming the positive.

"Nope, a NIC knifed the moonshiner in a squabble rolling dice." McConnell shrugged, "That's the wild card on the street. Seems like just when were ready to get the bad guy some other bad guy kills him. You watch. If we don't get Blue Shoes tomorrow – sooner or later 'the street' will get him."

"Peabody will have that bus stop address as soon as I get it. I'll tell him I want his plan in the morning. You'll have it when I do."

Midmorning the next day Parker reported back to McConnell. "Peabody took two men and cased the bus stop late last night. This morning he picked six plain-clothes from the colored detail – no whites on the street, two coloreds for the close in work and the other four to manage the street. I know them. I trust them. We are the wrong color for the neighborhood; I have four of our uniformed whites for out of sight back up. No matter what happens afterwards any citizen that comes on the scene will want to see a uniform. Everybody understands that Peabody is in command. The whites I picked have worked with the coloreds in the past. No problems there. You and I will also be out of sight in a building down the street we will have a phone, ice tea and a bathroom. We have a sliver of a view of the bus stop – no more. Just as well, we don't want to get caught peeking."

"Anything else?"

"No. Specifically, Peabody picked Marlin and Bodine to be at the stop. They'll look like day-laborers, they'll be in close."

McConnell chortled, "I had Bodine on the street one time and didn't recognize him at all. I gave him two bits to move on. He looked up at me and said, 'Captain it's me – Bodine.'"

Parker laughed, "I bet he kept the two bits."

"Yes he did." The two officers smiled and tried to ease the tension of the upcoming operation.

Parker continued, "Once Blue Shoes or one of his gang makes a move for the decoy, Peabody will call for their surrender. Marlin and Bodine will try for the arrest. Construction signs around the bus stop will direct pedestrians away. I told them to pull up a few of those six-sided sidewalk pavers and rope it off and add some yellow cones around the sidewalk to make it look like real construction – but no workers."

McConnell commented, "Nice touch. It will look like preparation for something under the walk waiting for another crew. Workers should be gone by late afternoon anyway."

"Yes, sir. The other plainclothes policeman from the colored detail will be on hand to steer innocent pedestrians clear of the area. They have mug shots of the men we want they will be allowed to pass. We don't want one man taking on three and we don't have enough evidence to get an arrest warrant."

"Yes, I understand that." McConnell shook his head.

"Our detail of four white uniformed officers will standby across the street in the back of a rental windowless van. The uniforms will pile out when called. Peabody said he would lean several sheets of plywood up on the street side of the van; a stray bullet would come straight through the sheet medal."

"Peabody is smart, thinks of everything." McConnell was relaxed and confident, "It's your case. Tell me where to stand."

Parker warned, "If shit hit's the fan we should be out of the splatter zone, but we are guns-out backup for the side street. We can be on the pavement in seconds if things go bad."

"Understood, and I like the plan. But trust me, notwithstanding Peabody, we're in charge and we'll be in whole other splatter zone if things go bad." McConnell said flatly.

Parker gave his boss a knowing nod.

"I'll be in my office. Come get me when your ready," McConnell added.

"Yes, sir. We'll leave after lunch. Peabody's plan calls for every one to be in place by two thirty in case Blue Shoes has a lookout."

***

Dad had been working from home and planned to stop in on Mack on a trip down town. When Dad called, Cheryl could not say where Mack was. Dad thought for a moment and called the emergency number.

"Captain McConnell please, this is Harry Lee McKnight, Nancy Creek Road. I'm on his emergency contact list."

"Yes, sir. I have your name...Captain McConnell is on a stake over on Ashby Street with his team. I can reach him by radio and he will return your call. I can also give you his back up here...Mr. McKnight?"

"Do you have a cross street on Ashby?"

"No, sir, what is your emergency? I may be able to offer a suggestion."

"No thanks, I believe the stake out is what I wanted him for. I'll call back later."

"Yes, sir. Don't hesitate, you are the top priority on his list."

"Thank you very much. Goodbye."

Dad called upstairs as he placed the receiver down. "Jeb."

"Yes, sir."

"Come down here."

'Oh shit,' I thought. Grown-up words had crept into my vocabulary and I had to be careful not to utter them out loud. I ran down the stairs from my bedroom lair – I was an indoor kid for the time being. I bounded down the stairs in my shorts, tee shirt and tennis shoes.

Dad motioned me close and talked in a whisper, "Jeb, do you think you can recognize those Negroes who came to the house?"

"Yes, sir."

"I may need you to point them out to me. You would not have to get close to them. You would be safe with me."

'Oh shit again.' I thought, but I answered in the affirmative. "Yes, sir."

"Kate! Jeb and I are going to run an errand. There is a police car at the end of the driveway." Dad disconnected the phone and brought it with us.

"Dad, I'd like the top up."

"Good idea and hold on."

We went out our driveway skidding onto Nancy Creek with such force the policeman on duty in his patrol car at the end of our driveway glared at us. We took Moore's Mill Road to a crossroads called Bolton stopping for gas and an Atlanta Map. Dad studied the map and then took off toward town on Marietta Boulevard, the car caught air as he drove over the median. The wheels touched the road, but I felt every sensation of flight.

There were no seatbelts in our Ford. I grabbed the door pull with my right hand and braced myself by putting my left hand on the glove box. Dad drove fast confident in his skills as a driver, his relationship with the police, and he thought 'it was damn important.' I prayed as my butt slid across the seat in spite of my death grip on the door pull. The V8 engine roared and whined through the gears as Dad throttled up and down. The tires squealed as Dad hit the breaks or went hard into a turn. I do not know where we were or how we got there, but I already knew I did not want to visit again.

Dad explained our mission. "Jeb, I believe the police have set a trap to catch those three Negroes. If we are there to witness they may get arrested and not shot. This is the law and I am an officer of the court. It's my duty to see the law is carried out." Every time I heard 'officer of the court' it meant shit hit the fan. Stan Wallace thought I had 'sand' for such occasions, however, the way my butt slid around on the seat I feared my 'sand' would fly out.

"OK, Jeb, start looking for those three Negroes or Captain Mack."

Dad went south first then north on Ashby Street. Although it was late afternoon traffic was light, probably because no one wanted to go there, I didn't. The area looked rough. I pleaded with Dad, "Don't stop the car."

After a little while I spotted three men poorly concealed as they looked over a brick wall. "Dad it's them. Don't stop!" Thanks Jesus, all twelve Apostles, several saints, and a hundred angels Dad kept driving as I sunk below the window.

At the second intersection past the bus stop, Dad hit the breaks hard, but missed the turn. He stopped and backed toward an oncoming truck. The driver honked and swerved around us. We were making a scene. Dad circled back to the cross street where he ignored the detour sign and parked the car illegally with two wheels on the sidewalk. An 'officer of the court' had violated enough traffic laws in thirty minutes to get thirty fines.

Dad got out and crossed the street and walked toward the bus stop. His eyes searched for any policeman. It was no use asking me to stay in the car, not in that neighborhood. I was right be hind him.

From nowhere a large Negro man wearing a sport coat without a tie stepped in our path. He pulled his badge as he spoke. "Mister, you look like you can read. The sign says no vehicle or pedestrian traffic. You and that boy are in the wrong neighborhood. Lucky for you, I am a policemen and I'll watch as you get in your car and drive away,"

"We need to find Captain McConnell, it's important."

The policeman gave Dad a puzzled look, "Mister, please keep your voice down." He pulled Dad into a doorway and I stood behind on the sidewalk. "Yes, sir, he's here on stakeout and I am not supposed to let any pedestrians up this street. Sir, you need to leave."

"Actually, I need to be here. My son can identify the men that Captain McConnell is looking for."

"You mean these men?" The policemen pulled out a sheet from his coat pocket with the three mug shots of the gang. "Sir, we know exactly what they look like. You should leave. Now."

Dad would not be deterred. The policeman was flummoxed by his persistence and knowledge of the situation. They continued to speak in hushed tones and I looked down the short block. On the east side of Ashby Street, the side closest to where we stood, a bus stop sign bent awkwardly toward us. I could see a small wall and part of an open space. A lone Negro laborer sat on the sidewalk along the side street with his back against the wall and one leg sprawled out into the sidewalk. His hat was cocked back on his head and a cigarette dangled from his mouth. He had a black tin lunch box at his side. Blue Shoes, Willie Rat and Boot Head eager for the kill waited out of our view.

***

The police had been in place since two-thirty as planned. Ida Mae's new bus stop was in an inner city neighborhood that transitioned from bad to worse. Occasional strips of retail broke up older homes, small multi-tenant units, and one story warehouses. The bus stop had a three-foot brick wall separating the sidewalk from a narrow yard in front of a vacant house. The wall looked as if a previous owner had built it to keep the people at the bus stop out of his small yard. The wall ran along Ashby Street and turned the corner down the side street. It had wide but empty gate openings at each end and there was a dirt trail in the sparse grass where pedestrians had cut the corner by walking in one gate and out the other.

Peabody and another member of the colored detail arrived in the windowless van with the four uniformed whites in the back. Peabody in the passenger seat spoke through the trucks partition to the men in the back. "OK we parked the truck. We are on the opposite side of the road from the bus stop. I know you all are smart, but we are on the point so I'm reminding you, If someone gets desperate to take a leak there are some empty milk cartons back there. Don't talk, whisper or move. When we call, come out the right side door on to the sidewalk. We'll cover for you if needed. The informant said the bad guys have at least one six-inch barrel .38. If they pull a gun - we shoot. Marlin and Bodine are on the street dressed as laborers, I'm not trying to be funny; but if you can't tell us coloreds apart remember - we will have our badges out and we all pack stainless .45's. So don't shoot a colored man waving a badge and shooting a stainless steel .45."

"Understood, good luck." came from the back.

"Y'all too." The Peabody got out of the truck and crossed Ashby Street to his spot in the doorway of the vacant house. The door was solid wood with a single pane window. The window had been broken and had security steel mesh over it. Peabody sat in a chair looking through one of a few holes in the door. He could see the bus stop. When the decoy got off he would have to open the door and show himself to call for the gang's surrender. The mission was on.

Close to four o'clock Blue Shoes, Boot Head, and Willie Rat followed the detour signs down the Ashby Street sidewalk. The street was deserted except for a grizzled old Negro who sat nodding off on the wide windowsill of a vacant store window. The stubble of his white beard stood out against his brown lined face and a bottle in a brown bag rested on the windowsill beside him. He was on the same side of Ashby Street as the stop ten feet short of the gate opening in the wall.

Blue Shoes ambled through the gate where the gang crouched or sat inside the wall along Ashby Street. They leaned low into the wall with each passing bus so no one on the bus looking down could see them. When the doors of the bus closed after letting any passenger off the gang rose to see if Ida Mae was on the sidewalk. They looked and acted like menacing wolves but they were invisible - no one in that neighborhood would see a thing.

The gang sipped their moonshine that had been funneled into store-bought bottles that fit nicely into small brown paper bags. Blue Shoes had the pistol tucked in his belt covered by his black jacket. Their car was parked down a cross street a block south of the bus stop for a quick get away.

"You sure this the right stop?" Boot Head complained.

Willie Rat was unconcerned. "Yea, this is it. My man don't lie. He knows Ida Mae; he hates her too. He said this stop be perfect for us on account of this wall. She won't see us until its too late."

"I ain't worried," Blue said flatly, "I fill her with lead y'all stick her with your knives. We can say, we all done her in."

"That will shut-up the people giving us shit," Willie Rat said.

"Ain't that the truth?" Boot Head bragged, "We'll tell them shut up or we'll do them the same way."

Willie Rat spoke, directing his comments to Boot, "Now people know we are for real. Ida Mae is a dead-nigger-walking on account of us."

"She ain't dead yet. She's a big country darky and she'll be caring her butcher knife. I'm gonna let Blue put some lead in her before I stick her. We gonna have to get out of here fast." Boot Head turned to Blue, "You know the nigger-in-charge around here? You say he's cool with us being here?"

"Yea he's cool. Smokey took care of him. He told me everybody wants her dead. He said nobody around here sees anything no how."

"What the NIC be called?" Rat asked.

"Smokey One," Blue answered. "He also has the numbers game. We gonna get a cut on what goes down on our turf. We don't do nothing, Smokey One gonna send a bagman with our cash every week."

"We are big time." Willie Rat beamed gently rubbing his slicked back hair. "Y'all need to style up. I'm looking too good. My hair been dyed, fried, and laid on the side. The peoples know I'm big time when they see me."

"Yeah, right." Blue Shoes ignored Rat's fashion statement; "Smokey One got a preacher on the radio that calls out the winning numbers like Bible verses. Boys, we are connected."

"Peanut told me he thought this was Slick-Stick's turf. We near there?" Boot Head looked around like he was searching for a landmark.

"Was Slick-Stick's turf. He got dead and Smokey One took over. You can ask Ida Mae to tell Slick-Stick 'hello' for Peanut." The gang chuckled at Blue Shoe's joke.

"How did Slick-Stick get dead?" Boot Head wondered aloud.

"Street got him," Blue said. "Don't be bringing bad luck on us talking 'bout it."

Willie Rat was feeling his moonshine, "I'm glad for two things. Ida Mae so big I can miss with my blade and Blue Shoes gonna drive my nigger ass away from here cause I ain't sure I can walk."

"Don't you get bad drunk on me," Blue Shoes ordered.

"I ain't. I'm just saying if you was counting on me to haul her fat ass to the car, I'd have to make two trips."

Boot rocked back and forth laughing. "That's right Rat have to break up that load so he can tote it."

Blue's gang was getting too loose to suit him, "This is for real! Tighten up, or I'll…" before he could finish he heard a bus diesel engine grinding down the street, "Quick here comes a bus, stay down behind the wall."

The large city bus creaked to a stop and the doors hissed open and clapped close after a hefty Negro woman stepped to the sidewalk. She clutched a purse close to her side and looked in both directions as if she was expecting someone.

She was expected. Blue's gang jumped from behind the wall and through the Ashby Street gate opening pulling their knives and gun. Blue Shoes aimed his pistol.

"That ain't her," Willie Rat called out as the woman dove for cover on the outside of the wall where it turned down the side street.

"Police! Drop your weapon!" Peabody's voice called from the open door of the vacant house. Blue Shoes swung his pistol level in the direction of the voice. Peabody slammed the door shut. Bodine jumped off his windowsill, his hands clutched a badge and stainless steel pistol. "Police!" Marlin, the resting laborer rolled onto his feet and appeared like magic above the wall with a stainless steel pistol in his right hand and a badge in his left. He too called out "Police!" The undercover cops fired their guns as they shouted.

Blue did not drop his pistol. Whatever thought passed through Blue Shoes' head, it was his last, the next thing through was a 230 grain .45 bullet from Bodine's pistol. A split second later he was hammered in the center of his back by another round from Marlin. His head rolled back before he pitched forward into the wall and the pistol clattered onto the sidewalk. When the shooting started Dad and I crouched against the building and watched the Negro laborer in front of me fire several shots from his 1911 stainless steel .45 pistol. The loud bangs rattled the windows and the spent brass shells glinted in the sunlight as they flew into the air.

Bodine had a clear shot up Ashby Street and he was protected from Marlin's line of fire by the corner of the vacant store building. Marlin fired across the small lot so the gang had no cover on either side of the wall. The woman decoy lay on the sidewalk protected by the wall on the side street by Marlin. Boot Head and Willie Rat panicked in the crossfire they dropped their knives and collided trying for Blue's pistol. The .45 slugs fired from close range tore through flesh and bone. Blood spewed out in all directions.

Blue Shoes and Willie Rat were dead before they hit the sidewalk. Boot held himself up on one elbow where he fell over Blue Shoes.

"Blue?..." He muttered. He looked over his own bloodied chest and collapsed dead.

The four uniformed policeman piled out of the van and joined Parker, and McConnell, all with pulled guns but the shooting was over. Blue Shoes and his gang 'got dead' in seconds. Their bodies lay on the pavement and their blood drained across the sidewalk down to the corner storm sewer. Nobody expressed any sympathy for the dead cop-killers.

Captain McConnell congratulated everyone. "Nice shooting Bodine and Marlin. No stray bullets. Good call Peabody and good decoy work Glenda. Everybody gets a good letter in the file for this one. And I want all the paperwork on my desk in the morning before you do another thing.

The uniformed policeman turned out but every living person on Ashby Street was a policeman. Grady Hospital was called to pick up the bodies. Bodine retrieved his brown bag with the bottle in it from the windowsill.

"Collecting evidence, Bodine?" McConnell called out.

"Yes, sir."

"Did A.P.D. supply that?

"Yes, sir." Peabody smiled as he answered for Bodine, "I felt it was an important part of Bodine's cover. I wanted his breath to smell like liquor in case Blue talked to him."

"I'm sure it does. Good work Bodine I do not think the Atlanta Police Department has any further use for your mouthwash. You can keep it." McConnell said.

"Thank you sir." Bodine answered.

Peabody interjected, "I am sure Captain McConnell intends that you share your mouthwash with the rest of us – not here of course."

"That's a good idea Captain, we don't want policemen with bad breath." Parker grinned his approval.

McConnell waved his hand, "I don't want to know about it. I think it's time for me to go." He called to Parker, "Good job Parker. May I stand down or do you still need back up?"

Parker beamed, "Yes, sir, you can stand down. You can take the unmarked car back in. I'll clean up here and have a report on your desk in the morning. No loose ends."

"Right, no loose ends. I'll tell the Sheriff my best man handled it."

When the shooting started Dad caught me and we crouched next to the building. After things got quiet on the side street; the smell of gunpowder wafted toward us. The colored policeman with Dad said, "Please leave. I can assure you there will be a bloody mess around the corner. Neither you nor your son should be here and I could lose my job if I let you pass."

"Thanks, I understand. I will communicate with Captain McConnell later." Dad grabbed my hand, and we headed for the car. Dad was not a happy officer of the court.

On the way home Dad turned on WSB radio; it was too soon for news of the shooting. Thanks again to prayers to the previously mentioned heavenly host. He drove slower and my sand remained intact.

At home Dad plugged the phone back in and fixed a stiff bourbon. I needed one too but had to settle for the sugar caffeine fix of a P.C.

McConnell's call to Dad came in as we sat down to our drinks.

"Hello Mack, thanks for the call."

"Hi, Hank, my team told me you came down. I won't cuss you for it, 'cause you stayed out of the way. I hope you understand that it was a real bad idea."

"I agree. I was hoping you could capture the men."

"No. Three bad guys dead, no one else hurt. Blue Shoes pointed his pistol, but never got off a round. The other two were shot to pieces as they went for the weapon. My men were right on top of them. The bad guys caught all the flying lead so there was no collateral damage." Mack's voice rang with satisfaction and he was too relieved to be mad at Dad.

"Thanks Mack, I won't forget all you have done for us. Let's have coffee soon and hopefully not for business."

A few days later Dad acquired a copy of the police report describing how the gang was shot. We learned all the gory details we had missed.

Chapter 25 Respite

Stan welcomed us into his home, "Sit down and have a drink. It's five o'clock somewhere and the bar at the Wallace house is open. Jeb, I told your Dad he could come if he brought you. I figured out I made a bad deal with your Dad. He brought the scotch, but I have to give your Dad my bourbon."

I grinned to be welcomed and included with the men.

Dad asked, "You heard those Negroes were shot to death?"

"Of course I heard. Probably, as fast as you did."

"I would like to ask you about the shooting," Dad did not tell Stan we were there and I was forbidden to.

Stan raised his hand to his head before spoke, "You must be joking. Go ahead and pour your drink. I think you're going to need it and I know I am." Stan and Dad fixed their drinks and Stan provided a Peachtree Cola for me. The familiar aroma of matches, tobacco, bourbon and scotch filled the room.

"Yes, Hank, I heard all about the demise of Blue Shoes and the other two. They closed the file on the retired policeman's murder and they got the woman who threatened your family on a receiving stolen goods charge. Didn't get something they could stick on her moonshining brother but he may be out of business. I hope you're not going after anyone else."

"No, I consider the case closed."

"Good. I got the suit against you dismissed." Dad looked puzzled but Stan continued, "Yes, Mr. Franklin, the Negro lawyer, filed suit. It was risible, Jeb that means laughable. No law supported any of his complaints. I looked him up to see if he had passed the bar, he had. His suit had to be thrown out but we had a hearing. I could not have timed it better, two days after the shooting. I told the judge, a different judge, that Mr. Franklin had no case because his clients, Blue Shoes, et al. had been shot to death by the police."

'You're kidding," Dad said in disbelief.

"No. I didn't want to bother you. The hearing was scheduled and Franklin tried to proceed as an injured party."

"What?...Injured party?...You're joking?"

"I kid you not. I asked how he had been damaged? He said he couldn't collect his fee. I argued it was not my clients but the police who shot his clients. I suggested he sue the police," Stan chortled. "Others in the courtroom appreciated my humor. I also noted that his clients were newly released from prison and had no money to pay him. I asked for a dismissal and the judge agreed."

"Thank Jesus," Dad sighed.

"I am sure thanks to Jesus are in order. But you can thank me too. And I will keep your retainer. What's on your mind now?"

"Don't you think it unwarranted that the police killed the three Negroes with one gun between them?"

Stan grimaced, "Go on, I did not read the report but I'll bet all my scotch, and that's a lot, they also had knives."

"They could not all have held the pistol at once."

Stan looked pained, "Hank,... This sounds like the bus shooting." Then he laughed, "Well, I guess there was a bus this time... Do you wish the criminals were better armed? Maybe the police did not want to wait and see how many guns they had or how many policeman they could shoot. It was not supposed to be a fair fight. They were justly shot in the commission of an armed felony."

Dad asked earnestly, "The police report, which I have seen, said the police opened fire when they saw one of the men raise a pistol and the other two were shot as they tried to get the pistol to return fire. How do they know they were trying to get the pistol? They may have been trying to help their partner."

"Damn it, Hank. And I mean damn," Stan took a frustrated puff off his cigarette and exhaled. "Two things, one, the police report represents the facts in this case. According to the report the eyewitnesses, the police, determined the deceased were reaching for the pistol. You are welcome to an opinion but you are not entitled to different facts. Number two, well, let me ask Jeb. You said you watch cowboys on TV. When the bad guys surrender what do they do?"

"They drop their guns and raise their hands." I said.

"Out of the mouth of babes,... Hank, I wasn't there but the only thing they could have done to avoid getting shot was raise their hands and quick," Stan raised his hands as he spoke, "the universally understood way to surrender. Instead they reached for a loaded pistol." He put his hands down and reached for his drink. "There is no confusing those two motions. They did not surrender and they died of their wounds instead of getting hung later. You don't like me saying this, but one less trial and justice was done."

Dad sat in silence and weighed Stan's remarks.

"Hank, I do not have the time nor do I wish to educate you. Get a job as a prosecutor and after five years you will agree with me. Two to three bourbons may make you more agreeable, but it's not the training you need."

Dad leaned forward as he spoke, "Stan, a 'shoot first ask questions later' policy helps to create scenes like this latest shooting."

"I disagree with your premise in this case but there may be something to your point. You're talking police procedure, not law. And I can assure you if I were a policeman I would want to shoot first rather than be shot. Address that with the Sheriff, not the courts. The gang had two choices: death by hanging after a trial or by a bullet. They chose the latter by their actions."

"I think the police are part of the problem." Dad said.

"And that's why they should be the ones to address it. If I were out to fix things I would work on the other side of the problem – the NICs. Blue Shoe's body wasn't cold before a new murdering NIC took over his territory, who in turn will be killed or prosecuted. Fix that one! The NICs think that crime pays – it's worth the risk to them."

Dad finished his drink and poured fresh bourbon into his glass. He sat back in his chair and took a long drag on his cigarette.

Stan continued, "You keep trying to make the case that Negroes are treated unfairly, I agree, but not criminals!" Stan leaned forward and hit the table with his forefinger to make his point. "Not criminals. I want to repeat for emphasis, criminals are not treated unfairly; they often get what they deserve. If anyone is treated unfairly it is the law-abiding citizen, waiting on the criminal justice system to work on his or her behalf. Let me ask Jeb, OK, Jeb?"

"Yes, sir."

"When the three Negroes came to break in your house would you have been grateful if the Klan pulled in your driveway and the three Negroes ran away?"

"Yes, sir."

"Now, Hank, don't get mad at the boy anybody would. No one in fear of their life cares about the politics of their savior. When the State Patrol came to get you in Magnolia did you ask them if they were Klan members? Communist sympathizers? Buckhead Business Club? Or anything else? - Before you allowed them to get you out of there? Heck no. You wanted to be saved and quick."

Dad shook his head, "Yes, but the Klan commits acts of violence."

"And the goddamn communist want to takeover the country. If armed hooligans attacked my home and the communist saved my family I'd give them all my scotch! I don't care if you catch my killer and he is convicted in the greatest trial in history with ten appeals – I'll be dead. I want to live, most people do!"

I wanted to ask how much that scotch was worth instead I interjected, "Great, Great, Granddaddy Jeb said that a neighbor with a rifle and dry powder was better than the whole British Navy."

"Really? Your Dad must have taught you that. I think when I was in the Pacific I would have preferred the whole British Navy. I wonder if Butterfield has a rifle and dry powder, that's my neighbor. But we are wandering afield of my point... too much scotch on an empty stomach." Stan glanced at Dad, "Don't let me get too far ahead of your Bourbon."

Dad added ice to his drink; "I hope I will not have imbibed too much bourbon to appreciate your point when it arrives."

"I thought I'd made at least one or two. Do you think other Negroes want those men on the street? Atlanta has a large number of middle class Negroes who own their own nice homes and have good jobs. They are well educated at Fulton Park University. I know a few and I like and respect them. Their lives could be better, but they are much improved from a few decades ago. Those Negroes are much more often the victims of crimes committed by Negroes. Ida Mae is not complaining the gang members were shot. What kind of chance did Cutler get? If Blue Shoes and his gang were white it would be the same result. Meet some middle class Negroes. They are intelligent and articulate. Ask them about their interests and dreams. I can assure you they do not want to be the perpetual victims of Negro crime."

Dad twirled the ice to cool his fresh pour of bourbon while he sat in silence considering Stan's point.

Stan paused for to sip his scotch, "I have offered you some criticism in private but I have none for Jeb. He has done better than anyone had a right to expect."

Stan and Dad looked at me approvingly but I said nothing.

Stan sprawled back in his chair as relaxed as his golden retriever on the floor in the foyer, "I suspect your guardian angel is slap wore out. I know I am. 'The Lord hath his way in the whirlwind and in the storm,' I believe that."

Dad nodded in agreement. I was ready for less whirlwind and less storm.

"I hate it that you bemoan the fact that the gang was killed instead of tried. Have you considered they might not have been convicted? Mistakes are made. I have seen mean bastards walk free to commit more heinous crimes. It depressed me as a prosecutor. Smile, all your loose ends are tied up."

"I do wish some things had gone differently." Dad opined.

"Don't we all. I wish we could have gone to trial on the house burning. I wouldn't care if we'd lost. I would have had a child testify in a case involving the Klan. I could have written a book and given speeches. I'd be famous, LIFE and TIME magazines, not the cover, but an honorable mention. I should write a book about Jeb's adventures, people would doubt me. I did take a picture of the burned out house. The truth certainly is stranger than fiction." Stan chuckled at his own joke. "Jeb proved himself to me. I'd have loved a shot at proving him to a jury."

"I agree," Dad said.

"I have thought about it way too much. You know, how I would handle the other lawyer, brief to the judge… I even talked to the psychologist about jury selection. If I pick jurors with children would they judge by their own kids or consider someone else's kid could do much better? We could only guess." Stan added, "Yes, I admire and share your ideals if not your methods. Dirk Lockhart told you and I agree with him, and for half his pay I advise you to choose another way to help Negroes."

"Stan, thank you; I have chosen another way. I have met a few Negro ministers. I am pitching in with them."

"Excellent, they would be worth listening to." But, I am afraid they dabble in politics."

"No comment. Thanks for everything. I need to get Jeb home for supper. Beside if I drive on one more shot of bourbon I may have to retain you again."

We stood and shook hands. Dad and Stan talked longer. I noticed some bright coffee table picture books in the living room and sat on the sofa for a better look. The strange forgotten feeling of relaxation came over me as I gazed at the bright illustrations of flowers and plantings.

Unconsciously tears began to roll down my cheeks. I didn't notice until they hit my blue jeans.

Stan noticed first, "Jeb, what's wrong?" He quickly covered the distance to the coffee table thinking a book was upsetting me.

Dad could not see. Stan turned to explain, "Jeb's in tears."

I looked up wiping my tears, "I feel safe here. I don't want to go home."

As I did damage control Stan said, "Jeb I am going to give your Dad my pistol he knows how to use it, y'all with be safe."

Stan pulled a snub-nosed revolver from his belt and handed to Dad who put it in his suit coat pocket. He looked at me, "Don't worry I have another pistol. I put a lot of bad guys in jail and the police encouraged me to protect myself. The things you have seen are quite unusual and our neighborhoods are safe and filled with the nicest people in the state of Georgia."

"I'm OK. Thanks for the Peachtree Cola." I did feel better knowing that Dad had an operational pistol.

Stan called out as we walked to the car. He tried to lighten the atmosphere with one last jab at Dad, "Drive safe. I don't want to defend you for driving under the influence of my bourbon; I could be an accessory before the fact. Besides, I don't want anymore of your money, at least for a while."

Chapter 26 Promise

At long last we were cut down from the emotional whipping post. A sense of relief and joy flowed over our home like a victorious football team after a hard fought game, happy to win but just too beat up for delirious celebration.

Many things from those days are better off 'gone with the wind' but not Miss Scarlett. In the fall I started a new era in my education at Scarlett O'Hara Grammar School. I liked two things from the get go: Tall Ed and Marvin were not there and Miss Scarlett was. I gazed at her life-sized portrait in the cafeteria everyday. She was easy on the eyes. Her white lace trimmed blue gown complemented her figure. Chestnut brown hair framed her fair skinned face. Sapphire blue eyes sparkled above rose accented cheeks and wine red lips. Miss Scarlett was drop dead gorgeous. But dang, unlike Mrs. Hewlett she did not come to school to talk to kids when they got in trouble. If she had - boys would have been in trouble every day.

Stan Wallace continued to be a friend, critic and supporter. Dad won some grudging admiration. Dad was never again assigned a pro bono legal case nor was he pulled over by police again in southeast Georgia. The Jekyll colored hotel became the meeting place for Negro ministers and leaders. On the beaches whites and Negroes enjoyed the same ocean a mile apart. Not one white person emerged from the Atlantic Ocean black because Negroes swam in it nor did any Negroes turn white. Jekyll was not all he wanted it to be but it was a bold start. Dad declared victory.

Ida Mae's life improved. I shared some of her fear of Nate's other friends or a new NIC. But the 'no damn goods' did leave us alone. Some thought the police were watching; the superstitious thought Ida Mae was protected by a super-hex. Laundry days became a small pleasure. She set the ironing board in the middle of the hall and opened the front and back doors to catch a breeze. Thanks to the new phone extension cord she could sit on the kitchen stool and iron clothes, while she listened to the radio, drank colas, and talked on the phone to an ever-widening circle of church friends. She still had struggles. She wandered in the desert but she was out of Egypt. She had a family; she had seen one anyway. She felt a measure of security and once again she dared to dream of the Promised Land.

www.ingramcontent.com/pod-product-compliance
Lightning Source LLC
LaVergne TN
LVHW051542070426
835507LV00021B/2367